In Mania's Memory

Trade paperback edition 2012
First published in 2010 by Read Leaf
an imprint of Simply Read Books

Library and Archives Canada Cataloguing in Publication

Birnie, Lisa Hobbs, 1928-
          In Mania's memory / Lisa Birnie.
ISBN 978-1-897476-45-1 (hc)
ISBN 978-1-897476-79-6 (pb)
          1. Holocaust, Jewish (1939-1945)--Fiction. 2. Holocaust
survivors--Fiction. 3. Concentration camp guards--Fiction.
4. World War, 1939-1945--Fiction. I. Title.

PS8603.I773I5 2009   C813'.6   C2009-906206-2

We gratefully acknowledge for their financial support of our publishing program the
Canada Council for the Arts, the BC Arts Council, and the Government of Canada
through the Canada Book Fund (CBF).

Book design by hundreds and thousands
Cover design by Naomi MacDougall

10 9 8 7 6 5 4 3 2 1

Printed in Canada

e-book edition also available

LISA BIRNIE

In Mania's Memory

Read Leaf

AUTHOR'S NOTE

The story of Mania Fishel Kroll is true. Because Mania was a child when her family was torn apart following the German invasion of Poland in the fall of 1939, a few of her memories are hazy and some are fragmentary. On the few occasions when this was the case, and the memories were not of historic importance, I took the liberty of fleshing out the social and domestic details based on the norms at that time in Poland. However, all the essential facts of Mania's life, such as being driven from her home, rounded up with her family in the Sosnowitz Athletic Field Aktion, and placed in a ghetto, and then in Auschwitz-Birkenau concentration camp before being sent to a slave labor camp, have been verified by documentation in Polish university and government archives.

It has not been possible to verify all the facts of Johanne Müller's life, nor the credibility of all she told me. Allied bombing raids, land warfare, and the actions of German authorities towards the war's end destroyed much official documentation. Administrators of concentration and slave labor camps were particularly successful in erasing all files relating both to personnel and prisoners. The files at Auschwitz-Birkenau were preserved only because of the secret work done by prisoners who were members of the resistance. Nonetheless, it has been possible to establish certain facts of Johanne's life. When details—peripheral and inessential to these facts—were missing but desirable either for readability or a better understanding of Johanne's actions, I drew conclusions from intimations and hints given by Johanne, sometimes with pride, sometimes unwittingly.

This book draws on my own longtime interest in the history of the Second World War as well as the extensive research done by Vancouver documentary filmmaker Maureen Kelleher. Without Maureen's tenacious work in Germany and Poland and her generosity in sharing her findings, this book would never have been written. ↔

The story that follows was told to me by two women, one a Polish Jew named Mania, the other a German Christian named Johanne. The facts recounted in Mania's story, such as the time and place of her birth, her imprisonment in Auschwitz, and the murder of her mother, are true and have been documented. Her memories cannot be documented; their value lies in revealing how, as a child, she experienced and perceived the world around her. These memories are still powerful enough to influence her life today. The power of memory to determine behavior for the rest of one's life is also reflected in Johanne's story. Set within the same time frame as Mania's, it reflects another but equally demented world. Johanne's tale is that of a beautiful young German woman passionately in love with an officer of the Third Reich. I have been able to verify some of Johanne's story, such as her birthplace and family life and some aspects of her love affair, but little else because of the destruction of documentation either by Allied bombing or the Nazi's attempt to cover their depraved behavior. Despite the differences in these two stories, the lives of both Mania and Johanne are linked. The extent to which they are linked is the subject of this story. I can only repeat what they told me and leave it to you, the reader, to come to your own conclusion.

My involvement with both women began in mid-2001 when I received an e-mail from Suzanne DePoe, a film agent in Toronto. I'd had contact previously with Suzanne, once during negotiations for the film rights of my book Uncommon Will: The Death and Life of Sue Rodriguez, and again when she and my former literary agent, Denise Bukowski, were in negotiations for the film rights of my book Such a Good Boy. On the rare occasions I received an e-mail from Suzanne DePoe, I paid attention.

This e-mail read:

Hi Lisa. A documentary filmmaker in Vancouver wants to do a book at the same time as a doc about a woman who is a holocaust survivor who was in various camps aged 7–12. In the last camp a nazi guard took care of her, gave her food and special care and offered to adopt her after the war.

Fast forward to 1976. The girl is now a woman living in Toronto. The woman hires a cleaning lady who turns out to be the same nazi guard.

This is all the info I have. Would you be interested in exploring it further?

At the time I was not working on anything. My husband had died the previous year and I was alone. My children, like those of many North American parents, lived thousands of miles away. I'd sold my home on Bowen Island, a short ferry ride from the British Columbia coast, and moved into a small waterfront apartment in downtown Vancouver. I was free to run the remains of my life as I pleased and was finding this freedom to be a wonderful, if seldom mentioned, part of widowhood.

I reread the e-mail and felt myself drawing back. I'd never considered retiring from writing, but a story like this, if there was any truth to it, would mean dealing with depressing material. I'd set up a cozy, comfortable life and wanted no part of anything that threatened it. Enough of my life had been spent asking the big and ultimately unanswerable questions. I'd been raised in Australia as a Catholic, a faith that formed my belief that life was essentially a spiritual journey and that I was merely a tourist going through it. As for ultimate answers, I'd concluded that the church didn't have them all by a long shot, and that trust under all circumstances was the only ultimate answer.

My previous two books had dealt with death, although the strange allure of that subject had played out in different ways. In one case, a seventeen-year-old high school student named Darren Huenemann, told by his mother and grandmother of the fortune he would inherit on their deaths, coaxed two high school friends to murder them.

Shortly after finishing this book, Sue Rodriguez phoned. Sue was a high-profile victim of amyotrophic lateral sclerosis (ALS) who, until her own death, fought up to the Supreme Court of Canada for the right of assisted suicide. Sue had "star quality" and, having become the icon of the Right to Die movement, wanted her story written. I was hesitant. Assisted suicide was a quagmire of moral and legal issues, one that provoked extreme emotional reactions for or against. I told Sue I disagreed with her pro-euthanasia stance but was aware I wasn't walking in her shoes. Even as I expressed disagreement, I felt that if I had a terminally ill child in exquisite, uncontrollable pain—pain that I have experienced through trigeminal nerve attacks—I would want a doctor to end it.

Finally I went ahead with the book, driven as much by Sue's desperation—her speech was becoming unintelligible—as by my need to find some sort of practical and moral answer: Were there extreme cases when mercy killing could not only be justified but actually be the right thing, the moral thing, to do? Sue put herself into the "extreme case" category. I did not. I'd known too many Darren Huenemanns to ever support state-sanctioned killing, known too many older people in severe pain who still chose life rather than death. I'd also watched for weeks while a friend died in agony, the pain of bone cancer impervious to the best medical and palliative care.

Watching the effects of ALS subtly and relentlessly embrace Sue's elegant body saddened me profoundly. Throughout the long hours of our talks, as the leaves turned gold and winter moved in with its own darkness, she sat rigid, imprisoned in her electric wheelchair, as if already mummified. I bit my tongue against the hollow words of comfort that tried to inject themselves into our talks. Sue wanted only for me to listen. Her mind was set on death. The only solace she sought was my tuning body and soul into her anguish. That's what I did. I let it become part of me.

After Sue killed herself, with the aid of an anonymous helper, and I had finished the book, I kept my eyes open for a subject that would challenge me without grinding me down. Ironically, for someone who regarded life as essentially a spiritual journey, I took for granted my right to opt out of other people's suffering. For a year there was nothing; then out of the blue came an invitation from Professor Michael Ashby, director of McCulloch House, the palliative care section of Monash University Hospital in Melbourne, to be writer-in-residence. Melbourne was my hometown. I jumped at it. From my months at Monash I wrote a book of observations about what makes for the best possible death. Called *A Good Day to Die*, it was published by TEXT in Melbourne. That experience left me inspired and energized.

Writing a story about a child victim of the Holocaust and an old Nazi guard would not. Unlike palliative care, where love and dignity fueled all activity and attitudes, I'd be going into a world of cruelty and madness. I felt my stomach tightening with the fear that I'd be seized by the same dread that had invaded me as I sat beside Sue. Thousands of books about life inside the Nazi death camps had already been written by those who had lived it. That world was outside my experience. Yet I couldn't keep my ego down and couldn't stop feeling flattered that Suzanne DePoe had asked me to write this book. Pride may be a base motive, but when it comes to writing, anything that kick-starts the process is priceless.

One day while sifting the pros and cons of the story, it struck me that the real or imagined experience of Mania, the survivor, must have happened to other people. All over Europe—as well as in parts of Asia and South America—hundreds of thousands of former prisoners and guards must still be accidentally rubbing elbows on city streets, at beach resorts, and in theaters and churches. Did former death camp guards scurry a little as they walked through the streets of Germany's cities, hoping the ravages of age would shield them from recognition? Were forgotten faces coming into focus as long-term memory surged and short-term memory faded? Were these faces filling out with youthful flesh and color and life again? Could the tormentor and the tormented still remember the details of the nose, hair, eyes, and cries of the other? And how often did such confrontations happen? And when they did, how were old scores settled? With words of contempt? Of rage? Acts of revenge, blows struck, faces slapped, arrogant denials, gestures of forgiveness?

What were Mania's real motives in wanting to once more confront this alleged former Nazi guard? Maybe she didn't even know.

I e-mailed Suzanne:

A former Nazi guard being hired in Toronto by one of her former prisoners sounds too strange a coincidence to be true. Are these verified facts? Can you get anything else on it?

The reply came from Maureen Kelleher, the woman developing the project. Maureen had been hired by an independent production company to write and direct six episodes of a series for the History Channel. But she had her own documentary to make—that of Mania Kroll, a child survivor of Auschwitz whose life had been saved by a Nazi guard.

Maureen had successfully raised funding and was planning the shoot in Germany and Poland.

Maureen's e-mail contained the news that she'd been in touch with Johanne Müller, the cleaning woman. Johanne told Maureen she had spent the entire war in Berlin working as a cook and had never been a Nazi. This denial was not unexpected. Maureen's research had revealed that of the three thousand female guards trained at Ravensbrück concentration camp, the only one to admit it was Frau Anna Fest, who was interviewed by Alison Owings in her book *Frauen: German Women Recall the Third Reich*. The average age of these female guards was the late twenties—Johanne's age at the time of the war. And the site of the slave labor camp where Mania was imprisoned was around fifteen kilometers from Johanne's hometown.

This coincidence cinched it for Maureen. She decided to one way or another woo Johanne into becoming involved in the documentary. Her hope was that Johanne would tell the truth. If she had been a guard, Johanne would become the first female guard to admit on camera to the role that she and thousands of other women had played as jailers in the Third Reich. For Maureen, this would be an international cinematic coup, every documentary filmmaker's dream.

Maureen's e-mail concluded:

In late September I will continue my research, travelling to Europe with Mania who will reunite with the guard 57 years after they first met. Who knows what will happen at this meeting, but Mania is determined to finally thank the woman whose kindness saved her life.

So Mania simply wanted to discharge a heavy burden of gratitude. Such a high-minded motive rang a warning bell. Would a normal woman fret for fifty years about some acts of kindness, even search Europe simply to say, "Thank you. I know you were in the SS. And weren't all women guards trained at Ravensbrück to be brutal? So God alone knows what you did to other women. But I was a child and you were good to me, so here's an armload of love and presents"?

It had all happened so long ago that I couldn't understand it. This was before I met Mania, before I realized that nobody who survived

Auschwitz was ever normal again. Or that a bowl of soup and a piece of bread indebted a sensitive soul for life. And between those edible realities and the rest of the world's idea of normalcy, the distance was infinite. And that from the suffering in the camps grew some souls that were bigger and grander than the cosmos, because there wasn't any closure. You dealt with it in whatever way worked for you and then got on with life, because the only alternative was a high-flying leap from the nearest building or stairwell.

Maureen had already interviewed Mania and Johanne separately and, with a generosity I came to know as typical, offered me a copy of her notes. A couple of hours later she arrived at my apartment building. I buzzed her in and watched as, clad in skin-tight latex and a helmet, she maneuvered her bike out of the elevator. She caught sight of me and beamed. Off came the helmet, down dropped an abundance of brown hair, damp around the brow after her dash through rush-hour traffic to deliver the package.

We surveyed each other across the hall and instantly knew we'd get on.

I took the interviews, poured myself a Scotch, dragged a chair onto my balcony, where I could watch the boats sail by in English Bay, and read them in one take.

From the ages of seven to twelve years, Mania witnessed evil and lived in terror. Usual Holocaust material; no surprises there, but they weren't long in coming. As I followed her journey from a warm, loving home, where as an only child she reigned like a princess, to her final imprisonment as a slave laborer, the story that unfolded was unlike any I'd read. Some of the twists and turns seemed unbelievable. The bizarre, the paranormal, and the abnormal were tied together in a tangle where all seemed of equal importance. I couldn't separate fact from fiction, and probable myth from possible truth. I reminded myself that Germany and Poland at the time of this story were like madhouses. Mania, like all the camp children, was not allowed any typical child's response to anything. Might not a child, living in terror for years, feel as if all around her diabolical and angelic forces were battling for supremacy?

If I were going to turn this assignment down, now was the time. But then I'd never know the truth. Somewhere in the messy tangle I sensed an intriguing story waiting to be told. There's a sort of euphoria in finding truth, in bringing to light something long hidden in darkness, more so when that darkness is wrapped around lives or acts that we cannot imagine ourselves doing or surviving. I find such stories irresistible. They tell us who we are and set us wondering: How would I have acted if that had happened to me?

I read on. By the end of Mania's story I could see the tracings of a pattern. Whatever forces had caused these bizarre twists and turns in her life—seemingly unconnected and spread out over five years—they had created a chain that resulted in her escaping death. I had to meet her; only then could I make up my own mind. She swore she was not Nazi hunting. Her only aim was to thank the former Nazi who had saved her life and, without doubt, that woman was Johanne Müller. "I want to treat her like I would my own mother," she said. I thought that a bit thick. "Like I would my own mother?" When her mother had fallen ill and was gassed? Didn't Mania have at least a little room for anger and revenge in her emotional life? Was she trying to pass herself off as a saint?

Next I turned to the notes on Johanne's interview, combing them for whatever strands of credibility or falsity I could find. My mind was open, but a life in journalism had taught me that almost all human beings struggle against looking face-to-face at their own reality. Her words fleshed out an upright woman, strong as a tree and sharp as an axe. I imagined her wearing blue pantsuits with flat brown shoes, thick grey hair home-done in a bathroom basin but carefully well-coiffed into a safe, familiar pattern. I dug around in the package to see if there were any photos of the two women, but no luck.

As I reread Johanne's seemingly spontaneous words, it became clear they'd been previously well thought out. Her mind was careful and disciplined. Her speech was courteous and now and then personal, even humorous. Occasionally she volunteered information, but such bits and pieces were trivia, little embellishments perhaps designed to distract from the few hard facts she seemed willing to share.

The next day I went to the library at Vancouver's Holocaust Education Centre, searching for stories told by other survivors from Katowice,

Mania's hometown in southwest Poland. I found an old but excellent video interview with Sigmund Sobolsky of Calgary, who had lived in that area of Poland and spent time as a prisoner in Auschwitz. Yet there was little in the video or library specifically related to the Nazi's treatment of Jews in the Katowice-Sosnowitz area. This lack of information added enormous value to Mania's narrative; it indicated how thorough the Nazi "cleansing" of that area was and how few Jews had survived. Mania's voice could speak for the hundreds of thousands of Jews in that region who had disappeared without trace. Her voice could record some of the facts and experiences surrounding their fate. It could provide these murdered innocents, voiceless for more than sixty years, with a memoir that would help offset the total silence of their airborne graves.

Questions about the enigmatic Johanne started to pile up. If she were the guard, she would have been an auxiliary member of the Schutz-staffel, the SS. Why would a member of the SS risk everything to help a Jewish child? Helping a Jew was an act of treason. When speaking to Maureen of her own life during the Third Reich, wouldn't Johanne have been tempted to suggest that she had never approved of National Social-ism, nor of Hitler, and that she had sometimes secretly resisted with sly little acts of defiance? As Alison Owens illustrated in her book, slithering out of a guilty past was common enough, with many interviewees hint-ing that at heart they'd really been anti-Nazi. But Johanne's words were free from any such insinuation.

Only one small thought now held me back: did we really have any right to bust into this elderly woman's life and dredge up her past? She'd never been listed as a war criminal. If she had been a guard, she was just one of a million aging barbarians getting ready to face God. Did she have any rights to privacy? I thought about that for half a minute. "Nope," came the answer. "Not any damn right whatsoever."

I was hooked. I e-mailed Maureen:

Okay. But must write totally independent of your documentary and retain total freedom as to any conclusions.

The following month Maureen flew to Germany and Poland to make preliminary arrangements. She planned to arrange and film a meeting

ing between Mania and Johanne at the site of the former Reichenbach slave labor camp. Johanne was told she would be meeting with
a Jewish woman and would accompany her for a half day of filming.
Johanne was told that she would accompany this Jewish woman (Mania)
simply as an ordinary German woman who had lived through the Third
Reich. The hope was that when Johanne saw Mania at Reichenbach it
might loosen her tongue and rattle the truth out of her. Was this plan
ethically flawed? It was weighted against Johanne because it implied
she'd been a Nazi, but so what? It might also prove that she was Mania's
savior. Mania would then not only thank Johanne, lavish her with gifts,
and perhaps even liberate her from past guilt, but most importantly
Mania would at last feel at peace: a debt that had become an obsession
would finally be paid. And if anyone in this world deserved peace, it was
Mania, along with every other camp survivor.

Obviously the meeting could go another way. Johanne might prove
herself entirely free of any link with the Nazis or the Reichenbach camp.
She might provide evidence she'd spent the war years as a cook to a private family in Berlin, as she'd claimed. She might blast Mania's belief of
a prior relationship right out of the water. In which case we'd pack our
bags, wipe a little egg off our faces, and return to Canada.

Late in the following April, Maureen and her partner/cameraman,
Neil Thompson, returned to Germany. Everything was in place.

I left Vancouver for Toronto in late April. I would meet Mania Kroll
for the first time in the Lufthansa lounge prior to the flight to Frankfurt.
We would spend two days in Frankfurt getting acquainted and then fly to
Katowice, Poland, and meet up with Maureen and her team. ↦

VANCOUVER

April 28, 2002

A half hour after the plane takes off I find myself brooding over the myths we invent to give some structure, some sense, to our lives. No proof whatsoever exists that Johanne served in the SS at a slave labor camp. Furthermore, she could deny it till hell froze over, because the Germans destroyed all the camp records. We have only Mania's word. And how much reality does that reflect? Mania's father died in battle when she was seven. When she was eleven the Nazis murdered her mother. From then on Mania no longer existed as a daughter until a female guard of her mother's age started to treat her in a caring, motherly way. Mania was twelve years old by then, but the way a child normally grows up is by learning independence and responsibility, and this was totally denied her. Maybe the only way Mania has of validating her own existence and keeping "survivor guilt" at bay is to meet once more with this mystic lifesaving guard who was to "blame" for her survival.

Staring out the plane's window at a pink-tinged cushion of cloud, I wonder if Mania has simply, and unconsciously, deceived herself. Her recognition of Johanne Müller as former SS guard Johanne Clausen could be a trick of her own mind. The distinctive accent, a German woman of a certain age, the blue eyes, the proud bearing—these elements had created a fantasy of reclaiming a lost childhood. Maybe Mania has done what I've done when I've needed something badly enough: talked myself into believing black was white. If only Mania wasn't so sure, so positive!

I have another problem, one of my own with nothing to do with these two ladies: I can see no way of telling these women's stories without intruding into them because World War II still soaks a large part of my own memories.

I'm not comfortable with Germans. It's not a matter of choosing to like or dislike. It is a feeling that arises automatically whenever I meet a German, a legacy left over from the war and a cultural background where a little racism provided the gist of many a good joke. I have German

1

friends, people I've taken the trouble to get to know, and people who've taken a great deal of trouble to get to know me. Yet whenever I meet a German stranger, a curtain drops within me in a way it doesn't with any other race. I am aware of my odious reaction, and I do social handsprings to avoid revealing the toxins stirring within me. In fact, I feel this reaction is separate from, and has nothing to do with, my "real" self. Still the process goes on unbidden; the filtering of everything said and done to find signs that this hapless German thinks of himself or herself as one of the Übermensch—the obsession with order, opinions rigid as cement, and the arrogant certainty of a mind in a lidded box.

Like most of my generation, I was brainwashed as a child. There was no television then, at least in Australia. I'd run out to meet my father coming home from work to get the newspaper before my siblings did. Then I'd crouch on the floor, bottom in the air, and read every word of it. Australia was still dealing with its horrific losses in the First World War, and the new World War consumed us. "Germans" to me meant swastikas, black boots, Nazi armbands, goose-stepping troops, and the rantings of a madman. They were "Krauts" and "Huns." Even the German-Australian farmers and their native-born sons were different—pleasant but un-Australian. They worked twenty hours a day, harvesting and planting their fields half the night by lantern light. All Aussies knew "they" loved sausage, the cheaper version of which we called "Fritz." They didn't lie on the beach all summer or play cricket or drink at the local pub—all of which offered proof they weren't one of "us." Then came the revelations of the death camps. It was easy to move from a sense of Germans being different to a reactive attitude of distrust and dislike.

I have another legacy from the Third Reich, a small loss compared to the multiple sufferings of millions, but a loss profound and painful.

My twenty-one-year-old brother, Robert, a bomber pilot in 460 squadron of the Royal Australian Air Force, was killed on a raid over Magdeburg. The news of his death followed three months of him being listed as missing. What happened after that had nothing to do with the Germans but everything to do with the culture of the times. Within my family there was no discussion of my brother's death, no grieving together, no hugs or holding, no body, no funeral service, and no details. After a few months a small box arrived with my brother's personal possessions: a few handkerchiefs neatly folded, a few letters, a rosary, and a diary. That's what remained of him.

My close family turned into strangers. My mother and father dissolved into each other, leaving my younger brother and me out in the cold, a brother three years older afflicted with a life-long guilt that he was not the son who died, and a sister who tried to hold us all together. My parents' stiff upper lip and carry-on response allowed my family no expression of our grief. It was not the "done" thing to make an issue of one's feelings, let alone give vent to painful emotion. That, in Australia at that time, would be considered vulgar and "Italian." "You're acting like an Italian," my mother would say disparagingly if I showed spontaneous emotion. Australia was racist to the marrow when I grew up. It was not an unwitting racism: the White Australia policy had few, if any, challengers.

There had never been what's now euphemistically called "closure," just a profound sense of loss all because of the Germans. Many years later, idly browsing through a book on the war, I came across a photo of the sky ablaze over Magdeburg the night my brother died along with fifty other Lancaster bomber crews and God knows how many civilians beneath. It so happened that at the time of my reading Queen Elizabeth II and Prince Philip were making a hugely successful and friendly visit to Germany. I knew then that anger was more appropriate than sorrow. I began to see my brother as a victim of British propaganda, an idealistic youth seduced into fighting in a war thousands of miles away. Yet whenever I traveled to Germany in later years I couldn't shut up an inner voice that persistently asked, "What in God's name was a twenty-one-year-old Australian doing dropping bombs on people who lived thousands of miles from his own homeland?"

By the time my plane lands in Toronto, my feet are puffy and my head is splitting.

I pull my carryon along and head for the international terminal, knowing that while I am after the story of a Jewish child survivor and a kind Nazi guard, I'll be going into a lot of dark, confusing territory, some of it inside myself. I vow to stay clear of my own memory bank. I'll need all my energy to tell Mania's story as well as it can be told.

It never strikes me that Johanne's story will also drain me, but in an unpredictable and surprising way. ↔

3

TORONTO

APRIL 28, 2002

The lounge in the Lufthansa boarding area is crowded with older couples, overweight, tired, and sour-looking. Some have sunburned skin; all slump in their seats. Their looks say they've been cruising in the Caribbean, toasting their skin and stuffing themselves until they fill their seats as if part of the chair. Bored to death with their long preboarding wait, their eyes follow me as I look around, trying to pick out Mania.

She seems to trot out of nowhere, clickety-clack, small feet daintily shod, a full head of dyed reddish hair complementing the beige shawl tossed over her shoulders, bright red lipstick, large blue eyes topped by brows as well shaped as a half-moon. She looks like a woman who's never had a bad day in her life. She holds out her hands to greet me, and a ring flashes on a hand with red-tipped fingers. She radiates warmth, energy, ease, and charm.

It is one of those bumbling meetings, awkward missed handshakes and half hugs, both of us talking half sentences at once. I smile warily at her; she beams at me. We look around for vacant seats but there are none, so we stand, each doing a split-second assessment one of the other. Mania vibrates with energy and the potential for a large dose of chutzpah. This energy translates into a matronly flash and allure that made me feel plain dowdy. ("When you're past forty, never dress as though mutton were lamb" was one of my mother's mantras.) I utter a silent prayer of thanks that I didn't wear my Birkenstocks. Then Mania says, "Let's get out of this spot before some of these fatties—may they have good health!—squash us to death." She doesn't bother to lower her voice. She dominates the air around us, tugging me into a corner while the bleary-eyed tourists watch with surly interest.

"We're going to be great together, God help me, I feel it," Mania beams. "I live from the heart, Lisa. You know my story? You read the interview?"

I tell her yes, and it's a very good story but I'll need a lot more. I shrink a little inside when I realize what some of that "more" might involve.

Mania senses this, but she says, "Listen, that devil Mengele didn't kill me. I'll survive again. This won't kill me either, and we'll have a good time doing it."

Mania doesn't lose any of that time. No sooner have we boarded the plane and strapped ourselves into our seats than she plunges feetfirst into our new relationship. I'm not quite ready for it, but there is a decided absence of choice. And it soon becomes apparent that Mania not only asks the questions but also answers them in the same breath, often with a few philosophic digressions thrown in, sometimes damaging her perfect English by the force of her emotion. She isn't above a little theological speculation either.

"I'm crazy, I suppose," Mania says. "I always have this feeling of hope. I'm so hopeful for this trip. Please, God, it works out. Why do I say that? God is just a word, just a word for hope. So if you say 'God,' it makes you feel better. You asking, 'Oh God, help me.' You're sick you say, 'Oh God, help me.' You're hoping…so I'm hoping now."

Wow! We're already talking about God! This woman is not going to hold back.

"You're hoping what for exactly?" I ask.

"You want to know what for exactly? How can I tell you what for exactly when I don't know myself?"

After a few moments silence she looks at me again.

"One thing I know because I do know: that lipstick you're wearing, the color's wrong, like for a schoolgirl. You should do something with your eyes too. Red is what you need. Are you crazy? No, no, not for your eyes. Like this…for your mouth." She hauls her handbag from under the seat in front of her, her arm disappearing to the elbow as she gropes around in the semidarkness. Finally she pulls out an expensive-looking black and gold tube. "This is what you need. None of that sicky damned pink. Here, here, take this. It's nice, makes you look…no, no, take it. Keep it. I'll buy another. No, no, take it!"

That tube of bright red lipstick is the first gift that Mania gives me. The rest of her gifts are the kind money can't buy. ↔

FRANKFURT

We check into a small hotel in Frankfurt, a clean, inexpensive place called the Hotel Paris on Karlsruher Strasse near the train station. I am lucky to be given a room over the street. The white painted wood on the lateral-opening window is peeling, but I can shove the stiff glass panel back and fill the room with fresh air. Mania is in a small back room with a view of a concrete wall, but she is so exhausted that it doesn't matter. She sleeps all night and all day while I stretch my legs, visiting Frankfurt's public and private art galleries and strolling along both sides of the broad and beautiful Main River. I am into the project now, but whenever I think of Johanne I feel unpleasantly tense. And it isn't solely because "wild-goose chase" keeps leaping into my mind.

It's the second night, and Mania has fully recovered. We have dinner at a Persian restaurant a few blocks from the hotel. We are going to Katowice, Poland, the next day, and I am anxious to start work on her story before we join the rest of the team. I explain this, and back in my room I pull out my notebook and settle on the bed with my back to the pillows. There is only one chair in the room, and Mania has it.

"I'd like you to tell me how you met Johanne in Canada, Mania, and anything, any details of that meeting that you recall. Maybe if I ask a few questions—"

"Questions? Who needs questions? I remember everything. As soon as I saw her I felt—"

"Mania, where were you when you first met Johanne in Canada in 1977?"

"That's what I'm telling you, about how as soon as I saw her..."

And for three hours this night, and for the hour's flight to Katowice, Mania tells me of her meeting with Johanne. I'm putting structure and sequence where it is lacking and straightening out Mania's individual way of recounting, which at times is like wandering lost in a maze. But the facts of the story are as Mania tells them, and the dates of events check against credible historical sources.

The only thing I'm leaving out are the jokes and chitchat Mania shares en route to Katowice with her fellow passengers who are mostly young Germans.

I'm surprised by her easy warm attitude and maybe a little envious. "You've no hard feelings?"

"Hard feelings? Why hard feelings? I've no time for that; life's too short. Why should I regret things I can't change now? These good people can't help it if their grandparents were dumb stinkers." ↔

FRANKFURT

JUNE 1977

Exactly what happened that morning, I remember. Even the date—the last Saturday in June 1977.

At the time I was getting better from a serious illness. I lived in a three-level townhouse and couldn't cope with the work that had to be done. A friend had told me of a German woman, Johanne Müller, a housekeeper for a Canadian couple in Toronto, whose one-year visa to Canada was about to expire. She wanted to save all the money she could before returning home and was seeking extra work on a temporary basis.

My friend had obtained Frau Müller's number. I had phoned her, and she'd tentatively agreed to houseclean for me one day a week until she left Canada. We arranged to meet at a certain time at the Finch subway station.

I left my house early, drove to the station, parked nearby, and set myself up at the top of the ramp where the passengers emerged. I got there in plenty of time. I felt sure I'd have no problem recognizing the woman. My friend said she was "mid-fifties, grey-haired, and strong."

I was excited. I can't stand a dirty house, and having a strong woman to help me was what I needed. I'd liked the way Frau Müller sounded on the phone—positive and cheerful. And she didn't have a long list of things she wouldn't do, like windows or ironing. And somehow she seemed dignified, a nice person to have around. She had a way of expressing herself, a sort of old-fashioned, old-world courtesy, not too much but just naturally, lightly. Still, we felt it best that we meet each other before deciding, so we arranged to have coffee the following Saturday.

I stood by the exit ramp and waited. People streamed by, hauling shopping bags and kids, coming and going, everyone busy. Then from the edge of an exiting crowd I saw a woman move towards me. I watched her approach, our eyes locked, her mouth opened slightly in a half smile.

9

Suddenly I felt weak. I started to shake. I heard Frau Müller say my name, "Mrs. Krohl? Mrs. Mania Krohl?" but I couldn't speak. Not a word. My voice was gone.

This had happened to me before when I'd received a shock. But this time I hadn't had a shock. The woman had just said my name. Nothing else. No bad news. But my vocal chords had paralyzed. What had I seen that had so shocked me? The sun was shining and the world swirled happily around us, but I felt I was in another place, another time, looking at the scene from a vast foggy distance. My body was trembling. I held on to the railing to steady myself.

Frau Müller stood smiling before me. She was handsome, upright, and strong in a tasteful, sensible blue pantsuit. Her skin was pale and pasty, her eyes blue, concerned, and questioning. "Mrs. Krohl?" she said again. I touched the sleeve of her suit jacket lightly, as if to say, "Just give me a moment."

I recovered after a few moments. She must think I'm crazy, I thought, so I said something about still being physically weak and suggested we have coffee at a cozy nearby restaurant. Once seated I felt at ease. People were talking, smoking, leaning across the table in confidential chitchat, and chasing after their toddlers. Everything around us seemed safe and ordinary. The feeling of shock faded. We talked easily together, mainly in German, going into English just for a word or phrase. Frau Müller spoke with a North German accent, one familiar to me.

I explained that I worked on an on-call basis for the attorney general's department, acting as a court interpreter speaking Polish, German, Slovakian, or Hebrew. My husband had recently died after a long illness, and I had been the main caregiver. I'd fallen ill after he'd passed.

Frau Müller responded by saying that she had met her Canadian employers when they were posted in Berlin. She was the housekeeper and the head of the permanent staff of four. When the family returned to Toronto, they invited Frau Müller to accompany them. She had obtained a one-year working visa, and now that it was expiring, she would soon return to Germany.

By the time we parted, Frau Müller had agreed to start work the following Saturday.

I drove home feeling vaguely unsettled. I was relieved to have someone help me. Maybe I'd get better and even start enjoying my life. For the years of my husband's illness, a large part of my own life had been on hold. But why, for heaven's sake, had I lost my voice? It wasn't physical weakness. Something had happened that I couldn't understand, something to do with my first sight of Frau Müller. Yet when we'd had coffee, I was totally at ease with her. In fact, I'd felt a sense of comfort in being with her, a very faint sense of familiarity.

That was it! With a shock I realized we'd met before.

Frau Müller came to my home the following week, and the arrangement we'd made worked well. She was a hard worker. By the time she finished her work, her cheeks and neck were flushed, and her brow and back slightly sweaty. But she was content. She was a woman who couldn't bear anything but a house that shone with everything in order. That was something I liked too.

But during that week of waiting for her, the feeling of puzzlement, of slight ill ease remained, ready to pop up in the middle of the night or anytime during the day. Why had I lost my voice? And why did I feel that Johanne Müller and I weren't really strangers?

The first time Johanne did the cleaning she refused to take any money, saying she'd enjoyed doing it for me and didn't want payment. I insisted that wasn't fair and, finally, she took it. We set another date, and Johanne came again. Her voice, her gestures, and even the proud way she held herself when she walked seemed to resonate in my memory as familiar and reassuring. I told myself to forget it, but I couldn't. The sense of familiarity would not go away.

One day I told Johanne that she seemed familiar, as if we'd met before.

No, she said, she'd definitely remember if we had.

Johanne had a precise, sharp mind: I had had no reason to doubt her memory. But I couldn't let it go. Hadn't we met somewhere, maybe Toronto, maybe somewhere else? No, we'd never met. She shook her head and said she'd absolutely remember if we had. She was very firm, and the subject was closed, at least for her.

Night after night I lay awake, puzzling, rewinding the mental tapes of thousands of women I'd known in my wandering life. I'd even wake out of my sleep with her face before me. Where, where had I seen her? Maybe it had been in Sweden, where I'd been shipped to after the war with thousands of other Jewish kids who'd survived the camps. It couldn't have been in Cyprus, where the British interned me for a year. Maybe—was it Israel, where I'd worked as a field laborer, a cook, a teacher on a kibbutz for years until I left for Canada? But that made no sense. What would an old German woman be doing in Israel?

Then one night I knew. And I cried out, "Oh God" as if my heart had been split in two. More than thirty years dropped away. I could see her as if she stood at the end of my bed. I was a terrified child again, raising my eyes and seeing the grey, black-buckled uniform, the flat black shoes, the thick lisle stockings. I saw her blue eyes, the same blue eyes, the blonde hair now snow white, heard the same voice, the same soft accent.

My cleaning woman was former SS Corporal Johanne Clausen, guard at Reichenbach slave labor camp. I had been a prisoner in that camp in southwest Poland, a slave of the Third Reich.

There was no doubt in my mind.

I wept uncontrollably, heaving and choking while anger, relief, joy, hate, and fear poured out in tears. I got out of bed trembling and put on a dressing gown. I was suddenly cold and shaking. In the kitchen I turned on the kettle and made a cup of tea. I hugged my gown around me and put on all the lights. I wanted to keep the memories away, but my mind was dragging me back, back, back to Reichenbach, where I'd been transported after two years in Auschwitz.

The Nazis had killed my entire family. I was twelve years of age. I don't know what I looked like when I arrived at Reichenbach. But I remembered it was winter, and I wore some sort of coat over a cotton dress, and my shoes were flapping, and my tin bowl and spoon were, as always, tied around my waist.

Reichenbach camp was like the end of the earth, looming up walled and wired on the frozen, empty landscape. I was one of the youngest in the transport. We were herded into a grey building where about one hundred of us were to sleep. The ground was covered with wind-driven snow, and our stone building was an icebox.

The next morning after roll count, a woman guard appeared before me and ordered me into her office.

Trembling, I followed the uniformed figure into a small room near the entrance to my block. The guard seated herself behind a makeshift desk and, although I dared not look fully into her face, I saw her for the first time. She was blonde, blue-eyed, and beautiful. I was sick with fear.

She asked me if I spoke German, and I said yes. She then asked me my name and I told her. I trembled when she said crisply, "Hmm. I don't think it is Mania. I think it is Marie. What's your name again. Is it Marie?"

I was extremely frightened, so I just kept nodding.

"Are you a Jew?"

"Yes." Would they hang me now?

This beautiful Nazi shook her head. "No, you are not a Jew. Say you're not a Jew."

But I couldn't say it. I was so afraid. I had been through this before, having to deny I was a Jew although I really didn't know what being a Jew meant. I'd learned I was a Jew by being in Auschwitz. When was it that I'd denied that truth? I tried to remember, but all I could recall was the sick feeling in my stomach, a feeling of betrayal when I'd sworn I was deutschblutig (pure-blood German). So I stood silent. She asked me my age, and when I told her she remarked that I was very small for twelve. She stared at me for a long time and then became very businesslike and said something like, "You'll be going to work, and it's very cold early in the morning. You'll need a hat and gloves and some socks." She turned away and took some things from a box. "Here, take these. They'll help keep you warm."

I was too confused to speak. I'd thought she was going to order me hanged, but instead she was being kind! I was stupefied. She was a Nazi! Was it a trick? She looked at me again for a long minute and then ordered me back to my barrack.

And so began a relationship that was to save my life.

Now, more than thirty years later, SS guard Johanne Clausen had reentered my life.

Never can I tell you how I felt when I realized who she was! I sobbed loudly, hysterically, half laughing, half crying. I wanted to shout with relief, tell her how grateful I was, explain how for years I'd wanted to thank her, how I'd never stopped wondering where she was and what she was doing. The memory of this SS guard had haunted me all my life: she'd risked her life for me, and I'd left her at Reichenbach to her fate in the hands of the oncoming Russians without a word of thanks or good-bye.

Now I had a chance to make amends. I gulped down my tea. I had to tell her right away, hug her, bless her, look after her as if she were my own mother. I picked up the phone and was halfway through dialing when I realized it was past midnight. I couldn't phone her without waking up others in the household. Still shaking, I took the tea into my bedroom, sat up, and waited until morning.

But by dawn I was more cautious. I'd realized that maybe Johanne Müller might also have recognized me despite my age. I remembered how firmly she had brushed aside any chance we could have met before. But if she had remembered me, why hadn't she said so? Was she scared of being prosecuted? For what? For being a Nazi? Most Germans had been Nazis, and besides, only a handful of female former guards had been prosecuted in recent years, all of whom had been particularly brutal.

More likely Frau Müller felt that I could destroy her life. She didn't know that all I wanted was to thank her and do what I could for her. She was a stranger in Canada. For all she knew I could be a Nazi hunter. At the very least, admitting she'd been an SS guard would bring back her dark past, one that she was probably determined to keep buried in a place where nobody else could ever find it.

I'm a spontaneous, not a cautious, person. I usually say exactly what I think. But this time I knew I'd have to keep my mouth shut. I'd have to go cautiously and win Frau Müller's trust. Then she might talk. I had no doubt of her identity. I longed for openness between us. She was the major player in the most critical period of my life. Maybe it would help me in other ways. Like all Holocaust survivors, I've got to subconsciously block out a lot just to function normally.

I'd be nonjudgmental about her being a Nazi, even about being in the brutal SS. I knew the Nazis crushed anyone who opposed them. Then again, maybe she'd wanted to join them. What did I know? I didn't even care. I didn't want to wound or humiliate her. And she'd given me something else other than my life; she'd given me proof that goodness exists everywhere, even when evil dominates.

I thought of approaching the subject in many ways. Frau Müller was coming to clean the following Saturday. After she finished work I always made a light lunch and coffee, boiling the coffee in the German way that she liked. Then we would sit down together at the table and chat. I decided that the next time I would tell her a little about my life. I would say my name had been Fishel before my marriage. I would mention Auschwitz in passing and then Reichenbach camp, and see how she reacted.

The next Saturday after I'd served coffee, I mentioned that as a child I'd spent a couple of years in Auschwitz. Frau Müller shook her head in sympathy and said what a terrible experience that must have been for a little girl. She was very sorry, she said, that this had happened to me.

I waited until she had lifted her coffee cup almost to her lips. Then I said, "And after that was over, I went to a camp named Reichenbach."

Without drinking Frau Müller put down her cup. It rattled against the saucer. She did not look at me. Nor did I look at her, but went on talking, helping myself to more coffee.

"Yes," I said. "I arrived in a transport with a group from Auschwitz to work in the factories in nearby Świdnica." And then I started to tell her about this good guard who had called me in and given me clothing, and told me I wasn't Jewish, and that my name was Marie, not Mania.

Frau Müller sat silently and slowly sipped her coffee. Her hand was shaking but she spoke not a word. Finally I said, "Frau Müller, listen, I think you could help me. I want to find this guard; I owe her so much. She was so good to me; she saved my life. She always walked beside me when we went to work in the dark, just in case I fell, so I wouldn't be shot."

Frau Müller didn't move. Her face was like grey stone. She sipped her coffee, slowly, deliberately, wordlessly.

I was getting nowhere. I took another tack. "I know that the German people sometimes were forced to do certain work for the Nazis because the Nazis were so strong. But these people can't admit anything today because there are still people hunting former Nazis. But I wouldn't do that.

I would take this guard under my protection. If only I could find her! I'm not Nazi hunting; it's just between her and me. Maybe you could help me find her."

Now Frau Müller responded full to my face: "Leider kann ich nicht." (Unfortunately I cannot.)

"What a shame," I said. "I'll spend the rest of my life thinking of this good woman, looking for her...you're quite sure?"

Frau Müller stood up and said in a tone that put an end to it: "Es ist ganz unmoglich." (It is completely impossible.) She had never spoken so authoritatively. As she was leaving she said, "I will be going back to Germany soon." And then she added something like, "This has been a very happy time for me."

Before she left for Germany, I took her out to dinner. We were now on a first-name basis. Johanne told me that she had lived with a man for many years, and they had been very happy but he had died. I told her a little about my life after the camps. We had a wonderful time, talking and laughing as women do.

That night when she left me she cried, hugging me like she couldn't help herself. "I've liked you so much from the beginning," she said, leaving me to wonder what she meant by "from the beginning"? "The beginning" when I was a child? Or since she had started cleaning my house? I said nothing. I didn't blame her for not trusting me. I knew who she was.

After she went back to Germany, we wrote to each other for a while. With time that stopped except at Christmas, when we sent each other cards. She never admitted that she knew me as a child, but in her final letter Johanne wrote, "Sie weissen nicht wasfur ein Leben ich hatte." (You do not know what my life has been like. Or: You can't imagine the life I've had.) I couldn't imagine why she'd written something like that. She was the sort of woman who despised self-pity, and she'd never spoken in such a personal way before. I couldn't get rid of the feeling that she was asking me to understand, even forgive.

That seemed to be the end of the story except I couldn't forget her. As the years passed, my need to see her again never left me.

Then out of the blue I was given this chance to go with Maureen and meet Johanne again. Before I die I want so much to know why I lived, and Johanne is the mysterious part of that. If I were really smart, one of those great people you read about like a musician or a doctor, then I'd know. There'd be a reason for my still existing. All I'd like is a clue as to what I'm supposed to be doing with all the time I've been given.

You see, Johanne was the third Nazi who saved my life. Not the first or second Nazi but the third, like there was a chain made up of invisible things, good forces that even the worst Nazis couldn't get control of. When I tell my story maybe you'll see what I mean. Some people will say it was just good luck. But it wasn't. There's no such thing as chance or luck. Chance—it's the end of a long line of things that we don't know anything about.

Anyway, that's how I met Johanne in Toronto in 1977 and in Reichenbach in 1945. And it's why I'm in Germany now. Tomorrow I'll start telling you the whole story. ↔

MAY 1, 2002

I wonder whether Mania can sleep, because I certainly can't. This city of Katowice, a utilitarian mass of old grey buildings, was where Mania was born, lived, first went to school, played with friends, met her first Nazi, and lost her home and her innocence.

My room is again facing the street. It is small but clean with a bed like a boarding school cot, and I'd swear the mattress is made of horsehair. The street slopes, and the old-fashioned trams, built like tanks that could knock down a cathedral, keep grinding down the hill with their square wheels screaming. Is Mania like me, tossing and turning while her mind churns up old memories and new fears?

Shortly before midnight I slip on my gown and walk up to her room on the upper floor. There's no elevator in the building. The light shows under her door. I knock.

The room is full of smoke, and the ashtray overflows with lipstick-marked butts. I remark that the place stinks and I'm going to open the window.

"You think this stinks?" Mania says. "Okay, go ahead. Open the window, stick your head out and breathe in a lungful."

I do as ordered. Two floors below, a row of overflowing garbage cans buzz to high heaven. I close the window, Mania laughs, a husky, satisfied chuckle, and we sit looking at a blank TV screen in silence. She lights another cigarette, coughing all the time, stunning me between her hacks with the news that she'd already had cancer and part of her lung removed.

I don't like the secondhand smoke, but I weigh this against telling a seventy-year-old Holocaust survivor how to behave. I say nothing. After a while Mania remarks that she's wound up over what will happen the next day.

"Maureen said we're going to my old home, where I lived as a child. I want to go and then I don't want to go. Some things I don't remember exactly. Some things I remember like yesterday. But dates and things… God, I was a kid! My memories are patchy. I was thinking that just now, before you came, remembering the place we lived—it was an apartment, big. Big windows. There were heavy drapes but thin silky curtains in the middle, and the sun would come through them. The light would hit the carpet and move around the room, and then other places would become dark and shady."

Mania stubs out her cigarette and stretches for her pack to light another. "That's what my memory's like. Many things I remember as if the sun were lighting them up, but other things…it's crazy, isn't it? But even things that happened years later, I don't remember at all."

It's not crazy, I say. Most children who survived the death camps lived in such fear that their entire attention was focused on surviving from one moment to the next. Always on alert, they scarcely noticed the ordinary routines of life around them, and what they did notice they often had to forget in order to go on living.

"You seem normal to me, Mania," I say.

She looks at me as though I've lost it.

"Normal?" She snorts. "Ach, what's normal? To work, to drive, to mix with people? Yes, I can function normally, and it's not as though I try hard to work at it or that I don't show my real face. You want to know how to get through a life like mine? You make everything simple. Now listen to me, I'm telling you something. You say about everything, 'This is what I know. This is what I don't know. Some people, they are this; some people are not this.' But if I were really normal, I'd be crazy. Do you understand? It would be normal to be crazy. A normal mind with human feelings can't deal with what went on in the death camps. In order to, you must have a sick mind."

I sink into my gown and hug it to me, suddenly chilled as if the air has turned cold, as if Mania's words and memories have stirred life into some stagnant air that, after being sealed for decades in some dank cellar, is now being sucked out, blowing away the dust, revealing memories long buried and forgotten. ↔

20

MAY 2, 2002

The next morning is sharp and clear, with gusts of short-lived showers. Downtown Katowice, despite the busy shoppers and heavy traffic, looks worn out and tired. We finally find somewhere to park and walk to the area where Mania lived before the Germans came and evicted her family. She is quiet and tense as we enter the broad, paved mall with its gracious old buildings facing each other on either side.

Mania's need to come to some peaceful terms with the mystery of her survival is written all over her face. She frowns and searches, looking right and left, fearful she might fail to recognize the remnants of her past. She walks along the mall, feeling for her bearings. At the distant end she recognizes something, a configuration of buildings: the train station. She turns and her eyes sweep a large stone building before her.

"Look!" she cries. "Look! The fruit and flowers!"

Fruit and flowers? What is this? She raises her hand and points, and we all stare, trying to see what she sees.

"Look! The balcony! There! Look! That's it. That's it; that's my home."

Above the transom of one upper-floor window, its French doors opening onto a small balcony, is a concrete garland of fruit and flowers. We all turn to Mania, smiling, but she stands transfixed, unsmiling. Neil sets up his cameras, but a gust of wind brings a cold sweep of rain, and we scatter for shelter under the curved tunnel entrance of Mania's former home. Everything inside the large interior courtyard is dark grey and old—the thick stone walls, the wooden doors, the cobbled yard. A sign over one door advertises wedding gowns, another a pharmacy. We can't go upstairs; the iron gate at the foot of the stairs is locked.

Mania says, "There were no shops here then. But nothing else has changed."

Mania is wrong. The grey stone blocks of the walls and the cobbled courtyard have not changed, but everything else has. There aren't any yellow stars stuck to people's clothing, no signs forbidding the sale of goods to Jews, no armed Wehrmacht soldiers patroling the streets, no one hanging dead from a lamppost. There are no black-robed or black hatted men or kosher shops either. There are no Jews—none—in this once heavily Jewish-populated neighborhood.

We spend all day around the area. Mania strolls the mall, darts in and out of the storefronts, and stops elderly people to speak to them. "Wasn't there a coffeehouse here once?" she asks a very elderly man. His wrinkled face stares into hers; he follows the direction of her pointing hand, shakes his head, and walks on. While this is going on, Neil shoots and Maureen directs.

This afternoon Mania starts telling her story, one that will continue for weeks as we wind our way around Poland and parts of what formerly was Germany.

As Mania speaks, her words and memories often take circuitous routes through different times and places. Again, I've given some sequence to these memories and, occasionally, a date or name that Mania learned only later in life. Apart from this, the story is as Mania told it. For more than a half century these memories have lain hidden in the cortex of her mind. It is not surprising, then, that in dragging them out, the voice in which Mania speaks and the feelings she expresses are often those of the child who buried so much of her own small heart and soul simply in order to live. ↔

MANIA'S STORY

KATOWICE

SPRING 1939

The apartment in which I lived…well, you've seen that now, or at least the outside. It's in the heart of the city, and the railway station is only two blocks away. A very busy area. Even when I was a child there was a constant flow of nearby traffic — cars and a lot of horse-drawn wagons. You've seen what a lovely mall it is—just like when I was a child.

The shops at ground level were small and specialized then, selling things like poultry or coffee or perfumes and ladies' cosmetics. A thin line of trees ran down the center of the mall. There were one or two restaurants, and in the summer people would sit outside under the shade, drinking coffee and reading their newspapers.

Katowice has always been an industrial city, with its money coming from local coal mines. Many of the buildings were blackened with soot, but our four-storied building was well maintained, scrubbed, and grime-free. On our apartment building, as you've already seen, concrete garlands of fruit and flowers, or even symbols of heraldry, decorated the outside walls above the window transoms.

I know some of these things because my mother was very proud of where we lived and often pointed them out to me.

My mother, whom I called Muma, was proud and happy about everything in her life. She was seventeen and working as a waitress when she and my father married, and eighteen when I was born. Often when we were alone together she would point out to me the nice things we had—the thick rugs and the silver coffee set, the goose-down comforter that was part of her trousseau and the oil painting that hung over the fireplace in the dining room.

My father, Bernard Fishel, whom I called Papa, was a lawyer. Even then I somehow sensed Papa would never have made the fuss Muma made about our nice things, because nice things had always been part of his life.

My mother died before I grew up—she was twenty-eight when she was murdered in Gas Chamber 4 in November 1943—so I never had a chance to really get to know her.

Sometimes I find myself so sad, like when I'm digging around the memories of our ten years together, looking for clues as to what she was really like. I know she was very brave, and I know that before the Germans came she was elegant and stylish. She must have had other characteristics that I'll never know about. Still, I speculate, and little scraps of memory tell a lot. For instance, I think maybe my mother made much of our possessions because she was surprised to have such nice things, and because she thought it part of my education. If I appreciated quality, I'd expect it as a wife, and that meant I'd have to marry well. I know that my mother was extremely feminine, though I didn't know the word for it as a child. Despite being short and petite, I remember her in the mornings struggling and pulling, sometimes with my giggling help, as she laced herself into a stiff pink corset. Children sense things more than we think, and I intuitively knew that my father liked her that way, tightly corseted and bound up even in the summer heat.

When she went shopping, Muma would wear gloves and stockings and sometimes place a little hat at a slant, almost over her eye, on top of the curls on her head. Her shoes always had high heels, and again I somehow knew that's also what Papa liked. In cold weather Muma wore a fur with beady little eyes and a hard black snout around her neck, making sure it fell off one shoulder the way ladies wore it.

This was before the Germans came.

Muma wasn't much of a reader. She'd hardly gone to school. She was working in her uncle's restaurant as a waitress when my father met her. I don't remember anything much about my mother's family except they were very poor and might have been observant Jews. My father didn't want me mixing with my cousins. In fact, he despised Muma's family. He would say, "Gelcia"—that's how my mother's name sounded, but I don't know how it was spelled—"I don't want you taking Manuska with you." Manuska was the diminutive of my name. And Muma would tell him I could be just as naughty and bad-mannered as my cousins at times. My father would fling down the newspaper and say he didn't care;

I was not to go or I'd end up being just like "them."

Sometimes Muma took me anyway. I had more clothes than I needed, and Muma gave some to one of her sisters who had a daughter my age. It was the only time I knew Muma to do something behind Papa's back. I know from this that Muma was fond of her sisters and maybe even her parents. But doing what my father wanted, and pleasing him, meant more to her, so I always felt we were doing something wrong when we went. "Don't tell Papa," Muma would say, and I didn't, not because I didn't want to but because Papa's temper scared me.

I don't know if my parents ever went to plays or concerts, but I know they loved the movies and the theatre. The only magazine I remember my mother buying was a movie magazine, *Kino*. It sometimes carried pictures and stories of Shirley Temple, who was my idol. All the city kids in Poland knew about Shirley, and I daydreamed of being like her. I had the same head of curls, although mine were dark brown with a little red. I used to dream at night that I was dancing on the stage in a fluffy dress. I was certain I was going to have a magical life just like Shirley's. All I needed were a few dancing lessons.

Muma was very indulgent with me. She'd clip out pictures of Shirley's dresses and have her dressmaker reproduce them. I had several Shirley dresses and a coat and muff like Shirley wore in *Poor Little Rich Girl*. My favorite dress, and my last one, was the one with a little bolero from *Heidi*. It had a big hem, and Muma kept letting it down and out and patching it. This was the dress I wore to Auschwitz.

Although I was only six or seven, I knew that most of what happened at home and what my mother did was connected to my father. She had girlfriends whom she met for coffee—she always wore stockings and gloves—but apart from that, almost everything else she did in life was for my father.

My mother loved things that way. I understand now that she loved being a woman and a wife and a mother. She treasured the life she had. Her dressing table had a large round mirror, and she would sit in front of it on a little padded stool, looking this way and that as she put on a necklace or adjusted her hat or lightly patted her thick hair. Standing near, I could smell her, soft and sweet. She used face powder and lipstick.

When she emerged into the daylight of the street, women would greet her formally with a slow nod of the head, but the men sometimes would stop and kiss her gloved hand.

I was like all kids: we think our mothers are beautiful. I picked up on my father's pride by the way he looked at her when we went out for dinner, which we did every Saturday night. Muma would go to the hairdresser's in the morning and have her hair washed and set. The hairdresser would pull the sides of her hair straight and up, and then anchor the curls down with lots of bobby pins and a squirt of lacquer. At the time of these memories my mother would have been about twenty-three or twenty-four.

We had a woman working for us. Eva came into the city early each morning on one of the big clanging iron trams from an outlying area where she lived with her parents. She did some housework, but her main job was to watch over me, see to my meals, and walk me to the park every day. Sometimes when I wouldn't eat what was prepared, Muma would tell Eva to get me a ham sandwich on a big bun from a shop in the mall.

Sometimes Eva acted as if she were in charge of me. Most of the time I loved her, but when she became bossy I hated her. One day, when I'd been given another new Shirley Temple dress, Eva told my mother it was not good to give children so much. I always remember what my mother said: "Mania is our little princess, and I want her to have everything a princess can have." It should have spoiled me, but somehow those words strengthened me, and, although I'm an old woman now, I love to say them to myself.

I didn't know that we were Jews. My parents were totally assimilated and virtually nonobservant. I faintly remember my father going to the synagogue sometimes, maybe for Yom Kippur. I don't know exactly but sometimes he went, and this made his parents happy and that's why he did it. My mother was more ritualistic, although we weren't really religious at all. But I think she observed Shabbat in small ways because I remember her lighting candles sometimes, and when that happened we'd have cholnt, a sort of stew, and grated potato. Because other people in our building did the same thing, I didn't connect it with religion.

Nothing was ever explained to me about Yahweh or Judaism. If I thought anything it was simply that my mother liked candlelight and cholnt. Being Jewish or Christian meant nothing to me. All the children played together and went to school together, and all the public schools were Christian, mainly Catholic.

One day every week, it was probably Saturday, we had a late breakfast, a leisurely time with my parents that gave me a deep sense of security and peace. For many months of the year a coal fire burned in the grate. It was Eva's job every morning to empty the fine grey ash, which fell into a pan below the grate. In summer Muma would pull the heavy curtains halfway across the French doors to keep out the sun and heat.

Each season had its own small memories and sense of peace. One scene stuck: I can see the three of us in the dining room, my mother standing to pour my father's coffee and my father looking down the table at my plate to see what I'd eaten. I never ate enough to please him. Often I could hear my playmates in the courtyard below, skipping rope, and the only thing I wanted was to join them.

"Eat your breakfast, Manuska," Papa would say. Then Mama would add, "Eat, darling, eat." I'd take a nibble of cheese or break off a crumb of bread roll and then push my plate away. Then Papa would put some food on a plate and hand it to me and say, "March!" ordering me out of the room. It was supposed to be a punishment, but it was what I'd hoped he would do. I'd dump the food in the kitchen and dance down the stairs to join my friends in the courtyard below. I often did this. That's why it's a clear memory when so much else has been forgotten.

I knew what my parents would talk about after I'd gone because sometimes I'd stay outside the door, listening. This way I learned that my father had wanted a boy, not a girl. Knowing I wasn't as important as a boy didn't bother me. I adored my father, although I was scared of him sometimes because he'd explode. But I always felt loved. I didn't think boys were any better than girls, so I was very happy being a girl.

Often my parents would talk about things I didn't understand, but their talk was mostly about me; that's why I loved to listen. When my parents had an "adult" discussion, they always sent me out of the room, downstairs to play, or to my room if it was night. Normally they spoke

Polish, but if they had to talk in front of me they spoke Yiddish, which they refused to teach me.

"No wonder she's so small and sickly. She never eats," Papa would say.

And then for some reason my mother would mention her sister, Rosa, and say things like, "I don't know why you have to see Rosa so often."

And Papa would always reply, "Simply because she's a nurse, and Manuska is so often sick."

And Mama would say again, "But why do you have to meet her?" And Papa would reply, "Because she knows about medical things; perhaps she can help."

Somehow in my child's mind this connected with an image of my mother standing silhouetted against the long drapes, a strange expression on her face as she watched through a darkening window, waiting for my father to come home. "Papa's late for supper again" was all she'd say. I think this is probably the clearest memory I have of her, maybe because with the soft fading light and food set out on the lace-topped table, I felt so cozy and secure.

Years later, while I was working in the fields at a kibbutz and remembering times past, my parents' whispered talks about Aunt Rosa stirred in my memory. And I realized with a shock—for by then I was a young woman—that maybe my father had been having an affair with Rosa.

You might feel that a suspicion like this dishonors my father. But all I know of my family is from scattered images, and every scrap of remembrance is sacred to me. I remember when my father's two brothers, Vilek and Motek, came to say good-bye. They were going to a place far away called Palestine. They came at night. I was sent to bed after I'd hugged them, but I knew they were talking about the man called Hitler.

My uncles said Hitler was mad, that one day he would cause war in Europe.

The thing that brought Papa greatest pride was being a reserve officer in the Polish cavalry. (Years later I learned that a Jew could not be a regular officer.) Papa said that if the Germans entered Poland, the cavalry would drive them back to Berlin in a week.

When Papa said that, Motek shouted, "Can't you see what is right under your nose!" I thought that was a funny thing to say. What did it mean to have something right under your nose?

A few nights later Muma must have said something to my father about us going to Palestine too. I heard my father say he didn't want to leave Poland. He sounded angry and said things like, "Leave here? Leave Poland? Because of Hitler? And go to what?" He said he'd worked very hard and it had all been for Muma and me. "Am I supposed to just forget my business? To do what?" He then said something I couldn't understand about digging rocks up in the desert. Muma kept trying to interrupt, not as if she was angry, too, but as if she wanted Papa to stop talking about it.

At about this time Papa, who thought of himself solely as a Pole who loved the Polish cavalry, started wearing his officer's uniform a lot. "Glorious" was the word he always used when he told me about the bravery of the men and the beautiful, charging horses. Except for the horses, I wasn't interested, but I always listened quietly because I knew he'd wanted a son and a son would have listened quietly. Muma didn't like it when he put his uniform on, although before everything changed she'd seemed to be proud of it.

In the summer of 1939, not long after I'd turned seven and started school, my life began to change. Something was happening that the adults didn't want me to know about.

On Sundays we would go to my father's parents, whom I called Bubsha and Tete, in Sosnowitz, a town about twenty minutes away by tram. They lived on the upper level of a solid stone building, which they owned, at 199 Cesna Street. The building, on a broad boulevard not far from the Athletic Field in the center of Sosnowitz, is still there—even the shops downstairs, which my grandparents rented out. The tram from Katowice ran down the boulevard.

I don't remember how either of my grandparents looked, but when I think of them, the same feelings always swell up in me. When I think of Tete, I am filled with a sense of gentleness and calmness, and when I think of Bubsha there's a feeling of sweetness but also a sense that I should be alert, straighten my back, and get busy. Tete worked as a clerk in the courts, I think, but my grandmother was a businesswoman. She had built a good business with scrap metal. I remember workers with wagons loaded with all sorts of bits and pieces of scrap iron coming down the lane and dumping it on a block of land she owned.

Going to my grandparents' home was always a thrilling adventure. One particular Sunday visit stands out. I was wearing a new Shirley Temple dress, and I couldn't wait to show it to Bubsha. After we'd stepped off the tram, I skipped ahead, greedy for the kisses and fuss my arrival would cause. But Bubsha barely glanced at me. She kissed Muma lightly and seized hold of Papa, saying how glad she was to see him. I tugged at Bubsha's hand and said, "Look, my new dress."

"Yes, yes," said Bubsha. "It's beautiful."

Then she gave me a "special" coloring book and told me to go into the kitchen and make some pictures. I knew it wasn't special. Kids know right away when adults aren't being straight with them. I knew they were talking about secrets they didn't want me to hear. I closed the kitchen door with just enough noise to make them think I'd gone inside. Then I opened it quietly and crept to the parlor door.

My mother was crying, because I could hear little sniffs, and Bubsha's voice was very calm, telling Papa not to go. Go where? And then Papa's voice was saying he'd made up his mind. And then Tete said, as he always did, that everything that happened was God's will. Sometimes when he said that Bubsha would sigh; other times she would nod yes, yes, because she believed too.

In the kitchen I hurriedly colored in a picture. I wanted to know what was going on, but when I walked back into the parlor, holding it out for praise, the adults looked up, staring as if they'd forgotten I was there. My ego must have been bigger than I was because I burst into tears. Papa angrily ordered me back to the kitchen. Muma and Bubsha said nothing.

Something really terrible was happening.

Nobody cared about my tears anymore. ↔

KATOWICE

Sometimes when it became very hot, we left town and stayed at a lake in the countryside. But in the summer of 1939 we stayed home.

Eva and I still went for daily walks in the park, and Muma still had her hair done on Saturday morning and we still went out for dinner at night. But all the adults seemed tired and cranky, and all they ever talked about was trying to find meat or oil or coal. That and the Volkdeutsch, Polish citizens of German origin.

No one fussed over me anymore or took too much notice of what I was doing or saying. The adults still sent me out of the room or made signals to one another not to talk in front of me. I felt so angry and humiliated when they did this. I knew what it was all about. Everyone was frightened of the German army, the Wehrmacht. They said if it entered Poland there'd be a war. I imagined the Wehrmacht as a terrible monster, big and black, and although I wasn't sure what war was, it sounded exciting and terrible.

"If the Germans dared set foot in Poland, the cavalry would drive them back to Berlin in a week," Papa said proudly. He often said that, and it drove Muma mad. She never said a word in reply; she just sat there and looked at my father with her mouth shut tight.

One day notices were put up all around town telling men to join their battalions. These notices made Bubsha really angry. She said it was just a trick.

"The government didn't put them up. It was those German lovers, the Volkdeutsch," she said. "They want all our men out of the city so there will be no one left here to defend it."

Soon after the notices went up we left Katowice. My mother told me about it afterwards, and I can't separate what she told me from the few things I do remember. I do know one thing: the adults were sad, but I was jumping with excitement. My life had always been fun and this was another adventure. I was seven years old.

We left in the middle of the night. Papa locked up our apartment as we made our way down the steel stairs and into the broad tunnel entrance that opened onto the street. A horse and carriage—more of a buggy than a carriage, was waiting. We squeezed into it, and Muma covered our laps with rugs. Papa, in uniform, rode beside us on his motorcycle. I asked where we were going.

"East," my mother said. "East, to the Russian border."

We could have been going to the moon, I was so excited. I snuggled under the rug, so I could see little but the back of the horse and smell its warm, sweaty backside. Clip, clop, clip, clop. After a while the shops and houses thinned out. We reached a big road. Hundreds of people were pouring into it from all over the city, and our carriage slowed to walking pace. When Muma told Bubsha we'd left too late, she sounded scared.

I fell asleep, and when I awoke the sun had arisen. We were on a country road, stopping and starting all the time. The road was blocked with people and prams and carts and old carriages. The dust was so thick that we held cloths to our mouths. Old people were sitting on the dried grass by the side of the road. They seemed too tired to go on. Tete had put his blue and white shawl around his shoulders and held a book in his hands. Muma told me to hush, that Tete was saying his prayers.

Papa had gone on ahead, and I watched him as he bounced back on his motorbike across a dried-out field. When he approached, he ordered the driver to get off the road and return home. He shouted to us in the wagon something like, "We'll never make it. There's not a chance we'll get to the Russian border. We'll have to go back." So we went back to Katowice.

One day very soon after this I was in the courtyard when one of my playmates ran in from the mall and shouted, "Come and see what I see!" I raced down the mall to the street at the railway station end. A small crowd was standing, still and quiet, looking down the street.

Two motorbikes with sidecars had turned a corner about four blocks away. They moved slowly down the center of the road.

A woman ran out of a nearby apartment. She pushed me to the side, shouting, "The Germans are coming! The Germans are coming!"

Everyone I knew seemed to dislike Germans, so I was surprised this woman seemed happy. I stood staring while the two motorbikes moved along, slowly, as if they owned the place. By the time they'd reached us, the woman had a bunch of flowers in her hand. She threw it onto the road in front of the motorbikes and smiled and shouted at the two men in uniform.

I was very excited because now I knew something about the Germans my parents didn't know. I ran back home, bounded up the stairs, burst into the room, and shouted, "The Germans are here! The Germans are here!"

I felt important and happy and ran back down again to see more Germans. But before I reached the bottom stair, Papa had come after me and half picked me up. I didn't know what I'd done wrong and started to yell for Muma, but Papa had already undone his belt and pulled it from his pants and was slashing my legs and bottom. He told me to get upstairs, and I ran up screaming. Muma was coming down, and I flung myself into her arms.

Papa ordered Muma to keep me inside and not to let me out again. I didn't know what a scouting party was, but that's probably what the Germans were. Papa seemed shocked and confused, shouting at Muma to get his things out. He'd never beaten me like that before. He'd been angry occasionally and smacked me, but it was nothing like using his belt.

I ran up the stairs wailing, holding up my dress to show the red welts on my legs to Bubsha and Tete. But they didn't care because they were following my father as he rushed out the door, and we all ran downstairs after him to say good-bye. He was racing off, just a few city blocks ahead of the German scouts, to join his regiment in Lublin. He was still shouting at Muma not to let me out. He was frightened of something — I didn't know what. He kissed me, and that's all I remember of him—the softness of his cheeks, the deep purple-blue of his eyes, and the faint smell of tobacco and cologne.

Later that day or maybe the next, we heard distant deep rumbles like a coming storm. Soon after that German tanks and troops were in the streets of Katowice. What happened after that is a muddle in my head, but I remember Muma and Bubsha and Tete crouched over the radio because bombs were being dropped over Poland's western cities and all the airports had been blown away. Then Hitler declared war on us. ↝

KATOWICE

Mania is totally exhausted. She doesn't appear at dinner, so Maureen and I go to her room. She is already in bed. Already smoking. We arrange for food, but she only picks at it. I'm horrified when Mania casually says that it's her heart. She's not only had a part of one lung removed but her heart is also weak.

This night her sparkle has died down. We sit on the floral cotton cover of her bed and wait. Finally she says apologetically, blotting her eyes and half laughing, "Excuse me…just a moment…" as if she has no right to cry, no right to cause anyone the slightest discomfort. "It's just that Muma… her life was so short…if Papa had known what was ahead for her…"

After a long pause Mania continues, "Later on in Israel I asked my uncle if something had happened between Papa and my aunt Rosa. She was younger than Muma by about two years and very pretty. I must have been about seven, but children pick up everything. And my uncle, Papa's brother, said, 'Yes, your father and Rosa had an affair.'"

Mania's intuitions as a child must have been exquisitely honed to have picked up on the triangle existing between her mother, father, and aunt Rosa. Yet I'm disgusted that Mania's uncle had revealed the secret sins of his dead brother. How did he think Mania would feel on learning for certain that her father, pampered and adored by his doomed wife, was unfaithful? And with his wife's sister! Couldn't he simply have lied and spared Mania the knowledge that her clearest memory of her mother, standing by the curtain, watching and waiting in the twilight, wasn't that of an adoring wife waiting for her beloved to come home but the pathetic picture of a loving woman experiencing the pain of betrayal?

I sit by Mania's bed and say nothing, inhaling secondhand smoke along with her silence. I reason I wasn't there, didn't know all the facts, and acknowledge that maybe Mania's uncle had done the right thing. Truth always has its own value, I told myself. It's best to feel its pain and find a way to deal with it rather than live with a false image that comforts. And in this case, if Mania's uncle had denied it, laughed, and told Mania she'd imagined it, what might that have done to her precious trove of ragtag memories and her reliance on the value of her powerful intuition?

Maureen and I walk down the dimly lit stairs back to our rooms. Finally I say, "Maybe knowing that her Dad was no saint, just an ordinary guy capable of cheating on his wife, gives Mania a truer, richer picture. You know, instead of a little girl's picture of a pure and shining knight. It's got to be worth something—truth instead of fantasy."

Maureen looks at me askance. "I wish. But I doubt it." ↦

KATOWICE

After the Germans arrived, a woman in our apartment building told my mother that the Germans were going to register all Jews. Bubsha came over, and she and Muma sat in the parlor talking quietly about Jews not being allowed to ride on the trams or trains any more. I listened to all this adult talk and thought it was silly.

"The Germans wouldn't do that," I announced. "How could anyone get anywhere?"

No one had ever told me, "We are Jews." No one had ever said, "We are Jews, and the German Nazis hate Jews." Instead, both Muma and Bubsha looked at me in silence. I felt that something quite apart from the war was happening that I didn't know anything about. When Bubsha told Muma to go to the bank and take out all the money she and Papa had, I knew it for certain.

"I'd have to ask Bernard first," Muma said.

"Nonsense, Gelcia. We're not even sure where he is or how to contact him. Do it now or you'll find yourself without a zloty."

Still Muma shook her head. I wanted to support Muma and tell Bubsha that Muma never did anything that Papa didn't like. I tugged at Bubsha's sleeve, but she ignored me and finally gave little jerks of her elbow to toss me off. She was getting really mad with Muma.

"Get your savings out now! Forge Bernard's signature if you have to. Yes, forge it! Don't look at me like that, Gelcia! Those devils are just beginning. They're going to take away all we have just as they've done to Jews in their own country."

It was new for me to hear Bubsha speak like that as she was always calm and practical. She often told Muma what to do and Muma always did it.

My mother dressed and went off in a hurry. Soon she was back.

"They won't let me take out anything," she cried. "Nothing. And it's our money! Those damned Germans—I have to get their permission, fill out a form, to get anything."

She started to cry.

I tugged at her hand. Nobody was telling me anything. I knew they were trying to "protect" me because I'd heard them saying that, but I felt left out of everything.

"Why can't you get Papa's money?" I asked.

Muma wheeled on me. "Stop it! Just keep quiet!" she snapped.

Day by day my world was sliding away.

One day, two weeks after the Germans had arrived, I was playing with friends in the courtyard when a neighbor, Pani Opolski, tapped me on the shoulder and told me to go upstairs, that my mother needed me. Going up I could hear my mother through the open kitchen window that was above the corner of the courtyard. I hated the sounds she was making. Once I'd seen a dog run over and it was the same sort of sounds.

Bubsha and Tete were in the living room. They were bent and clutching each other as if they were going to fall over. Bubsha let go of Tete and came at me with open arms, grabbing me and half-falling into a chair. She started crooning and I hated it. Crooning and talking and crying "oiy, oiy, oiy," like I'd heard peasant women wail when their barrow of vegetables fell over.

Papa was dead. Killed near Lublin eight days after the war started. I remembered a dead girl in a house down the street. She'd been laid out in the front room, all dressed in white like a bride with a crown of flowers around her head and candles lit on both sides. I tried to imagine Papa lying down, maybe with candles by him.

I wanted to wriggle out of Bubsha's arms and run back downstairs. I managed to squeeze out some tears because I knew I should, but I couldn't feel anything except wanting to get away because the noises the adults were making scared me—my mother yelping in the bedroom and Bubsha moaning in the living room, and Tete swinging back and forth like a piece of loose wire in the wind, saying over and over something I would hear so often in the future that I finally knew it by heart: "Yisgadal ve yiskadash shmei rabba." (May His name be exalted and sanctified.)

After a bit I went downstairs. Germans were in the streets. That made the streets dangerous, but I didn't know why and I couldn't understand why the Germans didn't like me. I'd never done anything to them. I stayed in the courtyard and knocked on one of the doors for my friends to join me in play. My friend's mother half-opened the door and peered out. Behind her stood my friend. And then the mother closed the door quietly and quickly in my face.

What was happening?

Since Papa left I'd been sleeping in my parents' bed with Muma, but that night she wouldn't let me. The dark scared me, but now there was not even a night-light. I thought about Papa being dead and wondered how long people were dead for. I couldn't connect "dead" with Papa.

Sometime after—it could have been a day or it could have been a month—I came across one of my father's jackets, probably in a closet. It smelled like him, and the smell made me cry. It was just the smell—nothing else, a mix of cigarettes and the cologne he used to pat on his cheeks—that made me cry. I didn't understand you were dead forever. My mother heard me and came out of her bedroom. She was crying, too, and that night I stayed in her bed.

A week later Muma received a letter from Papa. She sat with it for a long time before she opened it. A piece of a bomb had gone into his spine. He was dying when he asked a nurse to write the letter for him.

⚘

I'm fearful of interrupting but I must find out.

"Mania, this letter. Did your mother ever say what was in it?"

I'm wildly, stupidly hoping Mania might still have it, a locked-away treasure in her Toronto home. I'm hoping she'll say the letter was filled with love and that Bernard might have told Gelcia that she was his only true love, that Rosa meant nothing. Maybe even in dying he might have asked his wife's forgiveness.

"My mother never told me," Mania said. "Just that Papa had shrapnel in his spine and it was infected, and because he couldn't walk anymore he knew he'd die. Muma kept the letter and read it often. When we were driven into a ghetto, she sewed it into the hem of her skirt. But when we reached Auschwitz we all had to undress and we never got our clothes back."

⚘

I don't remember much else about this time, although I know that Muma sold Papa's brushes and all his clothes to get some money. There were men and women on the streets, selling things from their homes. The Germans would only let Muma take a few zolty out of the bank. Things hardly got better after we were issued ration cards. There was never enough food, but at least we got a share, even though Jews only received half the food rations the Poles did, and the Poles received only half the rations the Germans did.

Eva stopped coming, so Muma did the housework and she hated it—not that she was lazy but it meant she'd lost the life she'd loved. She worked at it like a madwoman, scrubbing and cleaning and half crying. We couldn't buy soap or cleaning stuff; it was just a matter of using water and rags.

There was a lot of talk about registering, and when Muma read that Jews who did not register would be "severely punished," she registered herself and me. It was then I asked her what being a Jew was. She said that we were Jews, but that we were really just Polish. Being a "real" Jew was something very special, but we'd never really been Jews "like that."

I didn't understand what Muma meant. I protested that I wanted to be something "very special." Muma sighed and said she'd explain when I was older, but I was in Israel by then and she was dead.

When Muma went out searching for food, she always took me with her. She never left me alone and, anyway, I'd become frightened of being by myself. Everything was strange on the streets. It was cold and quiet. The Germans had stopped Jews from selling anything. They strolled around as if they owned the place. Muma never looked at the Germans. She was frightened of them and despised them.

When we saw people we knew, we just hurried by without a word because the Germans wouldn't let Jews talk to each other on the street. I was used to going to the park, but Jews weren't allowed in. Years later I saw a photo of the notice they had stuck on the entrance. It read, "Juden Eintritt in die Parkanlagen Verboten." (No Jews allowed in this park.) We couldn't ride on the trams either. We had to walk everywhere, even if we were very tired while the trams went by half empty. One day we went to the library to get warm because our apartment was freezing, and a nasty woman stopped Muma from going in. Muma grabbed me and almost ran home.

After Hannukah and Christmas passed, we were thrown out of our home. That's one night I remember well.

Muma and I were in bed in the dark, dressed and covered with blankets to keep warm. We weren't allowed to put the lights on at night. Muma was telling me a story about Shirley Temple. I knew these stories so well that I'd correct Muma if she made a mistake. I loved hearing every word about this magical little girl who was just like me but rich and loved by everyone and lived in America.

I asked things such as whether Shirley had a pony. Muma always knew.

"A beautiful pony," Muma said. "Brown like chestnuts with a cream mane and tail."

I imagined the pony. I saw myself sitting on it. "Does the pony live with her? What's the pony's name?"

My mother ran her hands through my curls. I don't know whether she really did, but that's how I felt her closeness—a warm, reassuring feeling of her fingers running through my curls. "Star is his name. And he lives in a little stable at the back of Shirley's house so that every morning she can look down from her bedroom and wave hello to him."

"Is Star a boy or a girl?"

My mother didn't answer. She sat up and put her hand across my mouth. She listened. I heard it, too—heavy boots clanging on the stairs. A banging on our door.

"Out of bed. Out! Stay by me. Don't move!" Muma said.

The banging was loud and impatient.

"Ich komm, ich komm," my mother called out in German. Only Germans banged like that. "Ich komm sofort."

Muma felt on the bedside table for the flashlight, knocked it off, and crouched down on the floor in a panic searching for it. She half ran to the door and opened it.

Two soldiers stood there. One was an officer. Muma pulled me against her skirt, squeezing me so hard it hurt.

The Germans pushed their way in. "Pull the curtains and turn on the lights," the officer ordered. My mother did as she was told. Her face was white.

"Wo ist ihr Mann?" the officer asked. (Where's your husband?)

Muma just stood there. She couldn't speak. She had her hand on my shoulder, and her nails were digging into my neck. The officer in the grey jacket and pants shaped like the ones Papa wore for riding asked Muma again where her husband was. Muma still couldn't speak.

So I piped up, "Papa ist tot." (My father's dead.) I wanted to say, "You killed him," but I didn't think Muma would like me to. Besides, maybe this wasn't the same soldier who'd thrown the bomb.

Then Muma spoke, "My husband is dead."

The officer looked at her and checked his clipboard again. And then he said we had to leave our apartment. "You are to resettle in Sosnowitz."

Muma just stood and stared at him.

He went on listing what we were allowed to take. Our clothes and something to sleep on and some dishes and pots to cook with. We were given eighteen hours to get out. He finished with a warning that if Muma took anything else she'd be punished.

My mother was frightened but she was also angry. Muma had a lot of spirit, and in her own home she couldn't hold it down.

"This is my home," she said quietly. "I have a child. Where will I go?"

"Eighteen hours," the officer said and snapped the clipboard shut.

But Muma still stood there, staring at the man and then around the apartment. "But where? Where in Sosnowitz? You mean, just leave here? Leave everything?"

The officer looked at Muma, expressionless. "Haven't you heard the order? Obey it and you'll be all right." They were always like that, always sliding some threat, some fear, into everything they said. At the door he turned and said, "Attempt to remove anything other than what is permitted and you will be severely punished."

Muma, who couldn't bear to look at German soldiers, moved towards him.

"When will I get it back, my home…these are family things, valuable…everything I have is here." She looked around the room in a sort of wonder, as if she'd never really seen it before—Papa's chair by the fire-place, the black cigarette box, the rose-colored glass vase, the pewter candlesticks. Maybe she realized then she was going to lose it all.

The SS officer's eyes swept the room. He checked his clipboard again, satisfying himself, and then said, "We will see that your possessions are well taken care of."

Then he left.

We got back into bed. Muma was trembling, and this time I held her.

We could hear more banging on the doors down the hall. ↦

SOSNOWITZ

We have arrived in Sosnowitz. It's a perfect day for shooting: clear, crisp, and dry.

With Maureen, Neil, Mania, and I are Piotr, a local sports broadcaster whose perfect English enables him to work as a translator, and Mr. Szaniawski, a historian who specializes in the German occupation of this part of Poland. Both Piotr and Mr. Szaniawski are in their thirties, but they could have been born on different planets in different centuries. Piotr is magazine-handsome and single, and chuckles when asked about his girlfriend—a kind of "which one?" chuckle. He wears sweaters and jeans, often travels abroad as a sportscaster, and calls newly introduced people by their first name. Mr. Szaniawski is a black-suited academic who bends slightly forward respectfully to listen as you speak. He wears glasses and is soft spoken and given to kissing women's hands. He glows softly when he speaks of his wife, daughter, and home. "Very modest, my home, yes, modest by your standards." He goes on smiling as if he and happiness are intimates.

We stand in a small group beside a large grey stone building that fronts a broad boulevard and tram line. To its side is an unpaved lane with wild berry-bearing hedges on each side. Neil starts taking shots of the scripted name above the building's main door. The address is 199 Cesna Street, and the name reads "Fishel." The Fishels were Bubsha and Tete, Mania's paternal grandparents, and the top floor of this building was their home. The downstairs is rented out as four shops, and Mania says this was the case when she was a child.

The old trams clang by, packed with people sitting bolt-upright on the hard, stiff seats. The tram stop is not far from where we stand, but the few people who spill out hurry by our cameras without comment. But there is an audience of one. Upstairs, to the right across the lane from the Fishel's house, an old man stands in front of lace curtains, smoking and watching our every move. Leaning forward, he flicks the ash of his cigarette onto the street. Was he here then, a watching child, the day the Fishels set out in their best clothes and disappeared forever?

We walk about one hundred yards down the lane and come to a back road paved with scattered housing.

This is Vieska Street, and Mania wanders off to the right, looking for number fourteen. There is only one unnumbered house that could have served as an apartment, and it's a shoddy, rundown affair but it's located on the spot Mania's memory has chosen. She looks bewildered and protests, "This is the place; this isn't the house. It was better than this." Its shabbiness appals her and she falls silent. It's not that she's simply quiet; she seems to be somewhere else.

I look back down the lane at her grandparents' building. Trams clang by; people go in and out of the shops and stand under the plaque marked "Fishel" and chat and smoke. The life that hums around its grey block walls doesn't affect my feeling that I'm looking at a mausoleum. Perhaps Mania in her unusual silence is feeling this too, feeling that time is reaching out and pulling us back into a lost, unimaginable world that will leave, for better or worse, a lifelong mark on anyone who enters it. ↦

SOSNOWITZ

SPRING 1941

Bubsha found us a little apartment on Vieska Street, down a lane near to where she and Tete lived on Cesna Street. The apartment has two rooms with a kitchen sink and a tiny bathroom with a sort of tub for a bath. Muma said the Germans made twenty thousand people move to Sosnowitz, so we were lucky to have anything.

Life seemed almost normal except we were hungry all the time. I went to school every day, and my mother went to work as a file clerk in a tool factory, which everyone thought was an excellent job because the Germans could have made her work anywhere. The Germans ran everything, and Muma could type and wrote and spoke perfect German. After school, I waited for Muma at my grandparents' home.

Bubsha always gave me something to eat. Although I don't remember her face, that I do remember. I suspect she gave me some of her own food because sometimes I'd see her crouched forward as if she was having cramps. You did that when you were really hungry, before you started to actually starve.

I was nine by now but still wore two of my old Shirley Temple dresses. We had no money for clothes, but there was nothing to buy anyway. Bubsha had let out both my dresses and used some old fabric to create new hems. My "Heidi" dress was like a magical cloak: whenever I put it on I still felt the same flood of happy dreams. I could be like Shirley Temple, with no German soldiers and my own pony. Yes, Muma said, as soon as the Germans left I was going to have dancing lessons.

After a few weeks in Sosnowitz, the Germans closed all schools to Jewish children. So Muma and all the other parents got together and opened their own secret schools in private homes and tiny apartments. I found it hard. I'd liked the school I'd been at and had friends there. But even these secret schools didn't last for long.

One day the Germans put up notices "inviting" all Jews to register. I was at my grandparents when Muma came home and told Bubsha and Tete about it. I remember this incident very well because my grandmother put on such a fuss.

"An invitation? What does that mean? It's a trick!" she declared. She was very pink. "Stay away from the Germans! Don't register. We're not going, and you're not going either."

Bubsha clattered around the dining room table as she said this, shuffling dishes and moving this and that, breathing hard as if she were angry. Then she said to Muma as if thinking aloud, "I have some friends, Polish from the time of the Cossacks, Christians but real Christians. They live in a small village behind Sosnowitz. I want you to take Manuska and hide there while we wait and see what happens to the people who register. I'll let you know when it's safe to come back. But stay until you hear from me."

Muma said it wasn't possible. She'd be reported if she didn't show up for work and then the Germans would come. But Bubsha had already thought of that.

"Listen. Go into the office and see your boss," she said. "He's a cursed Nazi, but he likes you and he needs you. He won't want anyone going after you. Tell him your child has measles—something contagious so he won't want you around. It's unlikely anyone will check; they'll be too busy registering."

Late the next day Muma and I left. The sun was going down, and I hated the coming dark. Since I was a baby I'd been terrified. I'd lie in bed and scream if I had had a nightmare. I'd be too frightened to get out of bed and go to my parents' room.

Muma led me through side streets and then onto a country road full of potholes and mud. We didn't talk. Muma had told me not to say a word. The Germans had imposed a curfew, and she was scared of running into someone. But the only things around were fields and trees.

The village wasn't far. It was nothing more than a few wooden huts on the edge of the fields. No lights, nothing. Everything looked rickety, as if the whole village was about to fall over.

Muma went straight to a hut and knocked gently. The door partly opened and a hand pulled her in. Then the door closed quickly behind us. There was an old bent couple there—real peasants. I'd seen old people like them in town, pushing wooden barrows piled with vegetables. There was just one room in the hut, and it was all dark except for a flickery lamp that showed a make-do mattress on the floor. The old lady told us we couldn't go out except at night to the toilet behind the house. By now I'd learned not to trust anyone: if we were seen, someone might tell the Germans.

The darkness of the house terrified me. I had a strong feeling of being dragged into a hole. There was something awful in the air. Muma and I stumbled in the darkness to the outhouse. The smell told us where it was. Then we went back to the hut, and Muma told me to take my skirt and sweater off and she undressed as well. I suppose the old people had undressed because soon we could hear them snoring and whinnying like little horses.

I couldn't sleep and asked Muma where we were. She said she didn't know the village, but we had to be patient. "Bubsha will tell us when to go back."

All day we stayed inside. I'd never seen such a poor place—just a rough wooden table and chairs, a big bed, our straw mattress on the floor, and a wood stove. The water was pumped from a well outside, and the only other thing was a string of wrinkled roots hanging on the wall and a crucifix on the crossbeams. The crucifix with the dead man Jesus hanging there didn't bother me because almost every building had one.

I remember the old woman, small like me but with no teeth. She always had a broom in her hand, sweeping the dirt floor, but I knew she wasn't a witch. Her eyes twinkled when she smiled. I could feel her kindness, but the hut terrified me. She could see I was scared. In the morning she patted my head and told us we were safe, that the Germans wouldn't bother an old couple who raised goats and sold their cow's milk for vegetables.

When it got dark, the creepy feeling I had about the place grew and grew until I felt I was choking. I told my mother, "It's bad here. Something's bad. I want to go home."

"Don't say that again." Muma was sharp. She sounded scared. When

Muma said something like that, I definitely listened to her. So I tried to say nothing.

We stayed another day, and all the while this sick feeling was building up inside me, so I said to her the next night, "Please, Muma, don't make me stay. I'm going to Bubsha to find out if we can go back."

Muma got angry. "Are you out of your mind? You don't know anything. You don't even know where we are."

"I don't care," I said. "I can't stay here anymore."

The feeling of badness, of evil, was filling me up. I jumped up. I opened the door. Before my mother could move, I ran out into the dark. I didn't feel anything. I wasn't scared. I didn't know where I was going, yet somehow I knew where to go. So help me God, to this day I swear someone was running with me, guiding me, leading me. I ran down the street and flew into the fields.

I don't know how long I ran. I just went—past trees, over fields—with no fear of being alone because I didn't feel I was alone. I felt like there was someone at my side, someone as powerful and loving as an angel. There were no lights anywhere because of the blackout, but I could see the outline of a building against the sky, and then I was in town, still running as if a propeller had gotten into me. And finally I recognized a street and knew it was near Bubsha's street.

I ran up the back stairs and knocked on Bubsha's door. She opened it and gave a small scream.

"What are you doing here? Get inside. Quick! Where's your mother? What's happened? Who came with you?"

"Nobody. We want to come back. Muma's all right. What happened to the people who went when the Germans asked them to?"

"The people? Mania, who came with you? Were you followed? Mania …stop tugging at me! What people? Ah, those people. None came back, the Germans took them all. To a family camp. To work. Now a transport's gone. It's probably safe here for a while. But you must go back to the village as soon as it's light, just to be sure…for a few more days. Manuska, are you sure you weren't followed?"

"Yes." I laughed. I was so pleased with myself. "Bubsha, I ran too fast for anyone to follow me."

"I hope, I hope. Now listen to me, you bold little girl, my darling. You go back first thing in the morning and this time you stay."

"No," I said.

My heart skipped a beat. I'd never spoken to Bubsha like that before.

I got out of the house before she could stop me and started running. Again I had the same feeling—that someone was with me, making me run and taking away all my fear.

At the village, I crept into the hut by the back door. Muma was sitting on the mattress. She leaped up, shook me, squeezed me to her.

"Mania! God, where were you?" She was screeching. "What are you doing? What has happened to you?" She held me at arm's length and stared into my face as if she thought I was possessed. "Tell me, tell me, who's with you? Did you find Bubsha? What is going on with you?"

Questions tumbled out of her.

I said, "Muma, pack! Quick! Don't talk! I can't stay here another minute."

My mother started saying something, but I wasn't the same child. I was giving the orders. I was not possessed, as Muma thought. Yet a strange power seemed to be filling me. I said again, "Throw everything in the case. Just come."

And she did. But she said, "We must thank them." That's just a scrap of memory but so precious. Always give thanks; I learned it that night. I could see the old leathery couple, with the bent-over woman muttering a blessing, but I had no time for that stuff. I pulled Muma out of the hut.

Outside she whispered, "Where are we? I don't know where we are." She was scared.

I said, "Just come," and took her by the hand. Again I had this guiding feeling in me, which I don't understand to this day. And I'm sorry if I can't make it clear because I myself, and nobody else, can understand how and why I acted as I did that night.

We got to Bubsha's house. She made us some sort of hot water drink, and we went to bed and fell asleep.

I woke up with a start. It was still dark, but someone was banging on the door. Then came a shrieking sound. It came from the kitchen. Muma ordered me to stay in bed, but I jumped out and followed her.

The daughter of the old couple was sitting in a heap on the floor, sobbing and wailing, "They've killed them, killed my Muma and Papa. We were betrayed. Someone in the village betrayed us. They knew you were there. Those Nazi dogs came to our hut with machine guns and shouted for the Jews to come out. 'Raus, Juden, sofort! Raus, raus!' They kicked in the door and fired. Kept spraying their guns around and around. Killed Muma and Papa in their bed and kept shooting. Walked out and kept shooting…the cow, the goats…they just kept shooting."

She stopped talking. Then she added, "Then they just walked away, just walked away."

I didn't know that anyone who hid or helped a Jew would be executed. But these old people knew. These old Christians gave their lives for us. Some Poles helped us; other turned us in. That's the way it was then. ↔

RURAL POLAND

MAY 4, 2002

We park the car on a tree-lined road and wander into the surrounding unfenced fields. We're in the countryside outside Sosnowitz. There's no hope of finding the village where Mania and her mother had hidden. Dirt-poor villages inhabited by ragged peasants don't exist in Poland anymore. But we're here because we feel driven to get out of town and get into that area, walk around, be by ourselves, get away from the burden of the ordinariness of the present.

Maureen and Neil set up their equipment to catch on film a little of the peace and tranquility of the flat, fallow fields that roll back to the Czechoslovakian border about forty kilometers away. It was the flatness of the border plains and a searing summer that baked the soil rock-hard, allowing the Germans tanks to roll into Poland like a steel tsunami, their grinding treads cutting deep wounds into the sleeping land on which we now walk.

Around us the world looks newly created, all traces of the past wiped out. The trees are budding and the hedges green. Along the verge of the track we're following, our feet leave imprints in the long, dewy grass. As if on cue, a farmer plods by in a horse-drawn wagon and a small cat appears from nowhere, its stiff tail stuck in the air like a flag as it walks along with us, uninvited.

In the distance I watch Maureen and Neil taking shots of a moss-covered barn, its grey wooden sides leaning sideways with age. I can't get the thought of the two old peasants out of my mind. They knew the Germans forbade anyone hiding or helping a Jew. It's unlikely they could read or write, and they lived as hard a life as their animals. They owned none of the stuff we think necessary for happiness or well-being. Yet they possessed a moral integrity so sure-footed that the Germans couldn't touch it.

As I start wondering what I would have done if someone had asked me to hide a Jew, I feel Mania's arm around my shoulder. She asks me what I'm thinking and I'm too uneasy to say. So I tell her a different truth: I'm troubled by what happened to her the night she fled the peasants' hut.It sounds so completely unbelievable. It would be difficult to make this experience credible if and when I wrote about it. "I believe it," I said, and I did believe she had had some sort of psychological experience that touched on the transcendent. "But people are cynical. When you speak of miracles, of angels, people are turned off. They just don't believe it."

"So people are so smart today that they know everything?" Mania says. "They want to stay young, they get old. They fall in love with some disastrous nut and everyone throws them a party. They get old and it's a big shitty disaster, and their only hope is a face cream that costs them their rent. But they think the idea of angels is whacky? Listen, what happened to me that night, I can't understand, but it happened. So what's to believe, what's not to believe? It happened. That's what to believe."

I tell her I have no problem with angels, or with anything to do with life in a realm beyond our own, for that matter. I explain that it's one of the benefits of being raised Catholic: one foot in this world and one in the next. It's a sort of mild type of schizophrenia because it allows for belief in all sorts of mysterious forces, not to mention an invisible cast of thousands of souls hovering overhead as thick as flies in the Australian bush.

"Many, probably most, excellent rational people consider Catholics to be nuts," I said. "That's probably why you and I get on so well."

"We get on so well because you don't lecture me when I light up," Mania retorts. "But what happened that night, I don't understand any of it myself. I've asked rabbis and priests, psychologists and friends: what happened to me? I could feel the evil coming—actually feel it like it was a heavy fog. The next day I was as frightened of the dark as always, and when people asked me to point in the direction of the village, I couldn't. Because I will tell you the best way I can describe it is that I felt absolutely sure and safe, like there was an angel at my side. It's a mystery. What's not to believe about a mystery?"

It isn't fretting about the existence or nonexistence of angels that keeps me awake that night. It's those two nameless peasants machine-gunned in their bed, their old bodies blown apart by men who also had been raised as Christian. Four people. All Christians. How are we to understand the difference in the choices made? ↦

SOSNOWITZ

AUGUST, 1942

By August 1942, I was ten and knew a lot more. Adults said things as if I wasn't there. Everyone was too sick and tired to pretend anymore.

That way, I heard about the deaths in the Lodz ghetto and the Jews from Prague and Vienna being shot or gassed. I didn't know where these places were, but I knew the Germans put some people in the backs of trucks and let the bad gas kill them. I tried to imagine what that would feel like. Germans scared me. When I saw one, I started to feel sick in my stomach.

We were hungry all the time. Everyone had gotten skinny like me, but now I was worse. All people talked about were the transports: what happened to the people who were rounded up and then disappeared? An Aktion—that's what the Germans called rounding up Jews to be re-settled in work camps. Some Jews believed there were work camps, but others like Bubsha said the Germans were liars, that they killed all the people they shipped away. I remember that Muma didn't believe every-one was murdered and she hated Bubsha saying they were.

We were lucky in Sosnowitz; we hadn't been put into a ghetto. Ev-eryone said that was because of a certain rabbi. This rabbi was smart and knew how to deal with the Nazis. Even the top SS officers respected him. (Years later, in Israel, I think, people told me this rabbi was probably Moses Merin.) People also said that maybe the Nazis were getting scared because the Allies were bombing a lot of German cities. Those bombings made us think the war would end soon.

One day the loudspeakers said there'd be an "assembly" the next day at the Athletic Field. When the Germans gave an order, they always screamed as if they were having some sort of a fit, but this time the voice was pleasant, like a kind schoolteacher's. All Jews had to register and they should wear their best clothes. "Festive wear" is what the Germans said. It sounded like a party. Jews could walk on any of the streets to get there, and they'd be allowed to talk to each other on the streets.

What was happening? Maybe there'd be some food. That's what the adults thought: why wear party clothes if it's not a party? And being allowed to walk on any of the streets and talk to each other—it had to be a party! Maybe it was because they were being bombed that they were weakening. They didn't want to be seen as so bad anymore. They might even be beginning to realize that Jews were kind, good people. Now that I knew I was a Jew I wanted the Germans to know this.

Muma and I washed our hair in the tin basin over the sink and cleaned our shoes with water and a rag. Muma bent my hair around her fingers into corkscrew curls, just the way Shirley wore her hair. I still dreamed about being Poland's Shirley Temple and continued to nag Muma about dancing lessons when the war ended. She always said yes, she'd see to it.

It was August 12 and a beautiful sunny morning.

We went to my grandparents' house so we could walk to the Athletic Field together. Everyone was excited. Muma put on the dress she used to wear on Saturday night that she was now saving for the end of the war. Bubsha wore something with lace at the neck and cuffs. Tete was in his best black suit and big hat. I don't remember what I wore. Bubsha pulled the curtains across the window so the sun wouldn't get in and fade the carpet while we were away. Tete locked up.

Everyone was so happy, dressed up and dreaming of things like chicken liver on thick rye bread, although I was probably thinking more of ham on a kaiser. People smiled as if they'd been hoarding joy and couldn't wait to spend it. They raised their voices, now used to whispering in public, and shouted to each other across the street. It was like we'd been let loose from jail.

We were so crazy with hope, so ingrained in our tradition of celebrating life, that our brains had stopped working. The Nazis knew Jews, but the Jews didn't know and could never imagine the thoughts of a Nazi.

As we walked along the street, people kept asking where the Germans were. Soldiers were usually everywhere, but since we left home we'd seen only a couple of greenish-grey uniforms and not a sign of the terrifying black or grey of the SS. We felt so secure. No soldiers, no Aktion.

Where were they?

"Hiding," someone said. Everyone laughed. There were too many of us for them to hurt.

"They're leaving us alone," Tete declared. "They're thinking about the end of the war. A new policy, surely that's it. Bless Rabbi [Merin]. He's done it for us."

The blessing rippled out around us, and I felt very special because Tete was my grandfather and people thought he was so wise.

We got to the Athletic Field through a road off the main boulevard. The sun was hot. New arrivals poured in from the side streets. The people who lived in the nearby towns of Bedzin and Dabrowa Gornicza did not come because they had their own assembly points. This was so they could not deceive the Nazis by saying they had registered in another nearby town.

People pushed forward to get onto the field. I could hardly see anything except legs in the crowd. We were jostled and shoved through the gates. But there weren't any tents or brass bands. There wasn't any food. It didn't look like a party. There were only a few desks with SS officers standing by. It didn't seem like fun anymore. It was too hot and crowded, and there were too many people pressing against one another. We'd counted on there being something to eat. Kids started to cry and I wanted to cry too.

We lined up to register. Muma registered us first, and Bubsha and Tete followed. We all turned to leave. An SS officer directed Bubsha and Tete to the end of the field.

Tete needed to go to the toilet, and it must have been bad because he whispered something to an officer who nodded as if he were a kind man. "*Ja, ja.*" But unfortunately none were available. Tete must wait before permission would be given to leave.

"You," he said, turning to Muma, "you can go, but you have to leave the child."

Muma stared at him and said this was her entire family. "We're all registered."

The officer spoke quietly and politely. "You can go, but you must leave the child. That's an order. When only one parent registers, the child or children must stay. Leave. The grandparents will care for her."

"I have no husband," Muma said. Her voice was rising. "The rule's for when there are two parents, there's only me...I—"

"Gelcia! Go." Bubsha looked scared. "We'll take care of Mania. Leave now."

We were holding up the line. Other people were pushing by us to go to the back of the field as ordered. Bubsha had one of my hands, Muma the other. It hurt. I started to yell. I thought they were going to pull me apart. The SS officer stepped towards Muma, and she let go. I went with Bubsha to the back of the field.

People all dressed up still streamed through the gates anticipating a party.

We were divided into three or four groups. Nearby was a large group of young men, strong and healthy. Not like my group, old and sick. I looked at Bubsha. She had a hand spread full over her face. She looked ill. Tete looked ill. I knew he was desperate to pee, but it was more than that because Bubsha was saying over and over, "We've been tricked. We've been tricked."

I sat on the grass. What did it mean, that we'd been tricked? Maybe we had been tricked because there was no food and no band. Soon I had to stand because people's shoes were beginning to hurt me. I asked Bubsha when Muma was coming, but she just shook her head as if her voice were gone. Tete had wet his pants. Others had too. You could smell the pee.

I was angry at Papa for being dead. If he were alive I wouldn't be there. I could have gone home with Muma. It was terribly hot. Some of the women were crying, and the men were shouting aloud for water. Tete was praying. Part of my body was pressed against his, and I could feel a little swaying all the time. Tick, tock, tick, tock. He was probably saying how good God was, but I couldn't see it myself.

Bubsha's hair was stuck to the side of her face, glued there. Her hat was twisted in a funny way. She couldn't raise her arms to fix it because we were so jammed. Tete still had his hat on, and his face was greasy with sweat.

I couldn't help crying. I could hear babies screeching on and on the way they do when they're very hungry. But most people were quiet by now. I hoped that if we all stayed quiet the Germans would let us go home. But then the sun started going down, and everyone knew it would be dark soon and people started to get noisy again.

And then I don't know exactly what happened because I was small and squashed in. I heard the roar of trucks and a lot of shouting in German: "Achtung, achtung! Stehen bleiben! Wer sich rührt wird erschossen." (Stay where you are. Anyone moving will be shot.) The Germans sounded so angry, like they'd like to shoot us, and people started screaming. The screams spread around, and I started screaming too. Everyone had their mouths open, screaming their hearts out, and then the whole field moved like a tidal wave, shoving me along because people were trying to reach the gate where we'd come in. Tete half fell. Bubsha let go of me and held him up. Again he said something about the Lord being our God and the Lord being good, but his voice was like a moan. A gun went off while he was saying it. Then more rifle cracks, screams, and yelling and dogs snarling.

We stopped moving. We froze.

Hours passed. I fell asleep standing up. When I woke I could see stars and clouds hurrying over the moon. The chestnut trees were still, but a sound like a strange wind was blowing through them, a moaning rising and falling, rising and falling, sad and ancient and terrible. I peed down my leg with terror. Then I realized the moaning rising and falling was coming from us, from the hard mass of us jammed together in terror in the middle of an ordinary city. Did the people tucked into their beds in Sosnowitz hear it too?

In the middle of the night it started to rain hard. The ground got squishy and so did our clothes. We raised our heads and guzzled the cold, sweet water.

In the morning soldiers were all around us. They wore helmets and were heavily armed, as if we were dangerous bandits. The dogs were still there, German shepherds with thick, glossy coats. They lay on the grass with their paws in front of them, the way a cat watches a cornered mouse. Rags and purses and black hats were scattered everywhere. The air stank like an outhouse. People had gone in their pants. ↔

SOSNOWITZ

MAY 6, 2002

The Athletic Field is lush, green, and centrally located, a perfect site for the soccer games that are Poland's national passion. On the side near the main boulevard there's a long stand of chestnut trees and several rows of low-level bleachers. Opposite there's another row of tall trees on private property. This mass of leafiness lends a park-like touch. At the far end of the field there's a row of large two-story homes; the windows have an unobstructed view of the playing field.

These trees probably weren't there when this field was used as a trap. The bleachers certainly weren't. German officers would have been billeted in the spacious houses overlooking the field. Did these safe, well-fed men feel triumphant, ashamed, or simply good soldiers of the Third Reich as they watched the Jews walk trustingly into the trap they'd laid? When the joy of the crowd turned into terror, when old men held their hands high and shouted to God, when old women fainted and children screamed, did these men despise the abject powerlessness of their victims or did they feel disgust at what they themselves had become? Did they feel anything?

The side street leading onto the main boulevard is the same. The sky above is the same. The earth we're standing on is the same. I walk away from the field, stifling an instinct to fall on my knees, lay my cheek softly onto the soil, and stay like that until my heart stops pounding.

Mania is trotting on ahead, walking onto the main road, chic and pretty in her little high heels and tailored suit. When she turns and gestures for me to join her, I hurry ahead. I'm relieved I didn't put my head to the ground. Not because it might have smacked of drama—which it both did and didn't—but because I was unsure of the origin of the instinct. Maybe it had less to do with the sufferings of the Jewish people than a sense of personal guilt at the silence of all the Christian churches, particularly all-powerful Rome, while Hitler rose to power and allowed the Nazis a free hand in creating a thousand Athletic Fields with absolute impunity. ⇝

SOSNOWITZ

AUGUST, 1942

About the middle of the morning, the barriers at the entrance gates were raised. People started pushing forward again. Bubsha staggered, holding up Tete. People screamed, dogs snarled, and the Germans barked orders. We poured out of the gates and onto the side street and then onto the main boulevard. We made a sort of procession. Soldiers with guns walked by our side as if we were wild criminals.

People were walking along the sidewalks, coming and going from work or out looking into the empty shops. Some stood and stared at us. Others didn't want to see and turned their backs. Then I saw three girl-friends from the public school. They stood on the curb staring at me. I was going to wave but suddenly I stopped. They didn't smile and didn't wave, but went on staring at me, stone faced, their eyes searching my face as if they'd missed something, as if something was stuck on me they'd never noticed before.

I realized then that I was different from them. I was with a shamed group, dirty, stinky, stumbling along. That's where they and other people on the sidewalk thought I belonged, not with them but guarded by soldiers with guns and snarling dogs. I was like a criminal. Suddenly I realized I was a Jew. Jew wasn't a word anymore. I felt "Jew" with my whole heart and soul. And I burned with shame. God forgive me that shame, and God forgive my poor parents. Until today I've not forgotten that moment, that feeling, that hot feeling of shame. And with it comes a worse shame—that I was ashamed to be a Jew even though I still didn't understand why or what it was.

Why hadn't Muma told me the truth? She'd said I was really a Pole, that she and Papa were both Poles. Why were my playmates looking at me as if they hadn't seen me before? I couldn't understand it. I wanted to cry out that it wasn't fair, that I didn't cheat at games, I wasn't bossy, I'd always shared my skipping rope. I felt so ashamed, so dirty. I started to cry. I looked for Bubsha so she could explain things to me, but she was gone. I ran along the edge of the line, shrieking for my grandparents, but a man grabbed my arm and hauled me back into line.

"Do you want to be shot?" he asked.

What did he mean, want to be shot? Why would I be shot?

We filed in line past my grandparents' house. I looked up at the windows. The curtains were still pulled the way Bubsha had left them. We walked to another part of Sosnowitz. I knew the streets and the shops. Now the Germans took out whips and clubs and started beating the people ahead of us into the courtyard of the big apartment buildings at Targowa 4 – 8 and Kollataja 6. Then it was my turn. I was swept along in the crush into Mardrzejowska on Sixteenth Street. The screaming and shouts to God were terrible.

The courtyard was like the one at home except everything was dirtier and blacker. The walls of the building went up five or so stories and surrounded us. I scraped along the courtyard wall into the corner nearest the entrance. Nobody could trample on me there. People had rushed into the building, mad for a toilet and water, but the Germans had turned the water off. The upstairs of the building was already bursting, people pressed against the glass, more fighting their way in downstairs. People were going crazy.

Then I saw Bubsha, high in an apartment window, pressed against the glass. Just a glance. I tried to push forward. My throat blocked up; I couldn't cry out. Then she was gone. I never saw Bubsha again.

Late in the afternoon the Germans told the Jewish militia to bring in some nurses. The militia was a Jewish police force that worked with the Germans and the Council of Jewish Elders. These Jewish Elders thought that if they cooperated with the Nazis they'd have some say or at least a little control. The Nazis didn't ask for nurses because they cared about our health. They were going to kill us, but they had to have everything looking normal, the way it was in the outside world. That way they could lie to themselves; they could avoid having to face reality and acknowledge themselves as murderers.

Some people were sick and dying. I watched a nurse arrive. She knelt near me, hidden behind a sick woman. She took her uniform off and there was another uniform underneath. The sick woman gave the nurse something, maybe jewelry. The nurse gave the sick woman a uniform. Then they both walked out through the main entrance. That must be the way things work, I thought.

Then something happened that can't be explained. It was a mystery then and remains a mystery sixty years later.

I was crouched in the corner, flat against the wall near the entrance to the courtyard where I could see anyone who came in or out. A man dressed in an ordinary suit came through the entrance. I watched as soldiers saluted and people pulled back. He was obviously a big shot. He turned into the courtyard and moved in my direction. He kept coming, and people around me stepped back. He walked straight to me and took my hand.

All he said was, "Komm."

I went.

Gestapo! Did I hear the word? Did someone mutter it? Or after three years of having the Germans around did I simply know by the plain suit, the hat, the fear created by his very presence?

We walked hand in hand towards the courtyard entrance. The people around us drew back. The guards snapped to attention. An officer raised his hand: "Heil Hitler." The man released my hand and half raised his with an offhand salute: "Heil Hitler."

I didn't feel scared, although everyone else seemed rigid and stiff, the way they are when big shots are around. They pulled back and let us through. At the tunnel the guards saluted. We went out of the entrance and into the street while all the guards stiffened to attention.

We turned onto another street. People were doing things Muma and I used to do long ago. They were crossing streets, going in and out of shops, strolling along carrying parcels, looking at themselves in the glass windows. All this was going on a few blocks from the courtyard where people were screaming and dying of terror and broken bones and killing themselves by jumping out windows.

We walked a bit, and I knew I was on Pergova Street. That wasn't far from my home. The strange man said nothing. Neither did I. I wanted to talk because I liked to talk, but I felt I shouldn't. For several blocks we walked hand in hand.

Then the man asked me in German, "What's your name?"

"Mania," I said, and I added in German, "Who are you?"

"It's not important," the man said.

"Well, just tell me because my mother would like to thank you."

He didn't answer me. Then he said, "Just tell me where you live."

I wasn't frightened of this stranger. But I knew how tricky the Germans were. They lied to get their way, like pretending there'd be a party at the Athletic Field. Why did he want to know where I lived? My heart started to pound. Maybe he wanted to take Muma away. I knew Muma would have gone to Bubsha's house after leaving the Athletic Field. She'd wait there for us. But maybe no one else should know this. I'd learned the value of silence.

I walked by Bubsha's house as if I didn't know it. I led the stranger down the lane and stopped in front of our apartment on Vieska Street. I knew nobody would be there.

"It's here?" he asked.

I nodded. "Thank you very much."

"That's okay, child," he said, and walked away.

I went around to the back of the house and waited with my neighbors. And then I ran down the lane to Bubsha's. Muma was lying on the couch, her face all puffed and swollen. How could I explain what had happened?

I tried to speak. "Muma, I saw Bubsha. No, I didn't see Tete, just Bubsha, we were all squashed like flies. Everyone screaming and crying. I cried too, Muma. And then this man...no, Muma, I don't know. I've never seen him. He just walked straight for me."

I wrestled out of her arms and marched across the floor to show her. "Just like this, through everybody. He didn't go this way or that way. Just straight to me. And then he took my hand and we walked home. All the soldiers said, 'Heil Hitler.' They knew him."

My mother was weeping and trying to pull me to her. "But what did he look like? Try and describe him. Who was he?"

"Muma, I've never seen him before."

But Muma, white-faced and almost hysterical, couldn't stop saying over and over, "But they told me, all of them told me, they can't help me, they can't find you. So I gave up. Since yesterday night I've been lying here crying. I asked everyone, take my money, take this jewelry, but help me. Look for her, I said, look for her. She's my only child. Impossible, they said, it's impossible; there are nearly twenty-five thousand Jews being registered, so go away."

Muma looked soaked wet with tears and grief. All that night she demanded; who was the man? All I could do was shake my head and imitate the way he had come straight for me.

Two days later Muma and I left home very early when no Germans would be around. They drank a lot of vodka after a selection. We knew things like that. Muma's eyes were puffed up like red berries. She held my hand so tight it hurt.

We walked a long way to a field where you could see the railway track that ran from Sosnowitz Station. Everything was quiet and peaceful. Soon we heard a train coming and then a long, silent line of cattle trucks slid by.

Muma and I watched until the last one passed. ↦

MAY 6, 2002

Later that night I press for more details.

"If twenty-five thousand people were rounded up that day, Mania, that means several thousand were in your courtyard. Someone must have known the man who rescued you. What did people say when they saw you back with your mother? What do they think happened? Could he have been an ex-boyfriend of your mother's, a friend of your father's? Could he have been bribed; would that have been possible?"

"Listen," Mania says, "if the Germans could have been bribed, there wouldn't have been one Jew in any camp anywhere. I tell you, everyone in the district talked about my rescue. Nobody—listen to me—nobody knew the stranger who took me out. You think people didn't try to find out? Everyone lost someone that day. Whole families disappeared. Hundreds of kids disappeared. Disappeared forever. Everyone was asking, 'Who was the man who took out Gelcia's kid?' I'd been led out, rescued. Some people called it a miracle; others say there must be more to it, like someone we knew in earlier times.

"I've told it as it happened. An unidentified German, almost certainly a Gestapo agent, rescued me, a Jewish child, in the middle of a selection. So who rescued me? I don't know. I have to believe I was rescued by someone, something, for a reason. How else can I explain it? There were hundreds of beautiful kids there that day. They all died. Why me? It makes no more sense to me than to you."

I agree with Mania: her rescue makes no sense whatsoever. But it happened. Mania was rounded up that day and somehow she was rescued. Research done by various sources, particularly the University of Silesia, the Silesian Museum in Katowice, and the Katowice History Museum, confirm the Aktion that took place August 12, 1942, as well as the use of the apartment buildings cited by Mania as holding areas for the doomed Jews.

Privately I wonder if Gelcia had an affair after her husband's death with someone who later joined the Gestapo. Women did worse things than that in the hope of saving themselves or their children. Or had Gelcia's boss at the factory intervened? That's possible; he had a lot of connections and liked Gelcia. Or had she managed to bribe someone? Not likely. I say lamely, lost for anything else to say, "What a mystery!"

Mania raises her crescent eyebrows and throws me a look of—is it pity? "You're telling me it's a mystery? I'm the one telling you it's a mystery. Why I'm telling you is because life's full of marvels and mysteries, of things that make no sense, that can't be explained. Haven't strange things ever happened in your life, crazy coincidences, mistakes and illnesses that turned out to be the best thing possible? Haven't things that can't be explained by this"—she taps her forehead with her scarlet nails—"played as big a part in your life as things that can be explained?"

Head on one side, she pauses for a moment, looking thoughtfully at me. "I tried for years to understand what happened that day. I still can't. Now I listen to life, try to see life because I know now it's full of marvels. But it's too much for us. It only makes sense if you understand it makes no sense. What do you want me to explain? I'm telling you because I know. Life's full of secrets, and every secret has a purpose." ↵

KORDONOWA STREET GHETTO

After the Athletic Field selections, we were ordered to gather at the Rialto Cinema at 20 Warsowski Street in Sosnowitz. Then we were all ordered into a ghetto. Some went to a village called Srodula a few kilometers away, others to a second ghetto in Old Sosnowitz on Wiejska, Ciasna, and Kordonowa streets.

Muma and I went to a grey stone building on Kordonowa Street. I don't remember what the room was like except we shared it with people we didn't know and the air was always stuffy.

We never saw a newspaper or heard a radio, but people talked a lot now about "the camps." Death camps or work camps? Everyone argued about it. Many people said it was wrong to say there were death camps. To think the Germans would have places especially built to murder Jews was the sort of thinking that was offensive to God. No human beings could be so evil, so depraved. Muma liked it when people said this, not because she was religious but because it made her feel better. The dress she'd been keeping to wear after the war, she'd left at Sosnowitz. But she still told me I'd have dancing lessons as soon as the Germans left. She'd pull me away when other people would laugh in a nasty way and say things like, "You're crazy. Can't you see they want us all to die?"

We became used to dead bodies. Old people would be walking along and then they'd fall over dead. And children disappeared. They'd go outside to play and never come back. And when the parents kept them inside the Germans would come and take them. I don't know how I survived. I can't remember. I do remember the screams of parents during the day when their children were taken and then all night the wailing and murmuring of prayers. I didn't know any of the prayers, but some words soon became familiar. Often I awoke to hear someone weeping and sobbing and saying, "His actions are perfect. All His ways are just." And although I was only ten, I somehow understood these people were feeling a particular pain because they were religious, and not being able to do the usual death and mourning rituals broke their hearts.

We knew German cities were being heavily bombed, but at about the same time there was more fear than ever. Later I learned that the rabbi who'd protected us had gone with the Jewish Council to a meeting of the SS commandant and they'd all been murdered. The Germans had just used them to keep order among the Jews and then killed them when all the Jews were rounded up. There wasn't anyone to help us now.

For a short time Muma had a pass that allowed her to go out to work every day. Then I had to stay in the ghetto alone, terrified until she returned. I don't remember much of this time except early one morning Muma and I were lying on our mattress when we heard the roar of trucks. "It's an Aktion," people screamed. That usually meant the Germans would pick out a certain group—children or old people or sick people. But this was the third Aktion and they took us all.

Muma said to get dressed. She tossed things at me to put on. I was shaking so much that I couldn't do it. All the time the bullhorn was ordering us out onto the street. We could take one small suitcase. Anyone who tried to hide would be found and shot.

We stumbled onto the street. There were screams and shots and trucks and Muma pushing me up into the back of one while the Germans shoved us with their rifle butts. "Auf, auf! Schnell, schnell!" (Up, up! Quick, quick!)

Standing up, jammed in the back of the truck, we saw the last of Sosnowitz. ↦

SOSNOWITZ

MAY 11, 2002

The area around Targowa and Kollataja streets is active, busy with shoppers, and full of life. It's Saturday afternoon and traffic is light. We find a massive grey stone apartment building, about eight stories high that runs half the block, historically confirmed as part of the ghetto created by the Nazis. In talking with Mr. Szaniawski, he confirms that the unnamed rabbi, whom Mania had mentioned and who had managed for so long to protect the Katowice and Sosnowitz Jews from the Nazis, was the heroic Moses Merin.

Neil shoots in and around the courtyard for a while, and a score of young children come skipping up to watch the action. "Hello," they say, and a girl of ten says slowly and clearly, "I am learning English." They are eager, shy, polite, and beautifully cared for, most of them wearing starched pinafores to protect the "good" clothes underneath. Their old-fashioned healthiness, shining innocence, and unspoiled eagerness moves my heart.

We go to a nearby street with a coffee shop with outside seating and sit and watch the world go by. From where we are we can see the grey stone building where thousands of innocent people were held prior to their execution. Soon, out of nowhere, four skinheads appear, the same shaven-headed, black-jeaned toughs who would be just as much at home in Liverpool or Melbourne. They move in on us, so close that Neil, who has set up his tripod on the cobbled mall, folds it up and joins our group. I have a feeling these thugs know what our group is about. One points his chin at Mania and tosses off remarks that curl the faces of his friends in vile amusement.

I ask Piotr whether there's still anti-Semitism in Poland.

He looks past me, embarrassed, possibly shocked by the bluntness of my question. He finally concedes, "It's a very difficult question." Again he hesitates and says, "Like that building back there," pointing to the apartment building we've just left. "Lots of families live there and the rents are low. They're scared that one day the Jews might come back and claim it." He adds with a tinge of—is it defensiveness or a desperation to explain?—"It's not anti-Semitism. No one around here knows any Jews. There just aren't any. It's just that,"—he shrugs—"people are paying low rents and that might change if some of the Jews come back and claim ownership."

I'm lost for words. We're back to the threat of the Jews and their money. I look at Piotr, so smart, modern, well educated, and well-traveled. The words with their history of hell fall out of him so casually: "It's not anti-Semitism. No one around here knows any Jews. There just aren't any." But in an instant I tell myself not to be so damned sanctimonious and self-righteous. With my innate wariness of Germans I'm not exactly in a position to fly to judgment. When Piotr was born, the Second World War was already a subject for the history books. Why expect the antennas of this decent young man to be always attuned to the past? And I grudgingly admit that what he says makes a crude sense. The Poles are admirably thrifty. They live modestly, shop with care, and dress well but in fabrics and classic styles that are immune to the extreme dictates of fashion. A rise in rent could mean financial disaster for old people, people with families, the single and unemployed, and the disabled.

Still, this evades the core issue of right and wrong. If the property does belong to a Holocaust survivor or a descendant of one, shouldn't the point be to want to give it back to the rightful owner? Even if you can't? Am I being stupidly idealistic in believing there'd be happiness and even relief in thinking you'd tipped the scales of justice one tiny bit by simply wanting to return the stolen goods of a victimized people?

I think about the children we've just left—their striking beauty, innocence, and openness to strangers—and wonder what, if anything, they will be told about the Poles who happened to be Jewish and the Holocaust that took place in the yard they now play in. Have they ever been told that the building almost certainly belonged to a group of murdered Jews? It's strange that a degree of unexamined anti-Semitism lives on with some Poles, that in this country, of all places, everyone would understand that discrimination can turn into a pandemic that kills. Auschwitz was originally planned as a concentration camp for Poles, whose number of murdered victims by war's end was second only to the Jews. It's a matter of historical record that after Hitler had finished with the Jews, he intended to exterminate the whole Polish race.

I'm beginning to doubt that we'll ever find a way to preserve lessons from the past and integrate this information into the core of human behavior. Or that we'll ever find a way to pass all that we've learned from the slaughter of millions of people on to the coming generations. So far, historical evidence indicates that what we've learned from experiencing war and injustice simply fades with the passing of time and the common apathy of the human condition. The end result: we're doomed to endlessly replay all the tragedies of time past.

I'll change my mind on this, and surprisingly it's Auschwitz-Birkenau that does it. ↔

SRODULA

MARCH – AUGUST 1943

We traveled east. Auschwitz was east.

I was too scared to ask Muma where we were going. I knew now that she didn't know anything more than I did, that we were just like a load of dirt to the Germans. After about an hour, the trucks turned off the main road and went through a single entry-exit gateway. And we were dumped out.

Srodula! A ghetto! Not Auschwitz! There were no big apartment buildings, just houses and barns and huts and, beyond the high surrounding fence, country fields. We milled around in confusion and joy. Whatever happened at the work camps, we knew we wouldn't be killed that day.

Where to go?

The Germans laughed. "Wherever you want."

We were latecomers. Thousands of Jews had been trucked in before us. There wasn't anywhere to go. Every room was already stuffed with people. Then Muma saw Franek, an old friend of Papa's. Franek was a member of the militia. He said there were no Poles left in Srodula because the Germans had forced them out of their homes, just like we'd been forced out of ours. Franek took us to a house where there weren't so many people. This house had a hiding place in the kitchen ceiling. At the first sign or sound of an Aktion, Franek said, a ladder was pulled out from under the floorboards. Everyone had one minute to be up it and into the hiding place with the manhole back in place. Anyone who didn't make it was left out.

"Do you understand, Mania? And you, Gelcia? One minute. No exceptions."

We understood.

I don't remember much about the house we were in. I made friends with a girl next door whose name I've forgotten. Muma stayed in the ghetto all day. All the strong men were trucked off daily to repair and build roads in Katowice. One of them, an older man, had been our doctor.

One day, soon after we arrived in Srodula, Franek came to see Muma. Muma ordered me to go away and play. I'd become used to listening to the adult conversations, so I felt something was up. When I came back, Muma was crying. She wouldn't tell me why. The next morning she told me I was going away for a holiday. She pulled out my small suitcase and started putting my things in it.

She was getting rid of me! Sending me away! I burst into tears.

"No, no, Manuska, my darling." Muma was biting her lip trying not to cry. She started lying to me. I could always tell when adults lied because their voices became different. "Something wonderful has happened. Franek wants to take you on a small holiday. You'll stay with a nice lady who has a daughter your age. It'll be lots of fun."

I said I wouldn't go. I didn't care about a holiday or a nice lady. Muma went on packing, I went on screaming. I wanted to stay with my mother.

Muma looked close to shaking me. She told me to keep quiet. "Just for a little while," she said. "Remember the big buns with ham in it that Eva used to get for you? They'll be lots to eat like that. Now, hurry. Franek is coming soon. You must be ready."

I hated going but knew I had to. The adults had decided. I had no say.

Later I learned that Franek knew that everyone in Srodula would be sent to Auschwitz. He couldn't help Muma, but he'd worked out a plan that might save me. He lived with a woman, a Volkdeutsch, whose husband had been killed in the Wehrmacht. Because I spoke good German and didn't "look Jewish," he planned to pass me off to this woman as his niece, and to the community as German.

I knew nothing of that, just the terror of being separated from my mother. When she said good-bye she was calm, but I felt she was screaming inside.

Franek took my hand and we walked towards the gate. Then he stopped and bent down beside me. He asked me my age. Ten, I said. Almost eleven. And then he said something I still remember.

"Try and understand, your life depends on what I'm telling you now. You are no longer Mania. You are no longer a Jew. You are Maria. You are a German. Say that to yourself over and over, 'I am Maria and I am a German. I am Maria and I am a German.' Do you understand me, Maria?"

I understood. I hated him; I hated what he was saying. But maybe he was just joking. I tugged at his hand. I wanted to run back to my mother. Bubsha would be angry if I did this because she had told me never to tell a lie and Bubsha was a Jew. I didn't want to say I wasn't a Jew. It'd be lying. But maybe then the Germans wouldn't kill me. But then I'd have to say my name was Maria. But Papa loved calling me Manuska. Thoughts like this ran through my head until I finally burst into tears.

"Listen to me," said Franek. He was getting mad and he was a friend of Muma's. "If the Germans know you're a Jew, you're not safe. It's not forever, just a while. Now say it!"

"I am Maria and I am a German," I said.

He walked me out of the camp—don't ask me how—and took me back to Katowice, to the other side of town from where I'd lived.

I saw kids going to school. They were carrying schoolbags with books. They wore shoes, even socks. They were laughing and talking. The girls had big crisp ribbons in their hair. I went into a house with Franek. The room had furniture, there was a carpet on the floor, and everything was clean and shining. I'd thought the Germans had changed the face of the whole world. I thought they'd taken everything and every child out of school, that there wasn't anymore food anywhere, and that they'd made the whole world poor and dirty.

The lady of the house, whom I'll call Frau Kinder because I've forgotten her name, smiled at Franek and looked at me. Her daughter, Elise, skipped in and said she'd show me to her room. I stared at the room in disbelief. I had my own bed. Clean sheets. Warm blankets. There was plenty of thick soup at dinnertime, and bread, potatoes, and vegetables. Sometimes there was a small piece of meat. For a few days food made me feel slightly sick. Then I became hungry all the time. I told no one where I came from because Franek had warned me not to.

I was enrolled at the local school. I had no problem with any of my lessons. I'd never gone to school regularly but found it easy to read and write. I must have taught myself a lot or maybe Muma taught me. Anyway, I ached to tell Muma everything and started to miss her a lot.

After a few days I was invited to join the Jungmädel, the junior division of the Bund Deutscher Mädel, (BDM). That was the girls' equivalent of the Hitlerjugend for boys. I was thrilled because all the girls were in it. I was bursting to tell my mother about all the wonderful things that were happening to me. Within days my life had been turned upside down.

When I received my uniform of a white blouse and a pale blue skirt, I was ecstatic. I had friends and all my teachers liked me. When we walked home, Elise held my hand, and we pretended we were sisters.

I'd have been in heaven if I hadn't ached to see my mother. Every hour it got worse. I wanted to tell her about all the things the Jungmädel did—picnics, folk dancing, cooking, sewing, and lots of singing. The Jungmädel taught young German girls they were going to be housewives and have babies. We would build a strong Fatherland of pureblood Aryans. That's what the Führer wanted. It didn't sound like much fun to me.

My Jungmädel teacher was a tall, thin-faced woman. She liked me very much.

One day after being back in Katowice for about a week or two, the Jungmädel met for an afternoon session. My teacher praised me for my speed in running and willingness to learn. And then she said something that turned my new world upside down.

"Girls like Maria delight our Führer's heart. Everyone can serve the Führer. Even young girls can help build the Third Reich. Does anyone know how?"

Silence. No one knew.

"One way is that you can learn to recognize a Jew. You don't have to be absolutely sure, but if someone looks a little like a Jew, report them to the police."

My hand shot up. "How do you tell someone is a Jew?"

The teacher drew up a list on the blackboard.

"Jews often have wet lips. Sometimes their lips are also loose." She underlined "wet" and "loose" on the blackboard. "They have hooked noses. Some of them have big, round noses. Their food is different. They cook it in strange ways. The men wear blue-trimmed shawls like a woman, with tassels hanging down. The men usually have beards. They smell different. Girls, even if you just suspect, go to the police and report them."

This was news to me. I knew it wasn't true. I remembered Papa's soft, shaven skin, the faint, fresh smell of cologne, Muma scrubbing me in the tub, Muma bending over the little sink in Sosnowitz though it hurt her neck, washing her hair so that as it dried it glittered in the sun. And our kitchen, and Buba's, too, shone and sparkled because it was so clean.

I desperately looked around at the class. Should I put up my hand and explain about Papa and Muma? But then everyone would know I wasn't deutschblutig. Everyone thought I was "pure blooded." It was fun pretending to be deutschblutig, and I had a nice bed and I wasn't hungry anymore or frightened all the time. And I remembered the shame I'd felt after the Athletic Field Aktion, when my school friends had snubbed me. I couldn't bear to feel so different and dirty again.

I felt sick and confused. Why was my teacher saying these things? Teachers were good people; they only told you truthful things. I thought of different people's noses. Tete had a big nose, but so did the school superintendent, who wore a red armband with the Nazi swastika on it. Should I point this out to the teacher? She was talking shit. Muma got angry when I used that word, but I'd learned it in the ghetto and liked it. I was busting to put up my hand, but I'd learned to pause, to listen to a voice inside me. Sometimes when people spoke back to people who loved the Führer they were knocked to the ground.

The teacher was now saying that Jews were luftmenschen, lazy people who liked something for nothing. If they weren't lazy, they worked all the time and became rich and became the boss and controlled things. She babbled on, saying Jews also liked to trick people in business.

My classmates were soaking it up. Now I truly felt lost, as if I'd done something horribly wrong, like I'd hurt something deep inside me, like I'd snitched on a friend. I didn't know why I had the feeling, but it was as though I were the biggest liar in the world. I'd gone to some invisible place where I should not go and I had to get back to the other side. I had to get back to my mother. I didn't care what Franek thought. I didn't care about anything except finding a way back to Srodula.

I was small but I was eleven now. I'd also seen a lot of how the world worked and knew how important it was to be cunning. I realized that if I wore my Jungmädel uniform I could cross the city unquestioned.

Everyone would think I was a little German girl going off and learning about having babies for the Führer.

That afternoon after school, while Elise and her mother were inside, I left the house and got on a tram and went to the railway station. I have no memory of whether I had to pay or if I had any money. I had to get back to my mother, and the only way I knew how was to find the men prisoners from Srodula who were working near the station.

Nobody stopped me or said anything. When the men stopped working and the trucks pulled up, I got into the back of a truck with them. I have no memory of whether I was still in my Jungmädel uniform or not. I remember only my return, with my mother holding me and the feeling that I was home, that the ghetto was where I belonged. ↬

MAY 11, 2002

What am I to make of Mania's rescue from the ghetto and her short, false life as one of Hitler's "maidens"? How on earth could she have climbed into a truck in the middle of a busy street in Katowice and returned to the ghetto with the workers? I don't know. This isn't the sort of story one makes up: it's too irrational, bizarre, freakish. But then irrational, bizarre incidents are the stuff of all survivors' true stories: they flesh out a world gone mad. All that Mania has told me so far has been documented, not by popular, accessible books on the Katowice-Sosnowitz "Jewish cleansings," because so far I've found none, but by local Polish scholars and historians.

I sit in my pajamas in the dimly lit room and start to write, trying to get some sense of how this child endured. This once-spontaneous, talkative child had to play the role of the "enemy" seven days a week. She had to watch her tongue and hide every trace of her parentage, her memories of home on the other side of town, her experiences at the Athletic Field, and her mother in the ghetto. She sat in class, played in the schoolyard, spoke German, and listened to German, terrified of discovery yet ashamed of denying her own heritage, all the while remembering Franek's words: "If the Germans know you're a Jew, you're not safe."

I'm deep into this child's story when suddenly, clang clang, the phone rings. I leap from my chair as if shot, so lost in time that I confuse it with an alarm, a shouted order, an Aktion. It clangs again. I pick it up, and Mania's husky laugh comes running down the line. "I'm in bed," she says, "and I've been thinking about Srodula."

I pull on a sweater and dash up to her room in my pajamas. If I run into anyone, maybe they'll think that's how we go to bed in Canada.

The only time I've seen Mania cry is when she's spoken of her mother. Quick dabs of tissues to the eyes, lots of "excuse mes," and then a bright smile. All day she's been dwelling on her forced separation from her mother, and the powerful need and love that drove her as a little girl to go back into the ghetto. She wants to talk; I want to listen.

"I remember more my feelings in those times than what I looked like or did," she says. "When I went back to Srodula, that was the time I lost the ability to hope. Just like that my heart changed. I remember it like you remember any big inside change, like when people say 'my heart sank' or 'my heart leaped.' It took only a few moments after I'd returned to feel this shift inside me. I knew good things still existed on the outside—clean houses and food and people who weren't desperate for water to stay clean. But I knew now I was a Jew and these things were not for me. That's the awful part—how they'd degraded us into feeling that.

"I still believed Muma and I would survive. I couldn't imagine death, but once back in Srodula, all dreams drained away. I knew then I'd never be like Shirley Temple. The only dances I knew were little steps I'd made up myself, and I didn't want to dance them any more, even when Muma asked. Or she'd say, 'Please talk to me, Mania. What's happened to my little chatter-box?' She'd say these things, I realize now, to keep me going.

"Srodula is where every last trace of my childhood was sucked away. But I realize now that worse was being done to me and everyone else. I thought that because we were Jews this was where we belonged, in a place where everything and everyone trembled with fear—the trees, the men, the women, the earth itself. But not the children, not anymore, because while I was back in Katowice, they'd all been taken away." ↔

SRODULA

AUGUST 1943

I don't remember what happened when Muma saw me. Two days earlier the Germans had had a special Aktion. The soldiers had picked up all the children with nowhere to hide and trucked them away screaming. On our street only my little girlfriend next door had escaped. So there was wailing and sobbing all night, and the air was smelly and black with grief and terror. All the adults were digging holes to hide in. They were like little field animals, burrowing into every crack and crevice, creating them in sewers, pipes, and furniture, and putting up false walls so people could be stuffed behind them.

I don't remember whether we had food or water, or how we spent the long hours. I heard and saw but nothing registered, just the feeling of terror. At night Muma and I clutched each other and jumped at every sound. The worst sound was that of a truck.

A few weeks passed, and then there was a second selection. It came in an explosion of noise and light. The arc lights were switched on. Night turned into day. Trucks roared in, troops poured into the streets, ordering everyone out. "Raus, raus!"

On this night we all made it into the attic. After a few hours they finally left. We came down.

A young woman wandered into our house, a stranger holding a newborn baby. Nobody wanted her. After she'd given birth she'd probably been turned out from wherever she'd been. Babies cried and drew attention. One night the woman decided to bathe the baby in the kitchen sink. I stood watching her hold the small body, cooing at it.

Suddenly arc lights again turned the streets white. The Germans had returned: a surprise Aktion meant to catch us all.

"Up, up!" a man yelled. He jerked the ladder from its hiding place under the floorboards. "Everyone up! Up!"

The woman went on bathing her baby. Was she deaf? Couldn't she understand?

"Up now!"

She trickled a handful of water over the baby's head slowly, as if in a dream.

The man yelled at her to leave the baby. The baby started to cry.

I was at the top of the ladder. I saw the man knock the woman unconscious. He dragged her up the ladder. The baby was left in the sink. Still crying, it slid under the water. Then I was in darkness as the ladder was pulled up and the attic sealed.

I was lying under my mother, strangers crushing against me. I felt pain and wanted to move my arm but couldn't. I didn't want to think about the baby sliding under the water, flailing its arms, but the picture stuck in my mind. The darkness went on and on and the picture didn't fade.

Was it night? Day? I couldn't tell the difference. Muma and I breathed in and out together, small silent sips of sticky air. I was wet with sweat. The Germans moved away. We stretched, rolled an inch or two, but dared not come down.

The Germans came back. They saw the baby in the sink and shouted for us to come out. They pried out parts of the walls, ripped up floorboards, and tore the doors off the hinges. Finally we heard the order: "Genug gesucht. Niemand hier. Abtreten." (Enough searching. There's nobody here. Let's go.)

Sometime later, maybe a day, Franek told us that SS officers were speaking of another Aktion soon in Srodula. It wouldn't be a selection but a total Judenrein. After that the ghetto would be razed. Franek thought because of the Allied bombing that maybe our rescue was just a matter of time.

"Hide," he said. "Hide for as long as you can. Keep hiding; the Allies might come."

The Judenrein came on a very hot day. Afterwards I learned it was in August 1943.

The warning given by the roaring bullhorns was new: Anyone who hides will be found and immediately shot. "Sofort herraus oder du bist tot." (Out at once or you're dead.)

We scrambled up the ladder. Night came, and the Judenrein went on. The threats to kill us pierced through the walls, wood, and plaster. We were wet with fear, piss, and worse. My heart pounded and banged around. I breathed in small sips. The Germans were in our house, crashing through the rooms, and in the kitchen inches below us. An axe sliced into the wall; another split the floorboards. At the front of the house a machine gun splattered bullets around. Then again and again. The sound was close, perhaps next door.

Up and down the street the bullhorns roared: "You have not escaped. You cannot escape. If you hide we will find you and shoot you."

And then came a new warning: "Out now or we will burn you out."

Burn us alive? We knew they would do it. We gave up. We sobbed aloud. It was a relief to give up. One by one we scrambled down. The voice on the bullhorns said we could take one suitcase. We snatched them up and forced our wobbly bodies into the street. We forgot the threats of death. "If we're allowed to take a suitcase, it means the Germans aren't going to kill us." That's how adults thought, and it seemed so clever that everyone clung to it. Yes, yes, we were not going to be killed after all.

We lined up on the street.

I couldn't see my friend. I had to find her. I had to stop her from being burned alive. I darted out of the huddle and ran into the house next door, into the empty front room, down to the back with a guard shouting and Muma running and screaming at me to come back. Down the dark cellar stairs I ran, calling her name. She was in the cellar, her skinny arms sprawled out next to her parents' bodies. She looked as though she was breaststroking in a swimming pool of blood.

Muma seized my shoulder and dragged me up the stairs and back into line, screaming at me, "You stupid child!" She could hardly breathe. "They'll kill you! Do you hear? Kill you!"

Maybe these weren't her exact words, but she was mad with fear. Her fingers dug deep into my shoulders. We stumbled along through the darkening village in some sort of a file: the Germans would never let us bunch together. There were so many of us and so few of them. The doors of the houses were wide open. Glass was shattered, shutters torn off. We were the last to go. The ghetto was dead.

My memories of what happened then are like a black-and-white movie, a dream in slow motion.

Trucks were lined up neared the barbed-wire gate. We were butted into them and transported to Sosnowitz Station. A long line of cattle cars was waiting for us. The arc lights were blinding white, the dogs black, the air grey. Hands pulled us into a freight car. Hours went by in suffocating heat and darkness. Then the train jolted and jerked, the wheels ground around, and we moved.

About four hours later, the train stopped. Bolts slid back, doors were flung open. It was early morning, and the daylight was dazzling. We tumbled out onto the ground.

The date was August 3, 1943. Muma and I had arrived at Auschwitz concentration camp. ↔

OSWIECIM

The town of Oswiecim, or Auschwitz as the Germans called it, is an old village with well-established charm. It's not far from Sosnowitz, maybe two hours on a well-paved road, situated on a plain divided by the Vistula and Sola rivers. We approach it along wide streets with detached homes and tidy gardens and check into the Hotel Olympia, a low-rise building a little out of town. It's a clean, bright, utility place where the only other guests are Polish athletes, all gorgeous-looking hunks training for some international swimming competition. This trivia comes from the hotel receptionist. Like all the town women I've seen, she's meticulously groomed, expertly but subtly made up, a self-contained matron obviously free of any hankering to look twenty.

I kick off my shoes, flop on the bed, and start brooding about the direction this project is taking. The more I know Mania, the more I see her entering Auschwitz as one in a line of thousands of kids, some who'd gone before, others still to come, all scheduled to be systematically murdered within the hour. The mystery of how a race as cultured as the Germans could so easily turn into barbarians torments me. Are we all just a hair's breadth removed from savagery?

The question—and the possible answers—exhausts me. And when I'm tired, uncertainty seeps in. I have doubts now about Mania's identification of Johanne. Mania has no evidence; all her so-called facts are circumstantial. And the rest of it—the night run from the peasants' hut, the rescue by some mysterious man after the Athletic Field roundup, the escape and return from Srodula—it's mounting up. So much intuition, so much mystery, so few facts.

If I'm getting churned up just being so near the camp, what must Mania be feeling?

I soon find out. She knocks and opens the door. She's born-again fresh, a pink cashmere shawl flung over her shoulder, a soft, tailored dress, and on her feet a pair of walking shoes that manage to look dainty. She announces

91

that she's getting a cab and going to see the town.

"I'll tell you why," she says. "For two years I lived near this stinky place and never got to see the town. Because—I'll tell you why—they wouldn't let me out." She gives a husky chuckle. Mania appreciates her own jokes.

We get a taxi and start out for Oswiecim. Mania's large blue eyes sparkle. She's as chatty as a tourist on a deluxe tour won in a lottery. Halfway there she stops the cab, tells the driver to wait, and drags me into a pharmacy where we have half the stock on the walls removed and end up buying one Max Factor lipstick in Happy Scarlet. Then we continue on downtown and pay the driver a wad for what was a seven-minute ride and a forty-five minute wait.

"Ah," says Mania, trotting into the town's central square with the enthusiasm of an explorer, "so this is what we couldn't see!" The center, reached through winding, cobbled streets, conjures up Old Europe: dormer windows, peaked-roofed shops, and a beer garden laid out in the middle. The local high school has just let out when we arrive, and tables of young people, some chugging schooners that would send me reeling, fill the air with shouts and laughter. There are a few girls among them, mostly fair-haired, pretty, without makeup, dressed like teenagers everywhere but with no flesh or flab showing. They carry a load of books, so I assume they have homework to do after they've had their schooners.

Mania shops around for more makeup, but not for her, as it turns out. For me. She still thinks me, well, not dowdy, but too unvarnished, definitely an unfinished work.

"*Got im Himmel*, Mania!" I say in exasperation.

She retorts, "A little eye shadow, that's all."

But I'm getting cranky. "What for? To visit Auschwitz?"

Mania looks at me. "Why won't you put your best foot forward?"

Sheer shame drives me into the store.

The shop assistants, who use makeup as if Polish women are born with the knack of turning artifice into art, practice patient endurance as they take out one box of eye shadow after another. I stand and stare at the muddy colors while Mania examines them and then looks at my eyes like a judge at dog show. Finally she pronounces judgment. "What I am telling you is that this will look beautiful. You won't know your own face.

Why do you look like that? Because you went to a convent, you think you're a nun maybe? Soon—a movie star." Or a mutton dressed as a lamb, I think.

We sit in the square and have a beer in the last golden rays of the sun. Neither one of us mentions Mania's past. I have no idea what's going on in her head or heart. I'm surprised at her light spirits, her funny comments on the life around us, and her easy laughter.

It takes me forever to catch on. Dumb isn't the word. Later that night, recalling those moments, I realize Mania was doing what she has spent a lifetime doing: acting "normally," making everything simple, "practicing" happiness, guarding other people from her sorrow, making them laugh, keeping the past at a distance because the alternative is to create more sorrow, and, ultimately, to be unable to live. ↔

AUSCHWITZ-BIRKENAU

AUGUST – NOVEMBER 1943

The grownups had always talked about Auschwitz as if it were a scary place.

This place didn't look scary to me. There were small farmhouses nearby but no animals, and the fields were flat and empty. Everything looked peaceful, although there was a very bad smell in the air.

It took a few minutes for everyone to get down from the train. Some people were dead and had to be tossed out. The train was so long that I could hardly see the end of it. People stood around, scared and very confused. The SS officers were calm and courteous. The ordinary soldiers stood back. The officer at the front with the bullhorn spoke very politely.

Muma squeezed my hand and looked down at me. I'm sure she thought it was a work camp. We all watched the officer with the bullhorn. He gave orders that were something like this:

"Men and women, please form two lines three meters apart. Place your suitcases and possessions to the side. These goods will be delivered to the camp later. After admission procedures are completed, they can be reclaimed. Everything will be taken care of. First, however, the maintenance of hygiene requires all prisoners to shower immediately on entering the camp."

Those weren't his exact words, but those of us who survived remember that our arrival was calm and even soothing. Muma believed every word of it, and so did everyone around us. We wanted to believe; we had to hope. And we would have believed anything to have a shower. Not only were we filthy but our tongues were cracked dry with thirst.

The men went on one side, the women the other. We moved forward. I could see another SS officer ahead. When Muma and I reached him, he directed me to the left, Muma to the right. I went off and joined my column. I turned to see Muma in the other line watching me. There were trucks ahead for our line and people were getting into them. There were no trucks ahead of Muma's line.

Suddenly, I felt Muma tug my hand. She hauled me back to her line. An SS officer walked over. He cuffed my shoulder and shoved me back to the other line.

Muma flew after me, pulling me with her. She looked at the officer and said, "She's my child. She's coming with me."

The officer looked at me and said, "Over there. NOW."

But Muma had gone crazy like a tiger. You had to be crazy to talk back to an SS officer. And she wasn't all that much bigger than I, but she'd wrapped her arms around me so I couldn't move.

Then the SS officer bent slightly towards Muma. I heard him say in a low, clear voice, "Lassen sie gehen! Wenigstens kanst du vieleicht leben." (Let her go. At least you might survive.)

Muma replied in the same low, clear voice: "Nein! Niemals!" (No! Never!)

The officer and Muma stared at each other. She looked very surprised that he'd told her that. The officer looked very surprised at Muma. He didn't know what to do. He stared at me. His eyes were very blue, and I looked right into them. Then a strange look came onto his face. He kept staring and then, as if something had caught his attention, he moved away abruptly. He turned his back on us. He looked ahead as if to check on something.

I got between a woman and Muma, and we all moved forward. The officer did not come back. As an adult I realized that he actually had not known what to do. If he had shot Muma, there might have been a riot. As usual there were thousands of "us" and only hundreds of "them." But they had dogs and machine guns.

Later when we found out what Birkenau was all about, my mother told me that when the officer said, "Let her go. At least you might survive," she knew she was in the right line. Those in the other line were to be killed. The trucks drove straight to the gas chambers.

My memory of the weeks that followed is very scrappy. I remember that the bad smell was worse as we entered the camp. It was sweet but made me want to throw up. We were shoved into the "sauna," where we took our clothes off to shower, and we never got them back. The towel was soppy and disgusting because we all had to use it. Then a woman cut off all my hair and Muma's too. And Muma's pubic hair too. Then an ugly woman slopped a rag smelling of disinfectant over where we'd been shaved.

The women and men were so ashamed, so humiliated. Muma looked very different with her hair cut off. She seemed to be smaller, and when she saw my bald head and my coppery curls on the floor, she started to cry.

Then we got tattooed. I had to hold out my left arm, and a woman turned it palm down and jabbed it with a black needle. It hurt. I pulled my arm away, but she jerked it back and kept digging with the needle until she'd marked "52894" into my skin.

That's who I was from then on. Number 52894.

We were given grey smocks. Size didn't matter. We couldn't get them over our heads quick enough, even though they were dirty, even lousy. And then shoes. Wooden shoes. Mine were so enormous that I fell over. I was still such a child that I started to laugh. I tried to do a little dance like Shirley Temple, but Muma tugged at my arm to stop.

We stayed in quarantine. The Nazis were scared of typhoid, and there was a plague in the regular camp. Some of the women went mad and were shot "to keep order." After a month we were marched off to our place in Auschwitz, which was in the section called Birkenau, or Auschwitz II.

Until I was an adult, I didn't realize the size of Auschwitz, nor that it was a massive complex. Birkenau was one of four main sections, the extermination section. All I remember was going down a central dirt road. Spread out on each side was row after row of wooden huts, so many that they disappeared in the distance. More than anything I remember how stinky it was. Even the soil stank. You couldn't get away from the sweet rotten smell. Some days it was so bad that you tried not to breathe. That's when they were burning people, but I didn't know that right away.

Muma became very weepy when we went into Birkenau, like a heavy cloud that finally burst. We were assigned to Hut 14.

Today everyone knows about Auschwitz. We did not. We didn't have the images that everyone has now. We didn't know about the cruelty, the terror, the filth, the sudden death. So the shock was terrible. We'd heard stories and rumors, and had seen people shot or dying on the street or in the ghetto. But we still hadn't understood exactly how much the Nazis hated us. Normal people couldn't imagine it. But we learned it when we went to Auschwitz, because after a while we weren't normal anymore either.

For a while on the first night, Muma simply couldn't make herself get into her bunk, which was boards with dirty straw on it. A lot of the women had diarrhea, and we could use the toilet only at certain times. The toilet was a large shed that had a long board with round holes in it over a trench. Three other women were in the same bunk. There was one blanket for the five of us, and the seams were white with lice.

Deep in my mind are two memories of those early days.

The head of our block (the blockova) was also a prisoner, a Jew named Editka. She cooperated with the Germans by seeing that we obeyed the strict rules. In return she had many privileges. Editka did not enforce the rules herself. She had two assistants, very mean young Slovakian Jewish women who were also prisoners.

I was standing near our bunk one day when an assistant guard came up. Her name was Elushka. I don't remember what we'd been ordered to do—something simple, like line up our shoes in a certain way. Muma's shoes did not please Elushka. Elushka raised her arm and struck Muma so hard that Muma fell to the ground.

Elushka dragged her up, ordered her to stand still, and hit Muma again so hard that her nose bled and a gash opened up over her eye. Muma fell down again and Elushka kicked her.

I watched, terrified. The other women were still and silent. Something happened inside me then. I decided I didn't want to live anymore. I was too scared to even try to protect Muma. I felt so ashamed that I'd rather be dead than alive.

A good way to kill yourself was to "go on the wire." Two women did it the day we moved into our hut. The Nazis had taken their children from them. The barbed-wire fence had 380 volts. One of the women managed to hit it. I heard a sharp, explosive crack and then a quiet click-click-click that went on and on for days. The Germans left the woman there, spread out like a squashed black fly. The other woman was shot before she reached the wire and left to die.

I couldn't get over my shame that I hadn't tried to help Muma, so I begged her, "Let's go on the wire." I meant it, but Muma looked at me as if I'd stabbed her in the heart. She started to say something but then stopped. She often used to say that life was precious, and maybe that's what she was going to say. But we knew how silly that would sound because we could see the crematorium chimney.

Finally Muma said something that surprised me. She didn't usually speak about God or holy things. She said, "God created you. He gave you life. No matter what, as long as you live, you have to appreciate it."

I didn't want to hear that. I knew Muma but I didn't know God.

"I don't care about Him," I replied. "Where does He live anyway? I'm hungry all the time. I'm frightened all the time, Muma. I don't want to stay here. It will only take a minute. Please, Muma, we'll hold hands and run on the wire together. Please, Muma, let's just do it."

These probably weren't my exact words. But I remember how I'd felt and how I'd begged her to let us die, and these are the words that arise in my head with that feeling.

My mother knelt down and cupped my face in her hands. What she said then I remember:

"Listen to me. Listen, Manuska. I want you to always remember what I'm telling you now. Promise? Always—never forget! We are still breathing. As long as we breathe, we live. As long as we live, we have hope."

Those words, and the way Muma fought to save me, were my inheritance.

The days dragged on. Summer was over, the mornings and evenings became darker and colder. Winter was coming. The thought of it was terrifying.

The regular visits of a handsome SS medical officer was the only time I felt joy. He came to look the women over. We had to line up. I hoped he'd notice me as he walked up and down. He always seemed happy, because he often whistled a tune and sometimes smiled slightly. His name was Dr. Mengele.

I was bursting to smile at him. I thought he was the only beautiful thing in Birkenau. His boots shone like Papa's used to. He smelled faintly of cologne. His cheeks were freshly shaven, his nails clean and manicured. I wanted to wiggle, to catch his attention. Dr. Mengele would look at the lineup. He'd ask the women to open their hands and stretch their fingers. Then he'd walk along the rows, sometimes touching the hands with his officer's stick.

I didn't tell Muma I liked him because I could tell she didn't. When this doctor picked out a woman, that woman seemed terrified.

One day a group of midgets arrived from Hungary. I loved them all. There was a grandmother and grandfather, sons and daughters, uncles and aunts, and lots of children who looked like big dolls. All were musicians and had the instruments of an orchestra in miniature. For some reason the Nazis had let them keep their little violins and violas and drums and bass. So they set up stools outside their hut and put on concerts. Their instruments were like tiny toys. Their sounds entranced me. My heart sang. I knew if I lived I could still be like Shirley Temple. I felt hope. It was a strange feeling to be happy again.

One day they disappeared. Dr. Mengele took them.

I said aloud, "He likes music. He's always whistling. He wants them to play for him."

Some of the women laughed at me in a nasty way.

I felt humiliated and stupid when they laughed. That day I learned that Dr. Mengele tortured people to death doing "scientific experiments."

I was eleven years old and was expected to know such things.

One day I lined up for a zell appell. That's when we were counted. In the winter it was the worst part of our lives because the bell not only rang at regular hours but sometimes in the middle of the night. When you heard it you raced to line up. Sometimes we'd wait in line an hour or two before the Germans counted us. Sometimes after the count the SS officer wouldn't dismiss us. We'd be left standing stiff and frozen like trees in a park for as long as the Germans liked. If you fell over, you were taken away and shot.

Muma didn't show up at this zell appell.

When it broke up, I ran around on wobbly legs calling for her. I didn't know who'd taken her or where she'd gone. Within a few minutes the bell rang again for another count, and my mother still wasn't there.

I was certain Dr. Mengele had taken her.

"Your muma's been given a job." The woman who told me was from our hut. "She's working. As long as she's working, she's all right."

I was frantic to know when she'd be coming back, when would I see her.

The woman shrugged. "I've told you all I know," she said.

I felt so angry at Muma for leaving me. I knew it was the Nazis' fault, but I still blamed her. She'd always protected me. I was wild with grief and fear. I scratched the lice bites on my legs until they bled. Muma had always stopped me from doing that. I gave them another good scratch. Where was she working? Why wasn't she with me?

That night from another block came the sound of music. It was thin and sad but very sweet. "Gypsies," someone said. Muma would have liked it. Could she hear it too? I wondered if there'd be more the next night. I remember the gypsies played each night but not for long. One night it was so quiet that I couldn't sleep. We didn't have any more music or gypsies after that.

Where are you, Muma? Everything seemed so black and painful. I felt so miserable, all the pain inside me felt heavy and black. I was forgotten. Muma was forgotten. All the people who lived in nice places everywhere had forgotten us. ↪

AUSCHWITZ (OSWIECIM) EXTERMINATION CAMP

When Maureen, Neil, Mania, and I roll up to the Auschwitz-Birkenau State Museum, we find the vast parking lot packed with cars and buses from all over Europe. Hundreds of teenagers pour out of the coaches, filling the morning air with the languages of Europe, the accents of Britain, both plumy and dockside, the varied sounds of the American states—all laced together with a scattering of Asian voices.

In 1974, almost twenty-eight years before I met Mania, I'd visited Auschwitz with a friend. We took a train from Krakow to the small railway station at Oswiecim. Whether we got out there or went a station or two farther I don't remember. What I do remember is that, walking down an unpaved road with flat fields on either side, the landscape was empty. No humans, animals, or cars—not even any houses. I didn't know then that the Nazis had demolished all farmhouses within a forty-kilometer radius of the camp to ease the recapture of any escaping prisoners and to hide their bestial activities.

We had walked through the iron gates with the overhead sign "Arbeit Macht Frei" and went where we pleased. There was no large museum at the camp's entrance as there is today. If we were stopped or questioned I don't remember it. There were a few men about, maybe doing odd jobs, and a handful of other visitors. We stood by the railway track where the camp orchestra, some of the finest musicians of Europe, sat and played as the starving workers left and came from work. We stood outside Block 11, where Dr. Mengele did his experiments and where Maximilian Kolbe, a Franciscan priest who gave himself in place of another prisoner, and hundreds of others, including children, were put to death with a phenol injection into the heart or arm.

We went to the execution wall, where thousands of prisoners, mainly Poles, were shot before the Nazis built the gas chambers and crematoriums intended to wipe out the entire seed of Israel. I remembered that spot when other far more important details were forgotten. Someone had placed yellow flowers in front of the wall. The vase still contained fresh water, but every flower was dead, as if it didn't want to live.

I remember how ambivalent I had been about going to Auschwitz. It seemed in bad taste, peculiar, and morbid. And wasn't it a terrible invasion of privacy to stare at pictures of people naked, terrified, being driven with whips to their death? I was ignorant enough to wonder if an interest in such things wasn't unhealthy, wasn't tainted by a trace of voyeurism.

If it hadn't been for my friend's insistence, I probably would never have gone. He was one of the few people, apart from those directly affected, who'd woken up to what this particular camp meant, how it revealed how close we are to being a race of savages. I was like most of the rest of the world: I didn't want to think about the degree of evil required to apply modern industrial methods to achieve the murder of millions of human beings. And when those who'd grasped the meaning of Auschwitz spoke out, few listened. Nobody wanted to ponder the significance Auschwitz held for each one of us in our ordinary, daily lives.

So this morning, nearly thirty years later, the sight of hundreds of teenagers pouring in and out of the glass entrance to the vast one-story museum fuels my hope. Those entering are chatting and shoving each other like little goats, the way kids do all over the world. Inside they stand and stare, mesmerized by the overblown pictures, mouths slightly open, bright canvas rucksacks strapped to their backs, taking in everything that the German High Command had tried so desperately to hide from the outside world. Exiting a couple of hours later, the kids traipse back to their buses in silence.

We're told there's nothing unusual about today's big crowd. People from around the world arrive daily. "Around the world"? I see no white dishdasha or women in embroidered *jillabeeya* enfolded in black *abayas*. Still, aren't the crowds evidence that we're at last starting to learn the lessons of history? Auschwitz shows the end result of being terrified of "difference." Every weekday of every year, thousands of young people look at the pictures of the crematoriums that shout, "This is where discrimination leads. This is the end result of ethnic and religious hatred." A few Holocaust scholars say Auschwitz has taught us nothing. But not for one moment do I think these crowds count for nothing. ↔

AUSCHWITZ-BIRKENAU

NOVEMBER 1943

One evening, three days after she had disappeared, my mother returned.

We crawled into the bunk and lay together while Muma stroked the wisps of hair that now covered my head. She talked softly and brightly as if she were happy. I knew she was putting it on because she looked different, not because she had sores on her scalp but because of the way she stared at me with a dull and hungry look.

Muma had been sent to Block 27, Camp B, straight down the road from Hut 14. She had a job in Warehouse 2. Everyone, even the Nazis, called this warehouse "Kanada." Muma said that was because "everyone knows that Kanada is a big country full of food and furs and riches, and everyone there is happy." "Kanada" was where the Nazis stored everything they stole from arriving prisoners—food, clothing, baby prams, silver, toys, shoes, jewelry, watches. Prisoners sorted out the loot, which was then shipped to Germany. Warehouse 1 was at the other end of the camp. It was called "Mexico." That's where all the junk and refuse went.

Muma was pleased with her job because it was inside work. She felt sure now she'd survive the war. We didn't talk about these things anymore. When she defied the Nazi officer on the selection ramp, I knew she'd never give up trying to save me.

My mother came several times after that, but they were hurried visits. We were scared because the Germans liked to have surprise zell appells. I tried to look happy when she came. I didn't tell her how I hated her being gone, that I was terrified being on my own all the time, that I felt sick waiting for her to visit. I didn't tell her that nobody took any notice of me or helped me or even spoke to me.

I never went to see her. There was a passage between her area and mine that was open during certain hours, but I didn't know exactly where it was. A count was taken as soon as work ended. If anyone was missing, the sirens started screaming and the dogs came in. So I was too scared to leave my area.

One day I became very hot and feverish. I could hardly breathe. I was sick a lot anyway, always coughing and having trouble getting enough air. This time I had scarlet fever. Editka sent me to the hospital, the *revier*, they called it. It wasn't a real hospital, just a sick bay. It didn't have any medicines or drugs or equipment. The Germans didn't mind shooting us or starving us to death, but they liked everything to look in order. They loved telling visiting officials that the prisoners had their own hospital.

The women working in the revier were Polish. I don't know whether they were nurses. They wore red triangles, not yellow stars, so they weren't Jews but political prisoners. My throat closed over. I could hear the nurses talking about me as I heaved and choked. They wanted to give me water, but they didn't even have that. Then one nurse had an idea. She had an apple in a parcel she'd been allowed to receive from home. She chopped it up and squeezed the juice into my throat. She could have let me choke and kept the precious apple for herself. I've forgotten so much, but I remember things like that, the way people can be so good.

My mother came to see me after I'd returned from the revier. I was weak and lying in my bunk. She tried to smile but her eyes were watery. She'd come days earlier to see me and couldn't find me. None of the other women could tell her where I was or whether I was dead or alive.

Then she said, "Manuska, my little darling." She started to cry. I hated it when she did that. "Manuska, I'm not well at all. I'm really sick."

Muma had never said anything like that before. I looked at her face. It was puffy and her stomach stuck out. I'd seen women look like that and they'd died. But Muma couldn't die. She couldn't leave me. She took off her shoes and climbed up into the bunk and lay beside me and stroked my hair. Then she said, "I've brought you something." She gave me a piece of bread. It must have been her bread, but I ate it and she looked pleased.

Again she said, "I'm very sick, but I had to come and see you."

All of a sudden the zell appell alarm went off like a kick in the stomach. Muma had two minutes to get back and be lined up.

"Go back, Muma," I cried.

She'd have to run. It wasn't very far, but her ankles and legs were thick and swollen, and the ground was covered in snow and crusted puddles of water. She couldn't be even ten seconds late. Some of the young Slovakian girls were very cruel, like Elushka.

Muma kissed me quickly and got down. Then she gave a little cry. "Someone's stolen my shoes!" I can't forget the look on her face, even today.

I wanted to get down and put my arms around her, but it hurt me to move.

"Go, Muma, go," I pleaded. "Hurry, hurry." I was so scared for her.

Muma went out the door in bare feet into the dark.

The next day when the bell rang for the count, I couldn't stand up.

Editka asked me if I had anyone. I said I had a mother but she was in Camp B.

It's strange that I can clearly remember Editka. She had short red hair and a round face with pale, creamy skin. And yet Muma's face by our apartment window is more like a soft, cloudy dream.

"You know what happens if you don't make the count," Editka said.

I knew. The SS guard came in and dragged you off to be shot, like a dog that wasn't any good anymore. I said I knew but I still couldn't stand.

"Come with me." Editka helped me get down and walked me to her office. There was a female guard sleeping there. Editka shook her awake.

"You've got to take the count for this one," she told the guard.

The girl went outside to be counted. Editka told me to get into her bed, and she covered me up and stuffed the bed a bit and then went outside.

Editka told the count officer that one of her guards had been on an especially long shift and she was sleeping. The officer sent a guard into Editka's office to check. He saw the body in the bed that was me. It satisfied him that nobody was missing. That's all they worried about, that the numbers were right and nobody had escaped.

(One Birkenau survivor has since said that my memory of this incident was faulty, that this could not have happened because everyone had to be present for the count, the blockova and all her guards included. But it happened as I've told it. Much stranger things than this happened in Birkenau.)

The next day I was deadly sick with typhus. Editka said it was too risky to hide me again. She'd send me to the revier, where she had friends, doctors and nurses who had been transported to Auschwitz with her. They'd try to help me.

The revier was not far from Hut 14. I staggered there. Editka told me to sit on the bench while she talked to the people she knew. I waited. There was a woman beside me, swollen and newly shaved. On my left side was a Greek woman holding a cup of chai, a tea made with herbs. I was burning with fever and my feet were swollen and frostbitten.

I asked the Greek woman for a sip of tea. Just one sip, I begged. She shook her head. Then the woman on my right, the one all puffed up, made a movement as if she was telling this woman to give me something to drink, and I turned around and looked at her. I stared. It took an instant to recognize her.

"Muma?" I asked and then screamed, "Muma!"

I lurched towards her. My arms went out. Muma couldn't speak because she was so ill with typhus. At that second Editka moved over, grabbed me by the hand, and jerked me up.

"Up! Away! Get away. NOW!" she ordered and dragged me to the door.

I dug in my heels and screamed for my mother, but Editka kept dragging me to the door. I clutched at it, looking back at Muma, trying to hold on, but I was too weak and my fingers slipped off the wood. And then we were outside with Editka dragging me across the dirt and hissing at me, "Run, run!" And then I tried to run.

Editka put me in her office. I was only half conscious. When I got my breath back, I choked on my sobs.

"Why did you take me? Why? Why?"

She answered in a flat, decisive voice, "One of the doctors tipped me off. The SS are coming in five minutes to clear out the revier. Everyone in it is going to the gas chamber."

I went back to my hut and lay on my bunk. Soon I fell asleep. When I woke up in the morning, I thought about my mother being dead.

I didn't feel anything. ↦

AUSCHWITZ (OSWIECIM) EXTERMINATION CAMP

MAY 14, 2002

Maureen has already verified Mania's arrival date at Auschwitz but wants to film Mania with the SS documentation in her hand. And I need to see the evidence for myself. So before we leave Auschwitz for Birkenau, three kilometers away, we're going to the administration building where the records are kept. This two-story redbrick building had been artillery barracks for the Polish army until it was taken over by the SS as headquarters for the administration of the Auschwitz camp, which later extended into four massive camps, one of which was Birkenau, and more than twenty subcamps.

Mania easily recalls the stages of her journey from her home in Katovice to her bunk at Birkenau but has no idea when this happened. Fortunately for me, the Nazis were fanatical about keeping meticulous records, including the arrival of every prisoner they intended to kill within the hour, and did so almost to the war's end. By verifying the date of Mania's arrival at Auschwitz, I'll be able to accurately reconstruct her entire journey.

We walk up the broad wooden staircase of the building to the second floor and enter a spacious but sparsely furnished office. During the SS occupation, these offices were furnished with pieces looted mainly from their Jewish victims, but it's back to basics now—a row of hard chairs along the wall, a large desk and chair, a small table and chair. My imagination starts working overtime. I put faces on the men whose hands slid along the same banister, who trod up and down these stairs in their calf-high power-boots, worked in this same room, perhaps on the same books that now lay spread before us. Some would be wearing the skull and crossbones on their cap, some as a knuckle-duster on their fingers. I wonder how these psychopaths had been raised as children. Did they torture the little animals given to them as pets? Who were their mothers and fathers? I can't say, "What in God's name did they teach them?" because obviously they taught them nothing in God's name.

Introductions are made, and Mania takes the proffered seat at the desk. A book the size and shape of an old-fashioned ledger is placed before her. She sits up straight and silent, like an accountant about to make a difficult and painful audit.

The official is kind and efficient, with greying hair but young enough for Auschwitz to count as history. "You know we have no names, just numbers." His voice is quiet, sympathetic. "They gave up recording them. Just too many transports to worry about individuals. But the station of origin was recorded. Your number again?" he asks.

"52894," Mania says. How many years has it been since she last answered that question at Auschwitz?

"And from Sosnowitz?"

"Originally Katowice, then Sosnowitz, then Srodula."

"Sosnowitz, Srodula, ah yes." He turns a series of pages filled with long lines of numbers, not individual numbers but lot numbers, 22298 – 35642, 39098 – 46756 and so on and so on, genocide and mass murder hidden behind figures, so tidy, so neat, such meticulous hand-writing and straight lines. I'm thinking of the SS brute who had done this, imagining that he'd probably been the top boy in his class, the teacher's pet, and likely a fink to boot. But I'm wrong. Mania is talking, and I can't hear what the soft-voiced administrator is saying, but he's talking about the partisans. Afterwards Maureen fills me in. The book was a copy made secretly and at mortal risk by members of the resistance who were prisoners within Auschwitz.

"Sosnowitz," the administrator says. "Yes, here we are. You'll find your number within this group." He runs his finger down the page and moves the ledger in front of Mania. "There."

Black ink on white paper. That's what's left. Mania and her mother, invisible and unknowable between the first and last recorded numbers, lost along with some four thousand others in that single morning's transport.

"The date you came," —the official looks up— "was the third of August 1943."

For a long moment Mania stares in silence at the orderly numbers lined up in black ink. This is what is left of her mother, Bubsha, and Tete. Then she thanks the official, perking up to do it, smiling brightly. Selfishly my first reaction is one of relief: now I can document Mania's story in accurate sequence.

As we start down the stairs that bore the brunt of killers, Mania again turns to the official and sends him a dazzling smile and a good-bye wave. Again I wonder how she keeps it up.

Driving along the road from Auschwitz I to Auschwitz II, the alternate name for Birkenau, I ask Mania if she's ever met anyone after the war who'd been with her in Hut 14.

After a long pause she says, "I saw Elushka, the young Slovakian Jewish girl who'd beaten up my mother."

Mania stares absently out the car window. On one side are empty flat fields, on the other an endless high-wired fence. I can feel in the closeness of the compact car how close she is to pain and realize that, after all these years, she's still touched by the same guilt and anguish felt as she'd watched her mother being beaten.

"I was serving tables at my kibbutz, Givat Haim, in Israel, not far from Tiberias," she says. "I was twenty-two or so by then. I went to take orders from a group at a table and she was there. I recognized her at once. The shock was terrible. I turned away and went to the kitchen.

"I told the supervisor there was someone in the dining room that I couldn't serve, that she had beaten up my mother when we were in Auschwitz. I said nothing to anyone else. The supervisor told me to go to the head of the kibbutz. I found him and told him my story. He was very surprised because Elushka, who was staying as a guest with one of the couples at the table, had said she'd been in Auschwitz and had had a terrible time.

"The head went back to the dining room with me, and from a distance I identified the woman in the group. He said, 'She'll have to leave. She can't stay at this kibbutz.' I can honestly say I didn't want revenge. I just couldn't bear to have her near me. I said nothing to her myself. The next day she was gone." ↔

111

DECEMBER 1943 – DECEMBER 1944

I spent all my time lying on the bunk. There was no reason to get up except for zell appells. There was no one to talk to; no one was interested in anyone else. There was nothing to do. Nothing to think about except staying alive.

I knew that Muma wanted me to live. But everyone wanted to live and nobody did. "Tomorrow isn't for us" is what one woman was always saying. I knew that one day the Germans would swoop down and catch me when I wasn't looking and take me away and gas me. I wondered what it would be like. Would they hold me down and smother me with gas? Everyone said, "They were gassed," but what happened when they gassed you? I didn't want to die. I didn't want to live either.

I could read and write, but there was nothing to read and nothing to write with. Nearly five years had passed since I'd been to regular school. I could speak Slovakian, German, and Polish, but I really didn't know anything. Sometimes Editka called me into her office and gave me an extra piece of bread. She was kind to me and I liked her, but liking her made me feel confused. She'd watched my mother being beaten for nothing and she hadn't done anything to stop it.

I didn't have any plans or dreams. Then something brought me back to life for a while.

One day, months after Muma died, I was standing outside the hut and a young woman stopped and talked to me. Grown-ups hardly ever did that. She gave me a piece of bread hidden in her jacket. We exchanged names. Her name was Mala. After she'd gone, someone told me Mala was famous in Auschwitz. She was just nineteen years old but spoke several languages so well that the SS had made her their messenger. *Laufer* was the German word for messenger.

Mala went "laufering" all over the camp. The Germans trusted her. They didn't know she despised them. She carried small contraband parcels from one part of the camp to another. She also took messages from the men's camp to the women's. And later I found out she was committing the worst crime of all: she was in touch with partisan fighters on the outside.

Then Mala escaped. She was in love with a Polish prisoner, and they escaped together. His name was Edward Galinski. Their names ran through the prison like lightning snaking across the ground. Everyone was stunned. It was possible to escape from Auschwitz!

Days went by and then a week. People started smiling when they talked about it. Two weeks passed and there was no word that they'd been caught. People were now laughing about it. Mala and her boyfriend had beaten the lying bastards at their own game. She and Galinski would be over the border and into Switzerland by now.

Then Mala and Galinski were captured. I knew the Germans would kill them, but they'd torture them first. We were ordered to report to the parade ground that separated the men's camp from the women's camp.

Mala had been placed between two gates on the parade ground, one that was the entry to the women's camp, the other to the men's camp. The road on which she stood led to the crematorium. An orchestra of inmates had been set up on one side. The orchestra played. We all marched by Mala. On order, we were forced to turn our heads and face her. I could see Mala. Her head was freshly shaven. She was white-faced and black-eyed. Her hands were bound behind her back, and her head was slightly hanging down.

Then we stood while the indictment was read. An SS officer read it, first in German and then in Polish.

I don't remember exactly what he said, except that he went on furiously about Mala betraying the trust the Germans had put in her. She had been given many privileges but she had abused them. She had been deceitful. She had failed. Everyone who tried to deceive the camp authorities would fail.

We stood silently, all of us starving to death while the Germans talked about trust and honor. Suddenly the women in the front ranks sucked in their breath. It made a strange whooshing sound. The officer reading the indictment stopped and turned. Blood was dripping onto the soil around

Mala's feet.

Mala had slit her wrists. Someone had slipped her a razor.

The Germans went mad. A guard flung himself at her. There was no strength in her body. Mala went down. She struggled to her feet. She refused to die like a dog.

A ripple of horror and joy swept through our lines. Horror at the blood that dripped from her hands, joy at the shit she was creating for her tormentors.

"You Jewish whore," the guard shouted. Taking Mala's arm he broke it. There was a brittle snap and an anguished scream. Today I can still hear that snap, like a candy stick breaking.

Then Mala's pain turned into shouts of rage. She called the Germans pigs—that I remember because her courage electrified me.

"You murdering pigs!" she shouted. "All the world knows what you're doing and you'll pay for it, you pigs!"

I heard another loud bang or crack, and Mala was lying on the ground, still alive but being hauled off.

Edward Galinski was tortured and hanged. I learned that much later. And Mala was dead, but exactly how, I've never known.

While I've forgotten so much, I remember Mala and that scene, probably because I felt safe while it went on because all the officers and guards were focused on Mala. They had her to torture and kill, and they weren't going to pay any attention to the rest of us. I was free to watch and remember.

I drifted on from day to day, doing nothing, thinking nothing, feeling nothing but fear. It was good that everything normal and decent inside me was in a coma. I used to notice the crematorium chimney sometimes. Now and then around the rim you could see red flames and sparks at night. Normally there was just black smoke, but I'd learned that when there were red flames it meant some new people, who still had a bit of fat on them, had arrived that day and were being burned.

I mention this because it was my childhood, and even if you escaped with your life, you took this childhood with you because it's the only one you'll ever have.

Something else happened that summer that I'd like to forget but can't because, again, it is part of my childhood.

I was sitting outside on a hot day. It was midsummer, maybe July. I'd been in Birkenau for nearly two years and had just turned twelve. The Germans were yelling at the men prisoners who were using picks and shovels to dig a very large pit on the other side of the wire near the men's camp. The guards were all on edge and worse than usual. They walked around poking at prisoners with their rifle butts, yelling at them to hurry.

A lot of women came over and stood near me. Nothing like this had happened before so close to the women's camp. Everyone was interested because we had nothing to do. The Germans didn't care that we were watching. To them we were already half dead, half gone from the earth. Soon we'd die, too, so there was no fear we'd bear witness to what they were about to do.

The sun was setting when a line of trucks moved into the area near the pit.

We stared in wonder because the trucks were filled with men, women, and children, and they'd come from a world we'd forgotten. Young and old people, all sorts, clean, well fed, standing upright, looking curiously around. The men wore suits, the young boys caps and sweaters, the little girls coats and sometimes matching hats. One was holding a doll.

My eyes were glued on the women. I drank in the way they looked, for it was just like Muma used to look. They wore dresses and smart hats and shoes—real shoes. They looked around, calm and interested. They weren't afraid. We were close enough to see that. We knew from our own experiences that they'd been told they were going to a work camp. Relief was written all over their expectant faces.

Something was wrong. Something very horrible was going to happen. I couldn't imagine what.

Those still in the trucks saw us staring at them. They stared back at us and saw what we were: a bunch of ratty-haired, starving people in rags, a group so near to death that our legs dragged as we moved. The arrivals swiftly scrutinized their surroundings and with new eyes they took it in—the huge pit, the tall brick chimney, soldiers now on the outer edge with machine guns. Something clicked. They started to look confused and uncertain. They balked at getting down. This wasn't a work camp.

They realized where they were.

Those on the ground panicked. Those in the trucks wouldn't move. The soldiers had been like tense maniacs all day, and now they became as hysterical as the prisoners. They screamed and cursed. The prisoners refused to leave the trucks. The SS officer shouted at the drivers. The drivers started their engines and tipped the flatbeds as if they were tipping out garbage.

The prisoners slid off the trucks and onto the ground. They couldn't move. They were paralzsed with fear. Then the Germans brought out the dogs.

We watched these people, some clutching children, being beaten into the pit. Some were shot and thrown in. It went on and on. Hundreds of people on top of each other, maybe a thousand. Then the Nazis poured gasoline on them and set them on fire.

We watched in silence from our side of the wire. The sounds were awful. It was close by but it somehow seemed far off and unreal. I watched an old bearded man. His beard was burning and he was crying out, "Shma Israel! Shma Israel!" Then flame covered him like an orange blanket. A cry came from the blanket: "Shma Israel!"

Then nothing.

The pit smouldered during the night. The stench seeped into everything—our hair, rags, skin, and our mouths, so you could taste it on your tongue.

That night a woman in our block said they were Czechoslovakian Jews from Theresienstadt. I asked her what "Shma Israel" meant. It was Hebrew, she replied. A sacred prayer that should be said several times a day. It meant "Hear, O Israel, the Lord our God, the Lord is One."

I decided I wouldn't cry the Shma when I was burned or gassed. There was nobody to listen. Or if there was someone called God, he really didn't care.

I can't remember much after that. I didn't want to be gassed but I wanted to go to sleep forever. I hung on by a thin memory in my head: Muma on her knees, pleading with me to live. But life worsened. Our two slices of bread a day were cut to one. Women in my block died all the time. In the morning I'd watch them being pulled out of our hut by one leg and tossed into a barrow.

The adults were now whispering all the time about the Allies. They were in France and Italy and moving towards Germany.

None of this meant anything to me. Muma had always said that the English would come. But that was at the beginning of the war and they never came. I thought the talk about the Allies were rumors. The more victories the Allies had, the more Jews arrived to be gassed.

I waited for the SS to come to Hut 14 for me. None of us knew the Germans were too busy killing new prisoners to fit us in, although we could see the crematoriums going day and night. We'd all soon die anyway. The sore on my heel was now big enough for me to poke my finger through from one side to the other.

Then one day Editka told me there was a transport leaving Auschwitz the next morning and she had put my name down for it. I felt myself shrink. Editka was the only adult in the whole world who knew me and called me by my name. But I was a prisoner, she was the blockova, and she'd let my mother be beaten for nothing.

I said nothing.

"I don't know where you're going, Manjika," she said. She always called me by the Czechoslovakian variant. "But it's to work in a factory."

I must have looked terrified.

Then I realized Editka was trying to do something good for me. She added, "I just want to get you out of here."

The next day I left Auschwitz. ↦

AUSCHWITZ-BIRKENAU

May 14, 2002

We stop at the high double gates. Sky-reaching wire fences spread out on either side and fade into a thin perspective. Our guide, Miroslaw Obstarczyk, leaps out and swings open the steel and wire, and we drive into Birkenau, the extermination section of Auschwitz.

We get out of the car. There are no other visitors; the silence is total. Permission must be had to visit these parts, and it's not always given. A two-story-high watchtower still stands guard by the entrance gate, the swan-necked arc lights still run along the two parallel barbed-wire fences, the unpaved road in front of the huts still goes to the site of the warehouses and crematoriums, blown up near war's end by the fleeing SS.

The natural world around us is soft and pleasant. A light breeze blows, the sun pours its warmth onto the soil, the grassy fields move in the sweet air. But there are no trees, no birdsong. The hard, empty huts look real, the softness of nature feels false. The huts stand as before, many reconstructed but they are just as they once were, line after line of nineteen in rows two deep, gravemarkers bearing witness.

The sight of them leaves me silent, not wanting to move but simply to stare, to soak in the sight of these ordinary, orderly huts. And to grasp with mind and heart the truth that these huts were once filled with ordinary women who just wanted to have a husband, create a home, raise children, swap recipes, go to the movies, take a book from the library. But instead, because the ersatz "science" of ethnicity triumphed over all divine and human values, they were systematically murdered.

I look at Mania. How can she bear it? Not all the 181 huts that were here have been preserved, but she is walking slowly down the road, looking for a specific one, her jaunty walk gone, her shoulders slightly bent. And then she stops, pulls her shawl tightly around her small body, turns, and beckons to us: Hut 14 is still standing.

Maureen walks ahead to pick the sites she wants, Neil sets up his camera, Mania stands silent at the hut door. After a while we go in. We stare at row after row of jammed double-layer bunks in rough wood planks. Mania is confused, looking around, trying to remember exactly where she and her mother had bunked. She walks between the rows once more, shaking her head hopelessly. She doesn't want to stay. She has to get out. She can't stand it. Outside she breathes as if she is suffocating.

After a few moments we walk through the calf-high grass to the hut behind. A plaque, partly hidden by grass, states that all children left alive after the destruction of the Warsaw ghetto were sent here.

"This can't be right," Mania cries, looking at the plaque in bewilderment. "What I am telling you is I never saw another child." But there must have been children here: the dates given on the plaque cover part of her own imprisonment. Her inability to remember them frightens and confuses her. It's a glimpse into the sheer terror in which she lived, a terror so powerful that avoiding pain and death was the only reality.

We walk away from Hut 14 down the gritty road, past the large parade ground where Mala gave her last gift of defiance to the women of the camp, and finally reach the site of a former crematorium. It is a scene of rubble and destruction: only the stone stairs leading to a nonexistent underground gas chamber remain. Two ducks paddle across a small pool formed by an indentation of the ground where ashes from the crematorium were once tossed.

Neil films, Maureen directs, Mania, seventy, stands still, thinking of her twenty-eight-year-old mother. Miroslaw speaks of the number of people who died here, a stunning number for what looks like a small location. And then Mania does something that makes Miroslaw exclaim in shocked surprise: From the gritty soil she picks up a small piece of grey bonelike matter. Miroslaw looks horrified as Mania holds it up and asks in Polish, "Is this a bone?"

"No!" he says, taking it and throwing it away. "It's ceramic."

He tries to draw her away, but Mania bends to the soil again, unaware or indifferent to his distress. Digging with her beautifully manicured nails, she filters the soil through her fingers as if trying to find something. Then she straightens up, wipes her hands one against the other, and says, "The whole world is buried here, including my mother."

We leave and go back to the hotel. And now I'm sitting here trying to describe something that happened to me at Birkenau.

As I walked along the dusty road back to the car, I suddenly felt so infused with love and pity for all who had died there that I seemed to be outside myself. I seemed to split into two, and the feeling I had seemed to be of another quality, of another place. It went way beyond one of compassion and ordinary love, so intense was its sweetness and so endless its space. My sense of acceptance and love was for all men and women who'd ever lived and struggled and suffered, and it seemed at that moment that this love was the only thing that existed. This sense of a transcendent reality was woven into a fresh, awakened love for my long-dead brother, Robert. It was as if his death was connected with, was part of, the pain and death of all those who'd been here. I saw why he had died, "tossed his life away at twenty-one, the idealistic, foolish boy," I used to say. He had not wanted to give up his studies to become an architect nor have his body committed forever to German soil, so far from the sun and sand of his native land. He had not wanted to burn to death as his plane did a slow spiral to earth, as later records show it had. He joined the Air Force because evil had overrun Europe. He understood, without ever having heard it, the remark Miroslaw made as he stood at the site of the train ramp at the gates of Auschwitz: "In every human the beast is sleeping. And the problem of our life, the sense of our life, is to not wake up this beast."

I felt as if a burden lifted from the back of my neck, as if a shell of concrete was breaking up. Walking along that gritty road, I found myself saying to God and to my brother, and for some reason, to the whole world, "Forgive me." I wasn't quite sure for what, because what had I, as a child in Australia, to do with all this? Yet the need for cleansing, for forgiveness, was deep. I wasn't troubled or anguished. I just wanted to be purer, to feel more deeply, more often, the sweetness of the compassion that had just overwhelmed and filled me.

It isn't until now, back in my hotel room and writing about it, that I think of another reason for this sense of a need to be forgiven. Perhaps it was because I am a Roman Catholic, the most powerful and best-organized church in the world. It's failure to denounce Nazism as it started to take root in the early thirties, its failure to use its mighty, universal voice to shout for justice as the evidence of its evil grew, had always mortified and shamed me. I have read the reasons given by apologists and scholars for the silence of the Vatican, of Pope Pius XII, of the College of Cardinals, and remain mortified and shamed. The deaths of hundreds of Catholic priests and nuns who resisted the Nazis remain for me a tragic gift that sustains my faith in the face of the miserable historic reality of a deadly silence.

For the first time I know I have no choice but to record Mania's horrific yet intriguing story. I'm filled with awe at the faith of the prisoners who were observant—the parents struggling to accept the loss of their children, the old man with his beard aflame, still shouting praise to God. Their faith was something the Nazis couldn't touch, steal, or destroy. I'll write the story not only for Mania but also for Gelcia and all the other innocents who never had a chance to celebrate life. I know a million Holocaust stories have already been told, but each story has its own value. And maybe, just maybe, by doing so I can make my small amends to those who might still have had a life if Rome had chosen to use its mighty spiritual and economic powers to combat the evil it must have perceived. ↔

REICHENBACH

It was a bitterly cold day when I left Auschwitz, and about a year after my mother had died. We prisoners climbed into the open wagons of a train, the type that hauls coal, with wooden sides and no roof.

I found myself crushed up against some girls about my own age whom I'd never seen before. They smiled at me. Something in me stirred. A chance to have friends! I hadn't had a friend since the girl who died at Srodula. Standing upright in the rushing wind and rain, we shouted our names.

"Mania!" I cried.

"Zola!" "Irina!" "Dolly!" they cried one by one, making small hand movements and giving half smiles.

I wished my mother knew I was getting away from Auschwitz. I wished she knew I had friends. I wished she were alive and with me.

The train shunted around for days. We stood in the open wagons, piled onto each other like a load of coal, except our heads and shoulders were layered with snow. I started coughing my lungs out. The hole in my heel was wide open and running. I wasn't going to make it. I was too weak and sick. I remembered what my mother said: "As long as we breathe, we live. As long as we live, there's hope." I tried to believe it but couldn't. I'd escaped from the peasants' hut outside Sosnowitz. A Gestapo agent had taken me away from a selection. Muma had rescued me from the gas-chamber line at Auschwitz. But my luck was running out. A woman next to me died, frozen stiff, and we were forced to throw her out of the wagon and onto the embankment.

My angel had deserted me. Or so I thought. In fact, I was heading for the greatest mystery of all.

We stopped at last at a place called Reichenbach. We'd been shuttled around and sidelined for days to end up—I don't know—maybe 150 kilometers from where we'd started.

Reichenbach was a real work camp, a slave labor camp but not a death camp. No chimneys belching black smoke, no miles of huts and barbed electric wiring, no stench. A high wall, stone barracks, wooden dormitories, and miles of white countryside surrounded by frozen forests and hard, fallow fields.

We were given soup and bread. Some scraps of vegetables floated in the soup and we got two pieces of bread, not the Auschwitz single slice. In our eyes it was a feast. Dolly and I found bunks near each other in a two-story stone building that looked and felt like a stone icebox.

Other prisoners told us about Reichenbach being one of several camps in a network called Gross-Rosen, the name of a nearby village. The camps provided foreign workers, including prisoners of war, for the local German factories. That's what we'd be doing—working in factories in the town of Reichenbach about five kilometers away. Some Gross-Rosen prisoners were highly skilled. The guards weren't as brutal as at Auschwitz, but they'd still shoot any prisoner who fell or even stumbled on their way to or from work. They were punished severely if a prisoner escaped and took no chances of that happening.

This terrified me. I was weak and wobbly. I'd never worked. I had no skills. I would never have been chosen for a work camp if Editka hadn't put me on the list. So I was petrified the next morning when, after the count, a female SS guard gestured for me to go into her office. I stood in front of her small desk. I was trembling but couldn't take my eyes off her. She was beautiful. She was the Führer's dream woman: blonde, blue-eyed, tall, slim, and serving the Fatherland.

She asked me if I spoke German. I said yes.

"What's your name?"

"Mania."

"Hmm. I don't think it is Mania. I think it is Marie. What's your name again? Is it Marie?"

I nodded.

"Are you a Jew?"

"Yes." Would they hang me now?

The beautiful Nazi shook her head. "No, you are not a Jew. Say you're not a Jew."

But I couldn't. I'd been through this before. When was it? I tried to remember, but all I could recall was the sick feeling in my stomach when I'd denied being a Jew. So I kept my mouth shut. Then the guard sighed and she became very businesslike.

"You'll be going to work, and it's very cold early in the morning. You'll need a hat and gloves and some socks." She turned away and took some things from a box. "Here, take these. They'll help keep you warm." She looked at me in a wondering sort of way. "How old are you?"

"Twelve."

"Twelve? You're very tiny for twelve."

So I should be big and fat? Of course I was small and skinny, and it was the Nazis' fault. I stared at the plank floor and said nothing. Overnight I learned the guard's name: Corporal Johanne Clausen.

Over the next few days I saw Corporal Clausen around. Maybe she was watching me, I don't know. Then one day she ordered me into her office again. This time I wasn't so scared. I was enjoying my gloves and socks and nobody had hanged me.

"You can sit down, Marie," she said.

I stumbled into the low chair opposite her.

For a while she just looked at me. Then she said, "You know, I am not married. I do not have any children. I've been thinking. After the war—it will be over one day—I'd like to adopt you and have you as my daughter."

I didn't know what to say. She meant it, absolutely. I could feel it. I also felt the craziness of it. People like her had killed everyone I loved. And now I was orphaned and she wanted to adopt me? Why would she want me as her daughter? She had blonde hair and blue eyes, and I had blue eyes but red hair. Her daughter? She was a Nazi and I was a Jew.

It was an insane idea! A strange, unfamiliar feeling ran through me. The idea was crazy, but it made me feel good. SS guard Clausen was an adult. She knew I existed! She liked me! She wanted to be liked by me! Editka had liked me and I'd liked her. But thinking about Editka gave me a pain in my heart. She'd stood by and let my mother be beaten bloody for nothing.

Another day went by. Meanwhile I tried to keep one slice of bread for when I felt weak. Eat one and hide one. Twice I did this, and twice some woman in my hut stole the hidden piece. This woman probably had had kids of her own, yet she knew she was killing me.

I told Zola. Zola was shorter than I and very skinny and had big black eyes. Like me, she was alone. She was smart and, except for the Nazis, didn't take abuse from anyone. She'd already managed to get herself a job carrying the empty soup containers back from the SS mess hall to the kitchen. Sometimes there was some liquid and scraps of vegetables left in the bottom.

One day I ran into her carrying an empty container almost as big as herself. She told me to go with her. We crept around the back of a hut and, crouching down, cleaned out the scraps with our fingers. Sharing your food with another prisoner was acting like God. So I told her about the woman who was stealing my bread. Before I knew it, I had my share of bread back. Zola stole it from the woman who'd stolen from me. That stopped it. That was Zola.

Another day went by. I was aware now that SS guard Johanne Clausen had her eye on me. But she didn't ask anything of me until the night we started work. And then all she said was to obey the camp rules, march properly to and from work, don't try to escape, and work hard.

I was beginning to feel this Nazi guard was a sort of friend.

Dolly and I were put to work in the Telefunken factory in Reichenbach. Going to and from work was dangerous. Because it was winter, the five-kilometer march was always in darkness. The snow was packed hard and the winds were bitter. A long section of our march went through woods where the piled-up leaves were thick and slimy underfoot and the uneven path went up and down.

The guards watched us every minute. They weren't going to let a prisoner slip off into the dark and escape into the woods. So they shot to kill anyone who fell. We marched five abreast, sick with terror that we'd stumble.

After leaving the woods and frozen fields, we entered town. The factory was a two-story redbrick building in an area of large, beautiful homes. To get there we had to go down one of Reichenbach's main streets. Thousands of people saw us tramp, tramp down the broad street right under their windows, right under their noses. No matter what they said after the war, they knew about kids and slave labor.

Once I reached the factory, I sat on my bench in front of a machine for a shift of ten or twelve hours. I had very good eyes. My job was to measure and cut wires as thin as a hair. Halfway through we were served some soup.

One night I was sitting, head down, working. My soup was finished. Then I felt someone beside me. Without a word SS guard Clausen passed me a second bowl of soup. I didn't speak. She didn't speak. It was as if there was a pact between us. From then on, every night I got something extra—soup or bread or the hot watery mix called coffee. Later, without looking at her, I mouthed the words, "Thank you."

When important visitors came to the factory, SS guard Johanne Clausen brought them to my bench. As I worked, head down, knowing better than to stare at the visiting big shots, she would state my age, praise my abilities, and act as if I already belonged to her. Later she would come back to the bench, say some simple thing, and smile warmly.

I knew then it didn't matter to her that I was a Jew and she an SS member. She wanted to do everything she could to save me, and that thought split me in two—not because of the praise or the food. I pushed it in and gobbled it down without a thought about anyone or anything. I was starving; food was everything. And SS guard Clausen's flattering words made me feel stronger, like I was worth saving.

I was torn apart because SS guard Clausen looked forward to a future. SS guard Clausen and I were in it; Muma was not. She'd fought so hard to stay with me and the Nazis had killed her. How would she feel if she knew a Nazi was stepping into her shoes, claiming me, planning to make me her daughter and raise me the way she wanted to raise me? Maybe SS guard Clausen would even try to make me a Nazi!

I had no one to talk to. I went over and over Muma's words when I wanted to go "on the wire." "God created you," she'd said. "He gave you life. No matter what, as long as you live, you have to appreciate it. As long as we live, we have hope."

I talked to her in my heart: "Muma, it's a Nazi who's giving me life and hope. Do you mind, Muma? Do you mind?" I felt I had to talk to

Muma about it, but actually I didn't feel guilty. All I wanted was for the food to keep coming.

As the weeks passed, the flow of extra food from SS guard Clausen continued. I became a little stronger. I could march to work without feeling I'd pass out. The leaking hole in my ankle closed up.

Dolly, who was fourteen or fifteen, and I became friends. I never knew her surname. We marched daily in strict silence to and from Telefunken together. None of us ever talked about our parents or grandparents or homes or what our mothers or fathers did or what pets or clothes we'd had. Those things were all gone. All we ever talked about was how hungry we were and whether we'd live much longer.

But one night in the camp, Dolly came to me and stuck something in my hand and said, "Look what I've made you. Here, take it."

It was a little necklace made of wire she'd filched from the factory, with dried-up berries in it for beads.

I'd never had anything like it. I loved it. It could have been made of rubies and diamonds and I couldn't have loved it more. It was meant to be like beautiful jewelry. It spoke of another world, a world my mother had been in when she put powder on her face or silk stockings on her legs, or sat on her little chair before the mirror and looked at herself, first this side, then the other.

No one had ever given me any sign before that I was a young woman, a female. I didn't have any breasts. I'd never had a monthly period. None of the girls or women did. Starvation and terror dries a woman's body up and sends out messages to a young girl that she can't menstruate because her body isn't fit enough to bear a child. Now I felt a rush, an awareness of self that I'd never had before. I didn't analyze it as such, yet I sensed unknowable possibilities if I survived.

I threw my arms around Dolly. I didn't think about it; I just did it. I could feel myself slowly coming back to life. Then something wonderful happened to help this feeling.

When Muma and I had entered Auschwitz, we'd lost all our family photos. But one of the men prisoners working in the Telefunken factory—to this day I've never found out who—had recognized me. He had not been in Auschwitz because I suppose he was a highly trained technical specialist and had been sent into a work camp from the beginning. He had managed to hold on to some photos of prewar times.

One night I came back from work, and lying on my bunk was a photograph of my parents. There they were, shoulder to shoulder laughing with two other couples at a dinner celebration, looking at me from the world that was stolen from us. I feasted my eyes on it, stared as if it were a miracle. This is what my father looked like! This is what Muma looked like then—happy, sweet, full of life and tender dreams.

A few nights later as we marched home from work, Dolly slipped and fell. She was on the outside next to me. I wanted to stop and pull her up. But SS guard Clausen, who was one of the escorts, shoved me on the shoulder and harshly ordered me to "move, move."

Before Dolly could stand up, another guard shot her. I marched on and left her lying there, dead or alive I don't know. I suppose they threw her into the woods.

It all happened within ten seconds.

I don't remember Dolly's face, just the powerful feeling of love and hope I had when she gave me the necklace.

After that Johanne Clausen was always an escort and always by my side. I don't know how she managed this. I don't remember whether she had a gun or how she treated other prisoners. I never saw her beating anyone. However, she was a Nazi and had probably trained at Ravensbrück concentration camp, where women guards were taught to be brutal.

Frankly I didn't care. SS guard Clausen gave me bread. Nothing else mattered. ↬

ŚWIDNICA

In the spring Poland is a heavenly country—rolling pastoral lands, distant mountains, deep blue lakes, and small villages. Driving in two separate cars from Auschwitz to Świdnica we stopped for lunch at a small family-run café. Not much was available except the ubiquitous ham and sausage, and whenever I see either I imagine some poor doomed pig, just two or so rungs down from humans in intelligence, having its throat cut. I don't think this scruple makes me superior; it's just the way I am. So I had a bowl of excellent soup.

Now we've checked into the Hotel-Piast Roman in the center of this medieval town. I've washed up and taken off my shoes and socks, and am sitting on a chair with my feet on the bed, making notes.

Riding into Świdnica, I asked Mania something I'd been meaning to ask for days: had she ever seen Editka again after Birkenau?

Instantly Mania's eyes went watery.

"That is something I am so sorry about that I will never forgive myself," Mania says. "I never saw Editka again. I had the chance and I didn't take it. We got in touch after the war. She went to university, did medicine, and became a pediatrician. She married. We wrote several times. She said she longed to see me and I felt the same way, because I understood as an adult why she had not interfered when the Jewish Kapo Elushka beat my mother. Then I was in Europe and I had the chance. We spoke on the phone. She begged me to come. But my friend wanted to go to Berlin, not to where Editka lived. And I chose to go to Berlin. And a while after I got back to Toronto, I had a letter from Editka's husband saying she had died. She hadn't told me she was ill. I'll never forgive myself."

I want to ask Mania why she is so unforgiving of herself when she is incapable of harboring resentment against anyone else, even the Germans. But I say nothing. Maybe later, if the right moment comes. Maybe. ↔

REICHENBACH AND RESCUE

One bitter morning in late January or early February, work was canceled. We were confined to camp. It was a terrible winter—icy, heavy snow, our hunger worse than ever because our rations were halved. We were getting no more than we had gotten at Auschwitz. But we could feel something was happening. The guards rushed around, and the icy air crackled with tension.

We'd heard rumors that the Russians were heading our way from the east and that the Allies were closing on Germany from the north and west. I'd lived with rumors all my childhood; they meant nothing. But Zola, a kitchen worker, said that in the mess all the guards talked about was the Russian advance. They were very depressed, and some SS officers were even guardedly talking about possible defeat. An officer doing that a year earlier would have been shot for treason.

This was scary news. What would happen to us if the Allies came closer? Older prisoners said the Germans would kill us all—certainly the Jews. It explained why all the soldiers were rushing around in a panic. They sometimes went to pieces when they were ordered to kill everyone and they drank a lot of vodka too. In Birkenau I'd seen them go crazy before the Jews arrived from Theresienstadt. SS guard Clausen couldn't protect me if some Nazi somewhere signed a paper to kill us all.

We talked about there being no crematorium, so they'd probably shoot us in the woods. Maybe make us dig pits first. I'd seen them do that, too, but that was in summer when the ground was soft. Now the ground was too frozen for digging graves. Still, they'd never let us go. And if they did ship us out of Reichenbach, where would we end up? In a death camp?

We were ordered to collect our things. Our things? I was wearing all I had: a cotton dress, a worn sweater, a wool coat, and, tied at my waist, my tin cup and spoon.

Why would we take a cup and spoon if they were going to shoot us in the woods? Maybe they were going to let us live. Maybe they weren't. It would be easier to stop us from panicking if we were told to take our cups and spoons. I remembered how they'd tricked us into going to the Athletic Field. And the Czechoslovakian Jews—they'd been tricked until moments before they were burned alive.

I left Reichenbach like everyone, sick with fear. I marched in line into the woods. I waited second by second for a burst of machine gun fire that would kill me. The trees on each side were frozen. That's where they'd hide, in the woods. There'd be a terrible noise and pain, and then I'd be dead.

We walked on and on, legs trembling. Then the trees thinned out. We were walking across fields towards town. We were still alive. On the tracks ahead of us was a freight train. Fear turned into delirious relief. We climbed into the open coal wagons. Soon the train was moving.

And then I remembered SS guard Johanne Clausen.

I hadn't thanked her, hadn't said good-bye. What would happen if the Russians got hold of her? The Russians hated the Germans. Maybe she'd be transported to Russia. Maybe she'd be sent back to Germany with all the other SS troops to fight the Allies. Or maybe some other SS guard would betray her to a higher authority because she'd broken rules to protect me.

I really wished I'd said good-bye. I'd be dead without her.

We were all jammed into an open freight car. Zola, Irina, and I were together again. The train pulled out. I thrust my hand into my coat pocket and held the necklace Dolly had made me in my screwed-up fist. I swore I would keep it for the rest of my life.

The snow blew in our faces, whitened our heads, soaked our clothes, and swamped our shoes. Nobody knew where we were going; not even the Germans, it turned out. We weren't given any food. We had snow for water. We stood night and day, frozen as statues. No toilets. Anyone who sat down never got up.

I had a terrible pain under my arm, but I couldn't raise my arm because we were so jammed. After a few days there was room to lift it and have a look because several women had died and been tossed off. Under my armpit was a lump bigger than an egg.

One night the train stopped at a camp somewhere, and we stayed a couple of nights. The pain in my armpit was excruciating. A prisoner who'd been a nurse lanced my armpit, made a sort of drain, and stuck it into the pus-filled abscess. Then we were loaded back on the train. After a couple of days the drain had to come out. A woman made tweezers out of wire and pulled out the drain, and yards and yards of hard white stuff came with it. There were no pain killers, nothing sterile, and all of us were crawling with lice, yet the wound healed within days.

We kept moving. Each camp we came to was overflowing with thousands of starving prisoners. Sometimes the train was shoved onto a siding and we were stuck there for hours. One night we pulled into Bergen-Belsen camp. There was no room for us. No room for the thousands who'd arrived before us. No room, no food, no water. We were ordered back on the train.

We chugged along like a load of unwanted sick animals. The Germans didn't know where to dump us. Nobody could handle us. There was nothing in any of the camps for us, not even room to lie down. The wagon ahead of us was filled with gypsies. When one of them died, some bit their throat and drank the blood before tossing the body over the side.

A woman in our wagon recognized the area and said we were heading for Hamburg. But before we reached there the train stopped at an old siding. A pile of abandoned boxes stood near the track. There weren't many guards around. Most had been sent off to fight. Some of the prisoners got down and investigated. The boxes were filled with sardines packed in salt. We poured off the train, shoving and struggling. I fought the best I could, but I was a shrimp in a sea of starving sharks. Then we were ordered back on the train.

The next day most of the women who'd eaten the sardines puffed up and died.

I didn't think twice of the women who died. No room for that. Just relief I was such a shrimp that I hadn't gotten any. Maybe I was meant to live! The possibility burst on me and made my heart race. I was twelve and in three months I would turn thirteen. Thirteen seemed like a turning point. If I could just reach that magical age, maybe I'd make it.

Finally we stopped at a camp near Hamburg. I can't remember its name. Irina and Zola were put to work in an underground munitions factory. I was too weak to work. I was confined to my blockhouse. Now the old Auschwitz terror returned. What would happen to me? I was a sick Jew who couldn't work. I knew what this meant, I wasn't the innocent child who'd entered Auschwitz. This was the Nazis' last chance to kill people like me.

The prison camp was in chaos. The sewers were overflowing. A half cup of water for drinking, nothing for washing. Watery soup some days, nothing on other days. Dead bodies stacked like cords of wood. All around me was talk of Allied victories and the rumor that the Third Reich was finished.

The guards were kids or old men. The few SS who were left didn't strut anymore. They no longer kept records, held zell appells, or bothered about things being in order. Their faces were sour, disbelieving, as if they'd woken up from a magical dream and found themselves knee-deep in shit.

I had a new feeling, too, when I woke up each morning. I had a mad hope that maybe, just maybe, I would live. I would fulfill Muma's dream. I would survive the war. Of both my mother's and father's families, there'd be one person left on earth to remember them.

We were at this camp for about six weeks. Then one morning came the familiar cry: "Raus, raus!" Soon we were moving on in the same open coal wagons we'd been in before. But this time we could sit down because so many prisoners had died.

Everything was going to pieces. All the coarse-faced bullies who'd shoved us in and out of transports for the past five years had disappeared. Our guard was a very shabby, very old German, like a daddy from some poor farm. We could have taken the gun from him and shot him if we'd wanted. Having Old Daddy guard us made it clear the end was near. But still the Germans controlled us, and still our train wandered on and on, around and around. And still we lived in fear of sudden death.

Then one day the train stopped. Nobody knew where we were. Old

Daddy didn't know. Some people walked up to our train and started speaking in a different language.

"What's being said?" I tugged at the woman next to me, but she shoved me aside. She was listening; she could understand.

"It's Danish," she cried. "They're Danes!"

I didn't understand. I thought she said "Dunes." Who were the "Dunes"? I'd hardly been to school. I didn't know what Danish was or where Denmark was. I didn't know any of the things you learned at school. Then we left again and the train continued. What was happening? All the women were talking, but the grown-ups paid no attention to me, a kid. I made up my mind not to ignore kids if I lived to be grown-up.

After a while we stopped and were told to get down. We stood on the ground and this is what I saw:

On one side were German soldiers, on the other side were Danish soldiers. The Germans saluted the Danes, the Danes saluted the Germans.

The Germans turned around and marched off. Then the Danish soldiers marched off. A group of people in civilian clothes approached us.

"What's happening?" I asked.

"We're free," someone said.

We stood by the train, still and silent. Moments passed. Nobody moved. Most prisoners fantasized that one day they'd be free even when they knew they wouldn't be, and this fantasy seemed to be the same for everyone, a sort of worldwide subconscious, slow-motion movie. The Russians or the Americans would suddenly appear at the gates of Auschwitz. They'd open them wide and all the prisoners would pour out. Now we were somewhere standing by the side of a train and being told we were free.

We watched the retreating Germans; we watched the retreating Danes. Free? Free!

Suddenly I felt very frightened. I thought, "Now there's no war. I'm twelve. I haven't any family—nobody. How can I be free? How can I live if I'm not in a prison? What am I going to do? Where will I go?"

I couldn't remember the world before the Nazis came. I tried to remember what normal was. But I couldn't. ↵

ŚWIDNICA COUNTRYSIDE

MAY 16, 2002

We're off to the Gross-Rosen Archives this afternoon, hunting down anything that might illuminate Mania's life at Reichenbach and the presence or absence of Johanne Clausen Müller. We drive some four kilometers through narrow roads and old villages. I am reminded that this is not Vancouver as we pass a chimney sweep—black hat, padded jacket, knee-high boots, an armful of chains and brushes—and the occasional stork nesting atop a chimney.

At the archives we're met by archivist Aleksandra Kobielec—Ola to her friends. She's groomed with the elegance common to women here: platinum-grey hair, steel-grey suit with a peplum jacket, silver broach. The large building looks like a former manor house, sparsely furnished but elegant proportions inside and out. With Ms. Kobielec is a bright young researcher, Elzbieta Gibokova, and our English-speaking contact at Gross-Rosen, Magdalena Zajac.

An interview with Ms. Kobielec turns up no confirmed date for Mania's arrival here. All Reichenbach records were destroyed by the Germans. But from information derived elsewhere, Ms. Kobielec says that Mania came in November 1944, and was evacuated in February 1945.

I ask about the possibility of a strong, healthy twenty-seven-year-old local woman working as a guard at the camp in 1944. Ms. Kobielec gives a full but scrupulous reply, avoiding any words that would conclusively point to Johanne being an SS guard.

She says that as the war turned worse for the Third Reich, the male guards at labor camps were transferred to Auschwitz because the SS troops there were sent to the fighting fronts. Prison guards were then recruited locally. All guards lived in the surrounding areas. Women? Yes. In 1944? Yes. Probably this was their only work opportunity. Initially the women received their training at Ravensbrück camp, but later this stopped. They were simply put into uniform and sent to the camp.

Ms. Kobielec notes that the archive workers are in a race against time in

139

documenting memories of ex-prisoners. Interviewers have found out that the older ex-prisoners are, the less comfortable they are talking about this time. She remarks, "It's easier for the grandchildren than the children of survivors to come here. The first generation was poisoned by memories, the next generation less traumatized."

She mentions that she is the daughter of people in a similar camp, and it is extremely rare for a woman ex-prisoner to visit Gross-Rosen. "Men search for details about their past, but the women, more sensitive, are psychologically blocked," she says. Mania's visit is considered a very important one. "Until now, we had no knowledge there were children in the Reichenbach camp. Now at last we learn there were three."

We're almost back to Świdnica when I remember with a start—Dolly! Mania, Irina, Zola, and Dolly. Four children.

I look at the others in the car. Mania is happy. She's given the archives information, and giving away anything makes Mania happy. Not the time to mention Dolly. Not even the time to mention Johanne, whom she'll meet tomorrow on the former camp grounds at Reichenbach. And not the time to mention that in all our discussions at the Gross-Rosen Archives, the word "German," as in "the Germans were to blame," did not come up once. No desire for revenge in the hearts of those who work there—only a powerful wish to remember and heal. ↭

JOURNEY'S END

MAY 1945 – EARLY 1947

The Danes took us over and treated us like babies. They started feeding us very slowly with soft food so our bodies would get used to food again. Overeating killed starving prisoners. Half awake, half dreaming, floating along, that's how I was.

Don't ask me how long we stayed in Denmark. A few weeks perhaps. Then we were shipped to Sweden. Not only the Jewish kids but Jews and Gentiles and men and women. I went on floating along. Irina and Zola were with me. I don't know who took care of us, the Swedish government or private agencies.

We were isolated from other Swedes because nobody knew if we were carrying diseases. Very slowly the doctors increased our food rations. The Swedes, too, treated us like precious babies. I just let things happen to me. It was so nice to drift; what else could I do? I hadn't any idea what I would do alone, where I would go, and how I would survive once the kindness ended.

One day we were put on a bus and driven to a very beautiful part of Sweden—I have no idea where. Irina, Zola, and I and some of the other girl survivors were enrolled in a private boarding school. The warmhearted Swedes worked hard to give us a normal life. We celebrated every girl's birthday, went weekly to a nearby boys' school for a dance, wore school uniforms, and took art and ballet lessons.

When summer came we went to "camp" for three or four weeks. Swedes opened their homes to us and accepted us as their own children. In return we worked in their fields, bringing in the harvest, probably more a nuisance than a help. Everything—fresh air, sunshine, companionship, the smell of newly cut grains—made these farms like heaven on earth. In the fall we returned to our schools, our bodies strong and tanned.

The Swedes tried so hard to make up for things, to make us like normal kids. And by now we looked normal. Our hair was shiny and silky, our faces filled out, and our bodies even had some fat on them. I couldn't see my ribs anymore, and two little breasts sprouted. It was the same with all the girls: breasts started springing out of flat chests and we all got our periods. We seemed normal and looked normal. But we weren't and never would be.

One day some people came. They were Jews searching every school in Sweden for lost souls, for Jewish children who had nobody. They were going to give us home and community in Palestine, they said. We, in turn, would be going to build the state of Israel.

This was a big surprise to me. I didn't know where Palestine was or what they were talking about. Vaguely I had heard of Palestine before, but what I'd heard I could not remember. And what was this Israel we were going to build? I didn't want to go to Palestine; neither did Irina nor Zola. On the other hand, school was so boring. I was so far behind that I'd lost all interest in learning. If we went to Palestine, maybe that could be the end of school!

We went with these people to their center, which was a huge, beautiful home. I learned new words and took part in prayers and rituals I knew nothing about. The people in charge of this house were "pioneers" from a "kibbutz" in Palestine. They were "the elite," and everyone treated them with great respect. There were other people in this beautiful home, survivors about three or four years older than I was. They were waiting for a boat or some way to get to Palestine, and were prepared mentally and physically.

I remember one in particular because of what happened to him later. Benjamin, a beautiful young guy who'd been raised deeply religious and strictly orthodox. He was about sixteen, strong enough to work so he had not been killed, but his mother, father, brother, and sister had been. There were other kids there whose families had been assimilated like mine, and they'd never been taught much, if anything, about Judaism. Sometimes there'd be a clash between us as to how observant we wanted to be. But Benjamin's faith seemed to be in his bones. He spoke Hebrew, always wore the kipa—the skullcap—and a gartl—a cloth belt—which he said were necessary to always have in mind that the upper body was spiritual and the lower body physical, which was news to me. Although he was still a kid himself, he lectured us like an old man talking to bad children. He couldn't wait for his shaven head to grow *payot*, the long side locks, and although he was beautiful and sweet, he'd become angry, almost tearful, if we laughed at him or showed how ignorant we were.

↜

Here I interrupt Mania's story. If I don't ask questions when I think of them, they're often lost forever.

"Irina and Zola...where are they now, Mania? Are they still living?"

"Still living?" Mania asks, astounded. "Of course they're still living. Living it up is more likely. Both are in Israel. We phone each other all the time. Sisters, that's what they're like to me."

"And Benjamin?" I ask.

"Ach." Mania's face falls. "He left Israel after a few years and became a successful and very wealthy man, but his inside was just eaten away by anger. One thing he had was a terror of dogs. Spent half his time dodging dogs. Once I met him on a visit to France, and we were out walking when a German Shepherd approached us. It was with its master and on a leash, but Benjamin, the poor guy—he was about fifty at the time—started trembling and ran across the road, dragging me with him. But that's not the worst. His faith went up in smoke like it had been cremated. He believed nothing and would shout, 'Shit' when the name of God was mentioned."

Mania reaches for her cigarettes, light up, and repeats in her husky, throaty way, "Yes, 'shit' when the name of God was mentioned. He could never accept that God didn't rescue the Jews. The sufferings of the Jews, the injustice—he couldn't understand why God had allowed it. You know the story of Job? Well, Job he wasn't. He couldn't accept. After the war, when he learned of the numbers killed...listen, I don't know what really happened in his head or how long it took, but by the time I met him, he couldn't stand to hear God's name. One day when I mentioned God, he leaped up and started shouting, 'Shit, shit, shit! Don't ever mention that word to me again.' And my feeling was that he was like a bitterly deceived lover, because there was such a mix of passion and love and hate."

She sighed. "I'm getting tired. I want to finish my story. Let's get back to it."

↜

Zola, Irina, and I weren't prepared for Palestine. We had no skills, I'd never learned Hebrew. The "elite" saw we'd be practically good for nothing as new pioneers, so the three of us were put to work in a clothing factory to get ready. In the evenings and weekends we were taught Hebrew and Hebrew songs.

I was about fourteen by this time. I didn't understand half of what was going on around me, but at this center I found what it was like to be happy again. The home was full of young people from all over Europe, and we'd all survived. Somehow we could all communicate, and it was like the tower of Babel. We'd never been able to talk about who we'd lost and the things we'd seen. Now for the first time we could tell about our lives before the Nazis came. We could say our names out loud and speak of our parents and what they were like and what they did, and whether we had had brothers and sisters and cousins. We could name the people we'd loved, the towns we'd come from, the homes we'd had, and the things we used to do before "they" came.

I could say aloud that I was Mania—Mania Fishel—not number 52894 but Mania Fishel, daughter of Bernard and Gelcia Fishel of Katowice. I'm telling you, the joy of such a simple thing! The feeling of release just in naming yourself! Saying our names out loud was like opening a cage and flying off free. It brought us back to life.

Yet it wasn't plain sailing. Part of me was stuck in a concentration camp. I'd survived but I felt tied to those who'd died. My body was in Sweden, but all the time I felt I should have been ashes in Auschwitz. I was meant to die and hadn't. For the first time I felt a need to become part of something big enough to protect me, something big enough to make sure nothing like that would ever happen to Jews again. These were the feelings I had, although I would have found it hard at that time to describe them.

I began to feel interested in going to Palestine. Some of the local fervor was lighting up sparks in me. "The elite" were trying to organize a boat to take us there. They were also trying to get us passports, but there was no chance of getting any legally. All of us kids knew that "the elite" had a scheme to print phoney passports and documents showing we were going to a South American country. We thought that was very funny because we'd be heading in the opposite direction.

We were going to make a run for Palestine. That's what we did one day, boarding an old boat at some Swedish port, each of us clutching a suitcase and carrying phoney documents. By this time my idea of Palestine was slightly advanced but not much. I thought of it as a hot place where everyone sang Hebrew songs and clapped their hands and danced a lot of the time. I couldn't see myself doing that but thought I'd worry about that when I got there. I was fifteen years old by then, out of prison camp for two years. Life was an adventure. I didn't have a worry in the world. And I didn't have any idea about who I was or what I was. I was still doing what I'd been doing all my life: taking orders from someone else and never making a decision for myself. It wasn't a bad start for living in a kibbutz.

About six hundred of us got into this ancient warship that sat low in the water. We each had a bunk to sleep in, but, apart from the crew, I don't remember any other details. The captain was an old Italian who knew the sea. He was the only one who knew anything. The sailors were young American volunteers who'd just left school and were busy trying to tell one end of a ship from the other. The boss was an Israeli who felt that worrying about the ship and bad weather was an insult to God.

When we hit the Bay of Biscay, we ran into a storm that fell onto the ship like a mountain had collapsed. Walls of water broke over us, sweeping all our oil and water supplies off the decks and into the sea. Zola, Irina, and I crouched down in a low part of the boat. Sitting on our suitcases, we screeched with laughter as the boat crawled up mountainous waves and then slid like a roller coaster down the other side. The more the sea boiled and the more we slid, the tighter we clutched each other and the more hysterically we laughed. Never in our lives had we had so much fun.

We were practically underwater when our ship received a signal from another boat. The Israeli boss crawled around in the foamy deck water, looking like he was surfing, telling us to lie low and keep hidden.

"Identify yourself. Identify yourself," the other boat kept signaling. "Do you need help? Do you need help?"

We were racing full pelt for Palestine and we didn't have one legal document among the lot of us. And we were going to ask a British ship for help? We plowed ahead. Later I was told that two other boatloads of camp survivors had been caught by a storm in the same area. Both boats sank and everyone drowned.

We stopped in a port in Algiers to get some supplies. Then we moved on, full of hope and excitement. But—and this was not unusual—there was a spy on board: a Hungarian woman who'd informed the British Navy of our position.

Early one morning I woke up to hear shouting and yelling on the deck. Everyone came running. People along the railing were pointing and laughing and crying. I looked. Along the distant horizon lay a thin line of land with a faint blue haze behind it.

Palestine! Until that moment Palestine had been just a word, something that adults spoke about that seemed unreal. My heart started to swing with excitement and pride. All around me people were laughing and crying and shouting praises to God. Almost at the same moment someone cried out that a British naval ship was steaming towards us, moving to place itself between us and the shore.

It was hot and sunny. The sea lay as flat as a pane of blue glass. Now we could clearly see the port of Haifa. Our old boat strained and plowed towards it. We were so close to land that someone with binoculars could see a school. Children were pouring out of its doors to watch our struggle to reach the port. Around me people were shouting in desperation. We stood in our hundreds, staring at the promised land. We were now in shallower waters. A few men took off their jackets and jumped over the side and struck out for shore.

The British ship now stood between us and the port. Small boats were lowered down its side, and sailors raced after the frantic swimmers and dragged them from the water. From the shore came a faint sound. The schoolchildren were singing the Hatikvah, the national anthem. We all started singing too.

We could see the British coming towards our ship. Compared to us they were armed like the Crusaders. Irina, Zola, and I stood with our arms around each other, and as the British came on board and took us prisoner, we pelted them with potatoes, which was all we had. Load by load we were transferred to their boat. Some of the kids were quiet; many others were shouting and crying. We'd been so close that we couldn't really grasp what had happened.

In a couple of days we were all back in a detention camp, this time a British one on the island of Cyprus. Other detainees have since told me they weren't treated well, but I was. The food was decent, the climate was good, we had movies, and I was still discovering the fun of having girlfriends. One day, some months later while still on Cyprus, I received a letter from my father's brother Vilek, who with his brother Motek, had gone to Palestine prior to the war. They had traced me through an international agency, and now Vilek was offering me a place in his home in Haifa.

I remembered they had visited us in Katowice to say good-bye, but how they looked and what they were like, I had no idea. I'd always dreamed of being part of a family, but now I became very confused. What I'm telling you is that the idea of going to Vilek's home scared me. I didn't know him. I'd had no normal family life since I was six. In Sweden and on Cyprus I had all these ideas put into my head about community life. I'd never had to make any decisions or choices. My parents, then the Nazis, and then the elite of the kibbutz had made them all for me.

I chose to live on a kibbutz.

What's to say about the years that followed? That's another story, not the one I'm telling. It's enough to say that I learned Hebrew, and worked on Givat Haim kibbutz near Tiberias as a nurse, a teacher, and sometimes a waitress. I married an engineer named Micha Kroll, who had been born on a kibbutz. I had two sons. Like all babies, they were taken from me at the hospital and placed in the kibbutz nursery, and I went back to work just as my mother-in-law, Ruth, had done when Micha was born. In 1971 my husband, who was employed as an engineer by Massey Ferguson in Israel, was offered a position with the company in Canada, and we emigrated. He died less than six years later.

I became a court interpreter, made new friends, and did what I had to do to re-create my life. One of my sons returned to Israel to fight in the army and then resettled in Canada.

During all those years, Johanne continued to live as if she were alive in my head. At times I felt I'd somehow die unforgiven if I didn't see her and thank her. It's not smart to be grateful these days, but what do those smarties know? I'm a grateful person. She risked her life for me. I had to thank her. I know who she is. Why are you looking at me like that? You'll find out. No matter what she says, my heart and my mind tell me the truth. Ach, why won't she admit it? Why won't she give me real peace?

༺༻

Mania lies on her back, the fringed edge of her bedcover drawn around her as she finishes her story. Her voice is flat and her perkiness gone. In the shadowy room, her face cleansed of makeup, she looks haggard, like a small bundle someone threw onto the bed. I press her for more details about her life in Israel, but she gestures to stop. She's too tired. All she wants is to rest until the final moment when she'll meet Johanne.

I wince when I think of her dreaming of the moment when Johanne will say, "Yes, you were right all along, Mania. I was that guard, and I loved you like a mother. That's why I risked my life to protect and guard you," because I don't believe it's going to happen. I want to tell Mania this and maybe soften the disappointment ahead. Most of all I hate not speaking my mind because she trusts me. But she looks so fragile, so drained. I don't have the courage. I say good night, go to my room, and write up my notes, wondering why, with all the doubts I had about the project, I hadn't listened to my own heart instead of tuning in to everyone else's as I tend to do, because I was raised that way. Unless Johanne is the greatest actress, the smoothest liar that's ever lived, I don't believe she was ever a guard, was ever at Reichenbach camp, had ever met Mania before their meeting in Mania's Toronto condominium.

I'm feeling this way because two days ago Johanne arrived here in Świdnica, her childhood home. And for some of this time, backed up by much of Maureen's copious initial interviews, I've been with Johanne recording her story.

What Johanne has told me, calmly, good humoredly, and at times with stunning honesty for such a proper and redoubtable woman, has borne home the fragility of Mania's case. This morning, walking the streets of Sosnowitz, each one thick with cobbled history, I saw dozens of women Johanne's age all looking painfully alike as many older women tend to do

148

in a grey curly-headed sort of way.

All the "evidence" Mania has of Johanne's identity is circumstantial. Johanne has blue eyes and her facial bone structure suggests beauty as a young woman. She speaks with a North German accent, holds her head high, and walks with the ramrod dignity of authority. In Toronto Johanne seemed to be nervous when Mania spoke of her early life, and her teacup "rattled against the saucer" when Mania spoke of Reichenbach. But did the teacup rattle? Did the pale-skinned Johanne really turn paler? Or did all these little details enter Mania's mind in exaggerated form and emerge as hard evidence of Johanne's former Nazi life?

Since I put aside my initial doubts, I've trusted Mania's intuition and memory 100 percent for good reason. Although she was only a child, every main event in her story, when held against historical records in the social sciences department at the University of Silesia or the Silesian Museum in Katowice, has proven to be fact. How could she be so tragically mistaken about Johanne? How, being mistaken, could she still remain so sure? Is it simply because Mania's nature is that of an incurably joyous dreamer, a believer in the unknowable, in angels, and in transcendental plans and the sheer mystery of life?

Throughout my talks with Johanne, no mention has been made of her being a guard, no hint or suggestion that she might have been in the SS. She knows she has a role to play in the documentary. All she has to do is simply accompany Mania for a day's shooting to contrast the life that she, Johanne, had during the war years with that of Mania's experiences. She is happy to do it; she's a practical woman with plain dreams and a cautious, prudent lifestyle, one which, in this case, has given her a free, all-expenses-paid trip to her beloved hometown. As she was living on a small pension in a distant part of Germany, it is easy to see that this last chance for a visit home was irresistible.

The plan is for the two women to meet at Reichenbach camp for the first time since they met in Toronto more than twenty-five years ago. The hope is that this unexpected meeting at an unexpected place will release a flood of memories, loosen her tongue, and let the truth out.

Two women, two different stories, linked somehow by long-ago events, events that still live in their minds as if they'd happened yesterday. But how they are linked, and when that link began, I still don't know. At

At times I feel so frustrated at my own inability to make a decision that I don't even care. But I do care. Unraveling the little mysteries of relationships is to experience one's own human nature. That's what life's about.

I've recorded Mania's story as she told it, and now it's time to tell Johanne's. Ostensibly unaware of our suspicion that she was a Nazi guard, she's too shrewd not to have made some sort of tentative assessment as to what our project is really all about. That could account for the directness and force with which she launches into her story. ↔

ŚWIDNICA

We arrange to meet in the dining-room bar of the same hotel Mania, the film crew, and I are staying in. Mania is elsewhere in town, and even if she were to suddenly appear, there is little likelihood of her being recognized.

I had pictured Johanne as a healthy, strapping woman in a pastel-colored utility pantsuit and shoes made to tramp around in. I'm not far off, although she's slimmer and taller than I'd imagined. No makeup, but she gives an impression of a silvery softness, a motherliness—silver hair, silver-rimmed glasses, faded blue eyes but still sparkling. What I hadn't expected is her rare skill of listening in silence, fully present and generous in her occasional comments. She's a woman in calm control of her life, a woman who knows who she is, or so it seems.

We find a place in the corner of the dark paneled room. Johanne takes her time settling in, eyes me calmly but not unpleasantly, and says that she decided to talk to Maureen previously and now to me simply because she loves Canada, respects Canadians, and is intrigued with the idea of taking part in a Canadian project, even though she isn't exactly sure about its purpose.

I ask her if she would like a drink before we start, and she says she would, that she would like a beer with a Schnapps chaser. At that point her eyes become watery. She says that every evening she and her late husband had shared this drink together. I'd thought her too controlled for such a quick reaction. Besides, her husband has been dead for years. Then maybe her husband has nothing to do with her tears. Maybe she is simply emotional because she is back in her old hometown. Maybe her cool, though courteous, formality is a front and something else is going on. The maybes are endless.

The waiter brings the drinks. Johanne remarks that she's had a big day back in her hometown and that it's pleasant to sit over a drink and "talk about it with someone." I tell her I can't wait, and that I will be taking notes as I'm sure the visit has conjured up many memories. Soon after

Johanne starts, I notice how often she comments on the excellence of her memory. Maybe she's simply proud of it. Then again maybe her narration isn't as spontaneous as it sounds. Could she be trying to underscore the fact that Mania's memories are those of a child while hers are those of a woman? In other words, "You'd have to be unhinged to take the word of a child against that of a grown woman." And if she is doing this, it means that, without knowing exactly how it will unfold, she knows exactly what our project is all about. After twenty-five years of silence, does Johanne realize that Mania is still seeking her kind Nazi guard and is unshaken in her belief that it is her?

I believe she does. Otherwise why would she agree to my interviewing her? Maybe to better understand her own life. But if so, why reveal the most personal parts in such detail, as this self-respecting, modest woman does? Unless she believes that if you give enough intimate details—real or fabricated—they will cover the truth.

Johanne tosses back her Schnapps in one practiced mouthful and starts to speak. ↭

JOHANNE'S STORY

Before we begin, I want you to understand that, despite my age, I've forgotten nothing. The big happenings, the little—both I remember. You'll agree there's no point in us talking if you're wondering if this or that is true, if this or that actually happened. To talk about myself isn't my nature. So it's wasting my time and yours if you don't understand certain things about me. Not that memories make my life—don't think that. I have no time for old women who stay at home, glued to their seats, looking back sighing, ach this, ach that. Never will I be one of them. Life's to enjoy, and I do enjoy it. I'm content with what I have. That's the secret of happiness, *nicht wahr*? My apartment, a few friends, some plants along my windowsill where they catch the morning sun, and I can sit there and enjoy my morning coffee. It's enough. And my hour-long walk every day—that I must have. Wind, snow—matters nothing. Out I go. My parents taught me discipline—a good legacy, that.

I've decided to tell you about my life even though I've always been a private person and have kept my feelings to myself. Everyone has problems and sadness: why impose yours on others? But I will tell you everything, everything that we endured too. I was in Berlin, and those who weren't there had no idea and they don't believe it when you tell them. I'm not only talking about the bombings—night and day bombings. Or the hunger. Or the Russians and their raping of almost all the women and girls of Berlin. I'm talking about the pain of knowing that our young people, who have so much of everything, will never understand what it was like for us who had nothing.

+~+

At this point I try to interrupt, but Johanne leans towards me impatiently, saying she'd prefer I didn't ask questions. It is as though she has geared herself for some sort of ordeal that is not to be interrupted. She adds that if sometimes her eyes become a little teary, the cause isn't self-pity but simply a physical function she cannot control. I nod that I understand but insist that sometimes I have to clarify a point and must do it

153

when I think of it. Johanne looks at me in silence, with half a mind as to whether to stay or go. I know she'll close down like a steel door if I don't capitulate, so I do, assuring her I won't interrupt but adding a caveat: "Only if it's a very critical point." Finally she nods, if a little tentatively.

Despite her hesitancy, I think this chance to tell her story is more important to Johanne than she's letting on. Maybe this eighty-five-year-old woman just wants to let her hair down and talk about feelings and memories that, regardless of her real or pseudo relationship with Mania, are her own. Maybe she wants to weave a fantasy or get something off her chest. One way or another, a picture of the woman will emerge, and it should be possible to tell whether it's authentic or phoney.

Taking a sip of her beer, Johanne continues:

✦

I'll give you an example of how good my memory is.

It's been nearly fifty years since I was last in Schweidnitz—that's the German name. The Poles call it Świdnica, but it's my *heimat*. I was born here, grew up here, and for me it's Schweidnitz. Always will be. When I wandered around town today, I knew exactly where I was. I knew every twist and turn of every street and even remembered their old names—their real names before these people changed them. Even the rounded curve of the cobblestones under my feet felt familiar. If a stranger had asked me for directions, like a shot I could have given them.

I recognized the shops too. The old butcher shop, where my mother bought soup bones, sells cosmetics now. The money women throw away on luxuries—how amazed Mutti would be! Hardly ever could she buy meat. Some sausage maybe, and not every day. My poor, dear Mutti. And the barber shop—I recognized that too. Vati never went there because Mutti cut his hair. That's the way things were then. Now it sells electrical gadgets—all the stuff young people think they need to be happy. The grand old buildings need new paint; the Poles never keep things up. But the heart of Schweidnitz, ach, it's still the same. The street stalls—along the pavement in the same area—they're still parked there. The tables are still piled high with beets, potatoes, onions, and cabbage.

But one very bad moment I had today. Let me tell you about it. You are interested in me? The life I've had?

154

I nod so vigorously that I almost fall off my chair. I want her to go on talking and don't much care what she says. Behind the calm body language, the gentle voice, there's a different woman—a taut, emotional woman. There seems to be anger, or could it be sadness? Whatever it is, Johanne is stuffed with memories that she wants and needs to voice. More than a half century has passed since Germany was forced to hand this part of Poland back to the Poles, more than fifty years since this town was renamed Świdnica. Yet Johanne insists on "Schweidnitz" because it remains "my heimat." "Heimat" has a richer, more possessive sense in German than its English translation of "homeland," and the way Johanne says "my heimat" sounds more like a challenge than a claim.

Taking a slow draft of her beer, Johanne sets the glass mug back on a paper coaster, daintily mops her mouth with a lawn handkerchief, and continues.

I went to see the house where I'd lived as a child. I'd always carried a picture of it in my mind. During the war, the memory of my home kept me going. I hurried through the streets, scarcely able to wait to see it. The old buildings surrounding it were still there. But of the house—nothing! Half a wall and some rubble that marked where the rooms had been, that's all. Never had I imagined it might be gone.

When the truth sank in, I couldn't move. Everything lost, the dusty rubble, the ruined shell—I felt like I'd been struck on the head. For a moment I was muddled, confused about time, and actually felt as if I were back in the forties. I could hear inside my head the familiar noise, sirens, bombers, people screaming and running. "It's taken a direct hit!" When I looked at that blank wall today, that was my first thought. Within seconds I came to my senses and knew the house hadn't been bombed. What a stupid woman I am, I thought. The war is history, finished and done with for more than sixty years.

I returned to my hotel and lay down, exhausted. No more of that, I told myself. Don't look back; it's over.

You're from Canada, so you wouldn't know about the terror of the bombing, the horror. Our skies, *ja*, black they were with bombers, our streets white with dust and heat. Day and night no different: the earth trembling and roaring and all of us crouched in the earth, so frightened we were. Being here in Schweidnitz, it's brought so much back.

❦

At this point I interrupt to say I've never had a chance to talk one-on-one with an older German who lived through the Allied bombings, and if only for that reason I'm interested in anything she'd like to tell me. At the same time I'm saying this, I'm strangling a small, horrible voice within me that whispers, "You brought it all on yourselves." I hate that nasty voice and I do like this woman, but I hope to heavens she doesn't go on endlessly about how much she suffered. Not with Mania, not with the remnants of the Gross-Rosen camps so close by.

Eyes down, Johanne thoughtfully rotates her jug of beer in little circles, listening, tolerating my interruption. I pray she can't read my mind. After a moment Johanne continues with a great sloughing sigh.

❦

Ach, it's not only foreigners. Even our own young people wonder about us old Germans and try to fit us into a wartime box. They see war pictures, but pictures can't describe our feelings, how deeply we suffered in every way. And not one in a million knows how the Poles drove us out of our homes here in Silesia. Eight hours notice, the Poles gave us. In the middle of winter we were driven like beasts back into Germany, no food, no shelter, dying by the road in the thousands. Nobody speaks of that these days.

I had a silly thought yesterday when I was walking around town. I laugh about it now. I wondered if you Canadians thought, just because I'm an older German, that I might have been involved in the war somehow. A foolish thought for me to have, but that's the way many foreigners think.

I will tell you things now I've never told anyone. My life is good but almost over. Make of it what you will. Most likely what you'll believe will depend on who you are, rather than who I once was. ↦

156

ŚWIDNICA

MAY 17, 2002

It's late afternoon, and Johanne and I are back on the couch in the narrow hallway outside the dining room entrance. It's inappropriate but neutral territory. The dining room and bar are full, and there's nowhere else to sit. She hasn't asked me to her room, and I haven't asked her to mine.

Johanne looks relaxed and at ease in her open-necked crème blouse and a light dab of fresh face powder. Her nails are clipped short and buffed to a polish. After this morning's session, my feeling that there's more going on here than meets the eye is stronger than ever. Johanne is making such a point of how truthful she is I'm beginning to feel that "the lady doth protest too much."

ŚWIDNICA

1916 – 1927

Ja, I've told you I was born here, in 1916 in the place I visited today. That part of Germany was then called Schlesien; now the Poles have it called Silesia. We were six children; I was the fourth. Four girls, two boys. From the beginning, when I was a baby, my memories are clear and powerful. It was a happy time, but children don't ask themselves if they are happy, *nein?* They just bounce from day to day.

We lived on the second floor of a small house just off Burgplan Street. It stood between a big house that faced the street and an even smaller house at the back. Our apartment had two bedrooms, a living room, a small kitchen, and a toilet upstairs. The toilet was outside the apartment on the landing near the entrance to our apartment.

Downstairs in the backyard was a laundry room with a large copper boiler and a concrete sink for soaking things that were hard to clean. There were lots of things to soak in cold water before boiling. Vati worked in a factory when he had work, and we used rags for handkerchiefs. Paper tissues that you throw away, there was nothing like that. We didn't have sanitary napkins for our periods and used rags for that too. Mutti would fill up the tub with cold water the night before the big wash, separate things, and let everything soak there overnight.

In the early morning everything was put into the copper pot and a wood fire was lit underneath to bring the water to a boil. Mutti would stand over the boiler, jabbing at the puffed-up clothes with the long washing stick. Her face would be all sweaty and her hair damp with the steam that rose up. The copper boiler was a dangerous place. Sometimes babies climbed up and fell in and were scalded to death.

When the clothes were boiled, Mutti rinsed them by hand. And then sometimes my two sisters Elise and Trudi and I would help Mutti hang them on the line in the backyard. Then we'd string some things up in the laundry and put other things over a clotheshorse in the living room. A

159

long while some things took to dry. Sometimes when we went to school, the thick part of our clothes, the collars, and the hems were still damp.

The main street passed the front of the big house. It went over the bridge to Breslau on the left, and on the right to Reichenbach. When Vati had the money, we would take the bus to the small village of Saro about fifteen kilometers away on the road to Breslau. My grandparents lived there. There were gardens nearby and a little creek we could swim in. It was a big, exciting outing.

There was always a crowd of us because Mutti's babies came one after the other. We were all born at home, and when you gave birth at home you got money from the government. When Hitler came, he increased that money three times more. But Mutti had died by then. To clean house and cook, that was a woman's pride, and Mutti taught us girls well. A beautifully clean house with everything shining, everything in order —that we must have.

Whatever Mutti put before us, usually potatoes, onions, and turnips, sometimes a slice of sausage, we ate. When Vati didn't have any work, Mutti would send us out into the neighborhood to do odd jobs. We were small, but we'd knock on apartment doors and ask to clean the fireplace and remove the ashes, or if we could carry wood or coal into their house. Sometimes we'd earn five or ten pfennig that way, and then Mutti could do some cooking. When Mutti put ten pfennig into the gas stove, we'd have six to eight hours for cooking.

I started school when I was six. We didn't wear uniforms. We shared classrooms with the boys but sat separately. Every teacher had his or her own class, and you sat up and listened. There were quite severe punishments, depending on what you did. You either had to stand in the corner for an hour or you got the strap. If you tried to pull your hand away, then the teacher held it with one hand and with the other strapped you.

⁓

Here I have to interrupt. I'm thinking of the convent school I went to when I was very small. It was always the kids who were "different" who got the cane, kids who always had snotty noses or wax dripping out of their ears or were slow learners or slightly smelled. Not the Protestant kids, though who were likely to be treated as pets by the nuns.

Only a couple of the nuns were mean—the rest were kind and excellent teachers—but the mean ones seemed to have free reign to pounce on those kids who seemed perpetually bewildered, seldom bathed, asked too many questions, or hadn't been taught any manners.

I cautiously ask, "Johanne, were there any Jewish children in your classrooms?" She looks at me, surprised, and says, "I suppose there were Jew children there too. It made no difference. I wouldn't know who was Jew and who wasn't," which I don't quite believe because this is the sort of things kids know.

☙

School wasn't just school. The kids weren't flipped out like they are today.

One must be friendly, respectful, honest, and obedient. Only afterwards did one see how good this training was. There was a meeting held in the gym, and in front of the parents, the teachers told us how we must behave towards them—that you should honor and fear them. Ja, honor and fear. It was good to be made hard. It helped us be happy and not to give up because things go wrong.

Mutti also ran a small business on Tuesdays and Saturdays. She went around to the big stores and collected all the leftovers. Most store owners knew we were poor, and because of this they gave her things like wood, pieces of fabric, and soap for practically nothing. Almost all the stores and businesses in Sweidnitz were owned by Jews. They had a special talent for trading—that we knew even before the Nazi time. But generous, ja, they were very generous.

When Vati had a job, he left at four a.m. He worked in a factory, an iron foundry, or sometimes gardening. He took whatever work he could. We got up at six a.m. for school. When you come from a big family there are always duties. On Tuesdays before we went to school we had to assemble the stand for Mutti on the sidewalk. Sometimes Elise and Trudi did it, sometimes my brothers Dieter or Harrer and I. We took turns. Then at one o'clock we'd hurry out of school, take the stand apart and run it home, and then run back to school. On Saturdays it was easier. Sometimes Mutti would earn one or two marks, and this helped a lot.

In Silesia we were so lucky. The land is so rich and there were lots of

161

vegetables. In the big cities people fainted in the streets from hunger. Young people today can't understand how poor we were, what it is like to be so poor. They blame us for everything, but they've never gone through what we went through. Ja, not only during the war but for years before.

It was not permitted for us to bring friends home. My parents said my siblings were enough. Elise and Trudi, my older sisters, had to look after us, and I had to look after my baby sister, Brigitte. We called her "Gitta." I loved school, especially recess, when I got to play with other kids. We had a lot of homework, and it was forbidden to do it at school. So all of us children had to help one another. We went home from school, did our homework, and then we were allowed to go up the road to the Moltke memorial and play for half an hour. You haven't heard of Field-Marshal Helmuth von Moltke, nein? He was a great Prussian hero, a great man. We played at his feet daily. Then home, eat, wash, and bed. Words like "entertainment" or "leisure," ha! Those you never heard. A little radio we had, but a telephone? *Gott nein!* That we would not dream of.

All our clothes were hand-me-downs. New clothes we did not expect. But whenever the school had a day trip to the mountains, "Ja," my parents would say, "you can go," even though it cost a few pfennig. Some children never went. Mutti would give us a sandwich and maybe some coffee. We had nothing yet I was happy. We had great family love.

So much I remember! There was a bakery, and on Sunday morning they sold all the old bread. If we kids had been really good, we all got five pfennig. With that you could buy a big bag of cake crumbs. Sometimes there was a complete bun in it, but when that happened Vati got it. We were happy for Vati to have it. We didn't feel we were poor because such things made us so happy.

When I was ten Mutti died, I don't know why. The priest came and gave her the last rites. She died at home. We had permission to keep her in the apartment for one night. We placed candles around her body, and the next day we carried her out of the house. I remembered then that when she did the washing she'd often hum or sing some little song. "Ich geh aus dem Städtchen heraus." (I'm leaving this little town.) Sad, ja?

How old she was, I don't know—maybe thirty-four, maybe thirty-six. She was seventeen when she married Vati.

My oldest sister, Elise, who was fourteen, left school to take care of us. My brother Dieter, fifteen, got a job in an iron factory. When I'd come home from school and Mutti wasn't there, it felt like an iron hand on my heart. Ja, I know what it is to lose your mother when you are a little girl. The hole it makes stays forever. Vati told us to be strong, resolute. Always Mutti said that too: "Be resolute!"

After two years I got a big shock. Vati brought home a new wife. Magda. He hadn't told us, and there she was, younger than Mutti and very pretty. Such a feeling I had! "Call me Mutti," she said. She had a nerve! I never could. I don't know why she married Vati, a poor man with six children. From the start I didn't like her. Reading romantic novels was all she did. One after the other, her nose buried in love stories while my sisters and I did the work. But when Vati came home she'd jump up, and Vati would turn into sugar, then whoop de whoop between them. Elise couldn't wait to leave home. She got a job as a house cleaner and left.

We all went to church, the Evangelical Lutheran. At twelve years old I was confirmed. You ask if there were Jews in Schweidnitz? There were many Jews, and they had many businesses. And you could buy cheap at their stores. We had one such shoe and clothing store that was cheaper than all the others. My father went to the Jews when I needed a dress for my confirmation, and he was given one—a beautiful black velvet dress—for a very few marks. Everyone said I looked beautiful. I was tall and slim, a good waist then, not like today. My blue eyes, well, they were even bluer then, and my hair, long and very blonde. Beautiful. Even my sister said so!

To go to a restaurant after the church ceremony was something we couldn't afford, so we had coffee and cake at home. That was a great day in my life. Eight days later—it was a Sunday—I wanted to look nice, so I went to get the dress but it was gone. "Where is it, please?" I asked my stepmother.

"Vati took it to the pawn shop and got three marks for it," she said.

That was all. You remember things like that, nein?

163

During this time I was in a play that the school put on in a the-ater downtown—a fairy tale about a princess who died and when the prince kissed her she came to life. I was so touched that I cried. That became my favorite dream, that I died and a prince fell in love with my long blonde hair. He stroked it then kissed me full on the mouth. I rose up and he lifted me in his arms, and then we floated away. The director told Vati that I was a very good actress and beautiful and that I should learn acting as a profession. But Vati didn't want me to learn any profession. It's too late now. Sometimes in my mind I wonder, Vati, why? Why?

↢↣

Johanne's eyes become watery again. She takes a handkerchief from her purse, dabs her eyes, and gives an awkward laugh. Watching her as she removes her glasses and dabs her eyes, I feel amazed at how our lives are shaped, how small things like an attitude or word from one's parents or teacher can turn our little rudders into a stream of life differ-ent from the one on which, even as children, we felt destined to travel. Here is this formidable woman crying over something that happened seventy years ago! I don't feel like saying, "Get over it!" She's paid a price for always doing what Vati said and remaining constantly "reso-lute," and is entitled to her regret. Besides, I'm only assuming the source of these tears. There could be something else apart from the sadness born out of her repressed anger.

To get the interview going again I ask Johanne if her stepmother sur-vived the war. To my surprise Johanne laughs and says that Magda lived into her eighties. And, with almost a smirk but certainly with relish, she says Magda died in the bathtub while reading a trashy novel.

↢↣

Ja, that is life, died in the bath still reading about love and romance! This woman, my stepmother, couldn't wait to get me out of the house. She helped me find work, housecleaning for a teacher and wife and their three children. So off I went. I slept at the teacher's and got food, too, and the kids liked me. I stayed in school—I was only twelve years old—but after school and on weekends I did housecleaning.

Three marks I got each month for cleaning. Sometimes my brother

164

or sister came to my employer asking for money because Vati needed a mark. My boss protested, "But then there'll be nothing for you at the end of the month." But what could I do? I knew they were hungry at home. Once, after the third mark was gone, I went home to my father and said I would like to have at least one mark a month for my work. But he said no. I accepted it. One must be respectful of one's parents, nein?

Don't ask me if this teacher was a member of the Nazi Party. How would I know? I was a child; I knew nothing about politics. There was pressure on teachers to join the Party—one heard talk of such things. They taught children, they set an example, so some people thought it necessary to join the Party. Otherwise it meant no job or a job far away in a village with one telephone and dirt tracks for roads.

In my home there was no talk of politics, no talk of Hitler. We knew without being told that Vati liked the Communist Party and we were never to mention that. Adults became excited when Hitler's name was raised, but adults closed doors to children and whispered when they spoke of things like that. We learned early to be silent. When the Jew and his family disappeared from the store where Vati bought my confirmation dress—the store that gave Mutti scraps to sell—we didn't talk about it. They just disappeared. We knew but nothing was said. We were children; our father had to be careful. When things like this happened, I remember 100 percent him saying, "This doesn't concern you, so we don't discuss it." Or, "Say nothing if you're asked or say you have no idea." Like when the Jew children weren't allowed to go to school any more. Where they went, I don't know.

❧

I interrupt. "Some of these Jewish children who disappeared would have been your playmates. You must have missed them, wondered where they went, talked about it in the playground. Maybe asked your parents?"

"No, I wasn't curious. Ja, I suppose I wondered. But things like that we did not ask."

Johanne's tone is now brisk, businesslike. But it wasn't when she spoke of her stepmother or her confirmation dress going to the pawn shop. "You remember things like that, nein?" she'd asked and waited for me to nod

165

in agreement. You remember the dress disappearing but not your Jewish playmates? You felt nothing, not even curiosity, regarding the Jewish man who owned the store and gave your mother scraps of fabric that helped feed the household? When told that none of these things concerned her, she accepted it. But when Johanne's father took her earnings, she felt cheated and spoke up.

What Johanne has just described was a typical learning experience in Germany in the 1930s—the learning of the value of silence. Learning that authority deemed some people deserving of justice while others were not. Johanne felt she had the right to speak up to her father. She was one of those who deserved justice. The Jews were not, so their disappearance was properly met with silence. ↔

ŚWIDNICA—BERLIN, GERMANY

1928 – 1936

For three years, 1928 to 1931, I worked for the teacher couple and then I went to work for an old couple. Same routine: school during the day, housecleaning after school. On the old lady's underwear was a band that had to be ironed. And I burned it ironing. There was no electrical iron; there was a lid on the iron and you put coal in it and shut the lid. It was really hot, and I burned the band. She smacked me across the face. In that time such treatment was common.

I was powerless. I had to eat. But the one little power I had I used. I said *auf wiedersehn* to that old lady. Not right away. People could be nasty, could tell lies against you. Say you were for Hitler or were against Hitler, who knows? I hardly knew who Hitler was, but knew he had a big stick. So I waited a couple of weeks and then left. I went back home, although my stepmother was not happy about it. She thought I was a little fresh and spoke my own mind too much. In fact, I was a very obedient, disciplined child. At once she started looking for another job for me. She couldn't wait to be rid of me.

By then you had to join the Hitlerjugend if you were a boy or the Bund Deutscher Mädel if you were a girl. We had no choice, but I wasn't forced; I could hardly wait to join the Bund Deutscher Mädel. To be given a new outfit was a dream. Always I wore my older sisters' castoffs. The BDM uniform for a young girl was beautiful—a white shirt, blue skirt, and blue jacket. Everything so smart and crisp, our hair braided and in order, our faces scrubbed. I was thrilled to have new friends, to go hiking with them, to sing around a campfire and feel the love for the Fatherland filling my heart. Sometimes when I wear blue today I'm reminded of those times. They bring a smile to my face.

I was proud to be in the BDM. Canada or America it was not. It was Schlesien in the early thirties. To be a lawyer or a doctor or a professor, these things girls like me never dreamed of. Such an idea! How we would have laughed! To hear German women praised, that I loved. The duty to keep one's house shining, everything in *ordnung*, honored everything that Mutti had taught me. Poor Mutti. Nobody ever had praised her. We barely had enough to eat, but now we could be important. Ja, I felt strong, we could do something men could not. We could have babies for the Third Reich.

Some say we were taught to hate Jews in the BDM. That I definitely do not remember. Perhaps things were said, but I think not. All else I remember. But Jews, no. Maybe after I left things might have been said. Food or a drink was served at the end of our meetings, but I always had to hurry back to my housecleaning. So of Jew hating I know nothing. Jew girls, of course, could not be in the BDM. One must be pure deutschblutig.

I must laugh about one thing. Here was I, being told about having babies but I hadn't even had a period yet. I didn't have a period until I was sixteen, and then I did not know what had happened to me. I ran home and told my stepmother I was bleeding, and she explained it all to me. Not like today, when you learn everything in kindergarten, nein? We knew nothing about sex, and we all sat there being told about having babies for the Fatherland, but what did we know? What did we know about anything?

Stepmother Magda had two babies of her own by now. Later she had another two. The farther I was from her and Vati the better she liked it. In 1935 I answered an advertisement in the newspaper and got a housecleaning job in Berlin.

The Berliners knew 100 percent that the girls from Schlesien were good, clean workers, and they all wanted them. I was there half a year and wondered why my employers packed so quickly and sold everything and left. And overnight I was left on the street. Afterwards I found out they were Jews and had fled to America. You ask if I hadn't known they were Jews? No, I did not. They spoke well and were very clean. Sometimes one suspects, but these Jews were no different from anyone else.

My aunt Maria, my mother's sister, and her husband lived in Berlin near Alexanderplatz. They had only two rooms but said I could sleep in their corridor. I was very grateful. I had been raised to be grateful for any kindness, and even today I think that's a good way to be. Sometimes I felt very alone and lonely. Vati had his new family. I felt that I belonged to nobody. Always I tried to be resolute. It was just before Christmas, so I was able to get a temporary job at Woolworths.

When the holiday season was over I was let go, and I applied for a job I saw advertised in the newspaper. A couple who lived in a private house near the Wannsee needed a cook. To call oneself a cook one needed a two-year apprenticeship. But such formal training was beyond the dreams of someone as poor as I was. Apprentices earned nothing. Always I had not only to keep myself going but sometimes I had to send money to my family.

✦

"Did you resent that, Johanne, always having to send money home, particularly to your stepmother?"

"I could not bear to think my little sister, Brigitte, might be hungry. Kids I loved always. For a child to be hungry, ja, I knew what that was like. Nein, I never resented it."

✦

Aunt Maria insisted I try for the job. She was so kind. Again and again she praised my cooking skills to give me courage. Together my aunt and I took the streetcar to see the lady of the house. She interviewed me in her elegant and formal sitting room. Never had I been in a room like that, so it was hard not to stare. But I knew better.

The lady's name was Frau Freye Lachmann, and her husband, she informed me, was the director of a large tool factory whose products were known throughout Germany. This was my warning that second best would not pass in this household. Frau Director asked me many questions, and I answered eagerly but deferentially. I was longing to live in this world, so refined, so elegant, that I was seeing for the first time. It would be an honor to serve these people, so distinguished, so high-class. It was clear that Vati's secret Communist ideas had had no impact on me.

I had not learned to cook expensive food or sophisticated dishes at home. Potatoes, onions, turnips, beets—what can one do with that? Actually, a lot with a little of this spice and a little of that, but this was not

169

what Frau Director Lachmann wanted served at her dining table. That I intuitively understood. However, at the teacher's house I had done a lot of cooking and baking, and I had learned to make delicious dinners with modest supplies. When Frau Director asked me how much I would budget for a week's meals in her house—she mentioned that their son, Konrad, attended university and lived at home, but dined with them only once or twice a week—I did a quick calculation that made her burst out laughing.

"And what might one expect from that?" she asked, her head slightly to the side as if what I had said amused her.

My cheeks felt hot. Nervously I burst out, "Sauerbraten and spaetzles, creamed chicken livers in wine, Beef Rouladen, Schnitzel à la Holstein, Bodenseefelchen, Rehrücken mit Preiselbeeren…" My words stumbled on top of each other. I searched frantically for desserts. "Pancake omelet, Salzburger Nockerln—"

"Stop, stop!" Frau Director said.

Were these dishes not acceptable? Had I spent too much money? Did I sound wasteful, extravagant?

I blurted out, "But Frau Director, I know how to make do. A teaspoon of lemon juice equals half a teaspoon of vinegar, a cup of yogurt is the same as a cup of buttermilk, two teaspoons of arrowroot equals—"

"Please, Fraulein, please." Frau Director spoke quietly but held up her hands to halt my flow of desperate words. She looked at me and said, "You can come on January the third."

At that very moment Herr Director himself, a distinguished gentleman of about fifty, came downstairs. Glancing at me he said to his wife, "How can you be so sure that you can trust her when you have only just met this young woman?"

And Frau Director replied, "I am absolutely sure."

She said this so firmly. Ja, she was definitely in charge of this matter. Such authority she had! Then she turned to me and repeated, "Come on January the third."

I could hardly take in what Frau Director was telling me. No other duties but to submit my daily meal plan to her, shop and cook, and keep the kitchen in spotless condition! Occasionally there would be guests for dinner—important people connected to Herr Director's work. For this I was to create a special menu. There was a housemaid, Anna, who did the cleaning, a woman who came three days a week to wash and iron, and a gardener who came twice a week to maintain the premises.

Thirty-five marks a month and free food and drink! A fortune *and* a place in life! I would be somebody! No more ironing with hot coals and having my face slapped! Nein, I would be the cook for Herr Director and Frau Director Lachmann! "Very important people in Berlin." Ja, that is what I would tell my stepmother.

I felt like skipping but knew I should just bend forward slightly in appreciation, which is what I did. A different world—and I was about to enter it. "A special menu"! For "distinguished" guests! I would outdo myself and make the Frau Director proud!

My aunt helped me bring over my few things, and on January 3, 1936, I moved into my own room in this beautiful brown brick house in the Wannsee area, one of the loveliest parts of Berlin. Parks, trees, a huge lake with a sandy beach nearby. Mine was a small attic room with a window that looked over the gardens and roofs of other large Berlin homes. I was nineteen, and this was the first time I had ever slept in a room by myself. I felt I had moved into a palace.

Ja, the happiest time of my life began then. I was a servant, but so respectfully and kindly did Herr Director and Frau Director treat me that I soon felt like part of the family. I had my own kitchen, bedroom, and salary. At nineteen I had my own life. Fortunate it was that I did not need company. Anna, the housemaid, lived in a matching attic room opposite the narrow hall. When we met, her only words were to establish her superior credentials. "Ich habe die Lachmann famile für über 25 Jahre bedient." (I've served the Lachmann family for more than twenty-five years.) After that I related to Anna as if to a nice old workhorse. That she liked; it was all she wanted. ↔

171

ŚWIDNICA

Because of the noise in the bar area, we agreed that the hallway is no place to talk. So this morning we met in my room, an intimacy that neither of us really wanted. After breakfast I walked a couple of blocks down the cobbled street to where the fruit barrows were and bought a small bunch of yellow flowers, which I've put in a glass on my table.

Johanne has been laying down all the rules for these interviews, which has made it hard to be myself with her. But I'm beginning to like her enough to want to see her life through her eyes. I want to understand what happens to a hungry, helpless child who has been taught from birth that all authority is sacrosanct. Maybe then I'll have a better idea of why the whole German nation went mad.

Johanne, too, is a little more relaxed. When we met this morning, she said she'd enjoyed talking about earlier times because "usually no one wants to listen to old women and their memories." This moved me because it's true. To get things going I asked her what she did when, for the first time in her life, she had some extra money. My question made her laugh outright, and in that sound and moment were glimpses of how lovely she once had been.

BERLIN

1936–1938

The first thing in my new life was to buy a pair of pure silk stockings. I stood at the counter tormented by this pair, that pair, no, this pair. I'd always worn grey cotton lisle that was so serviceable. I almost ran back home and in my attic room I put these beautiful stockings on. I lay on my bed and stretched my legs into the air. My legs seemed magically changed—not my old lisle legs at all! I told myself I would keep the stockings for special occasions such as...I could not imagine. *Nein*, not true. For when I found a man. *Ja*, increasingly I dreamed of that.

The second thing was change my hairstyle. After a month I had enough money to go to a hairdresser. Never before had I spent money on things where I could make do myself. I had the braids I wore on my head chopped off. Shocked, I stared at the blonde woman facing me in the mirror. Whoop de whoop! I thought, where has the country girl gone? My hair I would wear tucked under my white cap while on duty, but ja, on Sunday, my day off, I would let it hang loose, free like me, and shoulder length.

Quickly I developed a routine. Once a week Frau Director and I met and planned the menu for the days ahead. Each morning I rose at 5:30, washed in the porcelain bowl in my room, and hurried down to the kitchen. I set the table, boiled some strong coffee, and laid out slices of brown or sourdough bread and slices of ham, cheese, or sausage. Breakfast was always the same. At 6:45 a.m. Herr Director entered the dining room. Serving was Anna's duty. I rarely went into the dining room.

You might find these details boring, but this was my life. The Lachmann house worked as precisely as a cuckoo clock, and I was more than happy to be the cuckoo. Work, order, and authority—that I understood, and with that I was happy.

At 7:30 a.m. the chauffeur arrived in the company's Daimler, and Herr Director left the house, arriving at his office "never later" than

8:00 a.m., Frau Director told me. When breakfast was over I walked six blocks to the local market to buy what I needed for the midday meal, the big meal of the day. At midday Herr Director returned home, walking through the front door at exactly 12:15 p.m. and going straight to the dining room, where the Frau Director was waiting.

By then I had prepared a soup, a main course of meat, potatoes, spaetzel, vegetables, and dessert. Sometimes fish—sturgeon they liked—and there was always a bowl of fruit on the table. The evening meal, served at 8:00 p.m., was light: salads, cold meats, and condiments. Wine was served only when there were guests, Frau Director told me. It would be a light Mosel, and Herr Director would choose it.

Because I had Sundays off, I prepared that night's dinner on Saturday evening and left it in the icebox. After I'd cleaned up I retired to my room, totally free until Monday at 5:30 a.m. Then I washed my hair and dried it with a towel. On Sunday morning I dressed in my good navy-blue gabardine suit and took the streetcar to the Kurfürstendamm in the center of the city, and met my aunt at Der Blaue Enzian for coffee and cake mit *schlag*. Then we discussed what we would do.

So many choices we had! The end of the Grunewald Forest was within walking distance, as were lakes and little beaches. And there were dozens of concert halls and live theaters, many art galleries, opera houses, and several very old castles. As for the stores on the Kurfürstendamm, one could spend a whole day window shopping, so beautiful the things were. After coffee Aunt Maria and I usually did a little of this and that, but always we ended up at the cinema. We both were mad about American films. Silly, nein? But they were so romantic and the endings were always so happy.

~

I interrupt, "About what year are we speaking of now, Johanne? 1936? Somewhere like that?" She nods her head, ja, ja, impatient to get back to her story, her energizing memories and myths. I want to hear more, but I need a larger picture. I say, "By then Hitler was in power."

~

Electrifying it was to live in Berlin then. The National Socialist Party, the Nazi Party, was in power. But I remember no talk of war. Nein, nein, nothing. I tell you the truth. People spoke about virtue, working hard, of being honest, of doing one's very best. These things I understood. This is

what Mutti and Vati had always told me and my teachers too. If the German people wanted they could build a Thousand Year Reich with such
good values. And our arts and culture! So superior, no country could
compare. Often in the city streets I heard a foreign language. Rich people
in America and England sent their children to be educated by us, that I
knew. I saw nothing wrong with Hitler's dreams.

Many old people today say, "Nein, nein, I never liked Hitler." But
they are liars. In Berlin I saw it all. The smiles, the cheers, the raised
hands, the marches, the streets filled with young people, with banners
and brass bands, brown shirts and black shirts, and the swastika waving
from every building. Twice I went to hear the Führer speak, and I was
nearly crushed to death by these old people when they were young.
He stood in the distance under lights, like a god shouting down into
our hearts, and love for him rose from every throat of these now old
people. You wanted the truth. Yes, well, this is the truth. They voted
him in, and, ja, they loved him like a savior. When they say now they
did not support him, they're either liars or senile. I am neither. That
you know by now.

Whether my Aunt Maria had ever voted I do not know. I had not.
I was not yet twenty-one, the voting age. During the first year of our
Sundays together Aunt and I never talked politics. We talked about films,
recipes, and family, but later on things changed, so eager was she to talk
about her life since Hitler became chancellor. "Like a miracle," she said,
the permanent work, good wages, health benefits. I told my aunt what
I thought, just like I'm telling you. I thought the Führer would be good
for all of us.

⁓

At the risk of cutting off the flow, I interrupt again. "Yes, I've read that
early on many people's lives improved under Hitler. But that isn't true for
all Germans. German Jews, for instance. You lived close to the center of
Berlin. Tell me what you saw, Johanne."

She looks at me calmly, but a pink flush moving up her neck onto her
pale cheeks reveals either anger or discomfort.

"I was just a cook. I knew nobody in Berlin except my employers, but
Aunt Maria knew many, Jews and Gentiles. She might have told me that

Jews were disappearing. I don't remember us talking about it."

"Never?"

A silence follows. Then:

"I do remember that one day I wanted to remind her how the Jews in Schweidnitz had helped her sister, my Mutti. So kind they were and all had disappeared. They had helped Mutti when no one else did. But for some reason I would not say it aloud. Vati had taught me long before the Führer became chancellor: 'Say nothing.' And there was in the Berlin air a kind of feeling that made one discreet, even with family."

"In Berlin there was 'a kind of feeling.' What kind of feeling?" I ask.

There's a long silence while she takes a thoughtful sip of beer. She continues with an edge of controlled irritation.

҂

One saw Jewish shops closed down one week, reopened the next, I suppose with German owners. I don't know. I was just a cook. I didn't get involved in things that weren't my business. I was a little…torn. The posters read, "Jews are our bad luck," or something like that. For me they weren't. Mutti would not have had her little business, there were days we kids would have eaten nothing, and I would have had no confirmation dress if it weren't for the Jews. I did not want to forget these things. I was raised to be grateful for all kindness. But these memories I kept to myself. Since I was a little child, I'd been taught to respect law and authority, and our leaders were important, clever men. In every speech they blamed the Jews for Germany's suffering. They said Germany must be "cleared" of Jews. It became clear to me that they knew many things I did not. I can't say I was bothered to see the Jews wearing a yellow star. One quickly got used to it, and it seemed normal to make the distinction.

I must have looked sour because Johanne burst out defensively:

I was young! All I wanted was to enjoy my new life. Selfish ja, but malicious, nein. One got tired of the whole thing. I knew Jews were different—that I'd always known, although I don't know how I knew. Never in my family do I remember Jews discussed. They'd helped Mutti, but I now began to understand how rich those Jews had been. I'd never run into any Jewish kids cleaning strangers' fireplaces as I did. But still

178

they were human beings. The more I thought about it, the more the whole Jew business got on my nerves. There was probably much more those Jews could have done for Mutti.

One Sunday night while I was going home, a Jewish mother and child were forced off the streetcar. Jews were forbidden to use them, but this woman had probably hoped to pass as Aryan. Someone recognized her, and others told her to get off. Until that moment, my heart was light and happy; I'd had such a wonderful day with my aunt. I could see the fear in the woman's eyes. As she left carrying her child, she looked at me. As if I could help her! I turned my head. It was her own fault; she'd broken the law. At that moment I decided one must trust one's leaders. From then on I did.

I tell you these things so you will know where I was and who I was. I was a cook then, and that's all I did during the war. That's what I'm going to show you. ↦

ŚWIDNICA

On this night before dinner I can sense Johanne is on edge, although I don't know why. I'm edgy, too, because it's hard to shut up in the face of Johanne's unexamined anti-Semitism. However, her discriminatory attitude towards one race of people has had the salubrious effect of forcing me to work on getting rid of any remaining traces of my own racism. No more does that unwanted but persistent voice with its "tough luck but you asked for it" arise when Johanne speaks of the horror of the bombings. Since my experience at Auschwitz, I seem to listen to others as if they were not "other" but—no matter what they are saying—as if they were part of me. And their pain somehow mine.

There's something else I've learned from Johanne, and that's how easy it is for terrorists of any ilk to take over a country where people are poor and authority sacrosanct. And, further, that the suffering caused by war perpetuates itself from generation to generation.

I ask Johanne to join me in the dining room. I order a vodka with beer chaser for her and Scotch for myself. After dinner we move to a table away from the others, and for half an hour I resist the temptation to order another drink. When Johanne starts talking, I order.

BERLIN

For nearly three years now I'd worked for the Lachmann family. Like Berlin, the family had changed. Neither of my employers was as lighthearted as before. They'd had big dreams for their son's future. However, he'd been called into military service immediately after graduating from the University of Berlin and was now in the Luftwaffe (Air Force) training as a navigator.

One day in late September 1938, Frau Director informed me that two special guests would be coming for dinner the following night. I made no comment but was surprised. On the rare occasions guests came for dinner, Frau Director and I planned at least one or two weeks in advance. So I thought that these guests must be very special and the occasion unexpected.

Planning a "special menu" with Frau Director was always a joy. She really liked me. I had never known this as a young woman. I'd never had any girlfriends except my sisters, who were far away. And my stepmother strongly rejected me. Being so close to Frau Director was like having a model, an example of what a woman should be. We mulled over this recipe and that, discarded one, chose another, and eventually put together a meal where the dishes complemented each other and the occasion.

On this day Frau Director was not her usual self. I knew her well by now and suspected it had something to do with the guests. As we sat down she patted my hand briefly as if reassuring me. She simply said that two gentlemen were coming. Far more quickly than usual, as if the meal were a duty and not pleasure, we decided on a plain but substantial menu centered around the main course of *Tafelspitz*. As she was leaving Frau Director said, "Herr Director will be offering vodka and brandy as well as wine."

Now that was interesting! During the week I'd noted a change in Herr Director's routine. As soon as he arrived home for lunch or for dinner, he and Frau Director went into the formal living room, or even upstairs to their bedroom, closed the door, and reemerged minutes later after what appeared to be brief and intense discussions. Obviously something was happening at the factory, and the two visitors were connected to it.

While I was busy in the kitchen the following evening, I heard the front doorbell ring, the muted greeting of Herr Director, the silence as Anna took the guests' coats, and the distant sounds as the guests moved into the living room for a predinner drink. I was not prepared for Anna's stunned announcement as she shut the kitchen door behind her: "Ein Obergruppenführer!"

A general? *Lieber Gott!* The idea of cooking for a general made me shake. And I had cooked a plain beef brisket!

"Well," I said to Anna as I poured the apple horseradish sauce into a heated pewter dish, "I can only hope the Wehrmacht does not cook Tafelspitz too often."

"Wehrmach? Nein, nein! Er ist ein Obergruppenführer von der Schutzstaffel."

An SS general! I went on working, swiftly, mechanically. Why was such a person in the house? Very close to the Führer were the SS. They took a personal oath of loyalty to him alone. And they had such authority! I had seen many in their grey and black uniforms on the streets of Berlin. They were the best of Germany's manhood—handsome, straight, with such proud bearing.

Fifteen minutes later the bell rang from the dining room. I spooned out the beef broth into the heated consommé bowls, Anna pushed her way through the door, and I set the asparagus beside the boiling water, ready to cook the instant Anna returned. The evening flew by—the beef ready, the hot plates out, the mayonnaise spooned lightly into two dishes, the apples baked, the caramel warmed, the used dishes rinsed and washed, and all the while Anna was pink-faced and moving swiftly to and fro with her habitual stony-faced dignity. I didn't have one moment to ask who the second guest was.

At 10:30 I heard sounds of the guests moving towards the front door. I felt exhausted. My head ached slightly with tension. Leaning back from the sudsy sink, I took off my white cap with one gloved hand and shook my hair free.

At that moment the kitchen door opened and I heard, "Enschuldigen mir bitte, Fräulein." I turned from the sink, and it seemed as if the whole world around me vanished and all that existed was the figure before me and myself. Ja, I remember exactly that's how it was. I could not speak. He stood silent, framed in the doorway. I stood with my back to the kitchen sink, my gloved hands dripping suds. Finally I blurted out, "Oh, General!"

My visitor smiled. "Nein, nein. I am one of the general's staff officers, definitely not the general." He bowed slightly then clicked his heels. "Sturmbannführer Kurt von X at your service, Fräulein." His real name he gave me, but that is for nobody else.

↜

At this point Johanne stops and turns her head away from me. "Excuse me," she says and sits silently, unable to continue. I say that I must give the Sturmbannführer a last name and ask if I can make one up just for clarity's sake. She nods in agreement, and I pick the name von Steiglitz. Years ago I had a friend with this name. I wait some more and think of the death's head insignia that some wore on the SS cap and the lightning strike on the rigid collar. And wait. Finally I say, "That was a very important moment in your life." After a moment Johanne speaks from memories sixty years away but memories so precious and so often lovingly mulled over in her mind that words flow without hesitation.

↜

Ja, that's what he said. "Sturmbannführer Kurt von Steiglitz at your service, Fräulein." Was he making fun of me? Foolishly I said what was obvious: "I am the cook."

My visitor frowned. "You have no name? Your friends just call you 'cook'?"

"Johanne," I said, "Johanne Müller, Sturmbannführer."

"Well, Fräulein Müller," he said, "the general declared your Tafelspitz the best he has had for some time. He would like his own cook to reproduce it and wishes to have the recipe."

I had no recipe. One put in a little bit of this, a little bit of that. How could I explain it? I noticed the major carried his greatcoat over his left arm and held his cap in his hand. He had been sent in the expectation of picking up the recipe and leaving.

"I am sorry, Sturmbannführer. I have no written recipe." With some embarrassment I added, "It comes from my head, from practice."

"Ah, so." He looked thoughtfully at me for a long moment. Then he said with a smile, "Then I will have to get it out of your head. Good night, Fräulein."

And with that he was gone.

I was just wretched in the days that followed. The nights alone were even worse. I could not sleep until the early hours. I'd never been in love, never even had a boyfriend, but now…My life—what had it been but work? I pinched myself to stop daydreaming and get on with my duties. The longing in me for love was like a sickness. You ask, was I uneasy that Sturmbannführer von Steiglitz was in the SS? Who thinks of such things when one is struck with love? And what did I to know about the SS? I'd heard they'd been formed to guard the Führer and his leaders. They had so much authority!

A million times I replayed my first sight of him standing framed by the door, so powerful and strong in his tailored grey uniform. He wasn't a very tall man but broad-shouldered and well built with very blue eyes in a fair-skinned face tanned by the summer sun. Was he married? The possibility came like a slap in the face. Ja, such a man would surely be married. Yet married or not, he'd liked what he'd seen from the hallway door.

An uneducated cook I was, a country girl, but I was no fool. I knew I was attractive; beautiful, my aunt and sisters said. And slim and shapely—*ganz schlank* like the young today. Still, I told myself that his surprise had nothing to do with my looks. He had expected an old woman as a cook, ja, that's the reason he had stared so hard. A thousand times I told myself this but it did no good. Just thinking of him made my heart race, my body restless. Never had I had this experience, nor had I understood what Elise, my oldest sister, had whispered to me in my late teens, that some women longed to make love with men, needed it, even craved it. I had never understood that until now.

I scolded myself for my silliness. A major in the SS and me, a cook, a servant! And the "von" in his name indicated he was from an old, perhaps aristocratic family. The women he knew wouldn't have their face slapped by an employer. They'd have only silk stockings on their legs, and they'd visit the hairdresser weekly, and would always know

186

exactly what to say and how to act. I was a little fool to hope to see him again.

But I did. I not only saw him again but he became the great love of my life.

Two weeks after the dinner, when I was almost cured of my madness, I received a note from him. If I were free on the following Sunday he would be "honored" to have coffee with me. And if the weather were fine, perhaps we could take a walk in the Tiergarten. He gave an address on the Hofjägerallee and said he would be there at 2:00 p.m. I held the note close to my heart and laughed with joy and relief. Ja, he was so confident I would be there!

When Frau Director remarked on my "merriment" later that day, I said I'd received a letter from home with good news. I was amazed how easily this little lie came to me and how readily my employer accepted it. I said earlier I never lie. Why should I? But sometimes it's for the best. I knew Frau Director wouldn't appreciate my meeting one of her "important" guests on the side. Besides, in this matter I was jealous of my privacy. I was about to learn that many strange discoveries came with love. The ease and acceptance of this deception was just the first discovery.

On the following Sunday I met Aunt Maria as usual at noon at Der Blaue Enzian. I was determined to be casual and discreet, but I couldn't keep my secret. Within a few minutes I'd spilled everything out. My aunt didn't look happy but alarmed. She knew how innocent I was. But her unwillingness to share my joy disappointed and then angered me.

Was he married? I thought she'd ask that and I was ready. "Absolutely not," I said. "You must understand, Aunt, Sturmbannführer von Steiglitz is not an ordinary man. He is honorable. That I know. He is an aide to a general. Never would he ask me out if he were married."

She sighed as if one of her worst fears had been fulfilled. "Just be careful, Johanne. Honorable, noble, you say. Sometimes, even with such men, the marriage vows can be forgotten." She could see her fussiness did not please me. But she couldn't stop. On and on she went. "And such a high rank. And in the SS, and his name! Oh, Johanne." She nagged on and on until I cut her off. "Aunt Maria, we are only going to have coffee and a walk in the park!"

"Ja, ja,'" she said, "and enjoy it, my sweet. But I want to remind you like your mother would. Ja, I'm not your mother, but listen to me. Such a thing could not work. Nein, society does not permit it. You are a cook, he is a major. He is well educated, probably from an old, distinguished family. And how old did you say he was?"

I had wondered myself. Twenty-six perhaps, or twenty-eight. "Twenty-six," I said firmly.

"Then he is married!" Aunt Maria's judgment came down like a judge's gavel. "And if he is not married, do you believe his mother would allow anything to come of a romance between her precious son and a servant? Yes, Johanne, a servant. A cook with a grade-eight education. This is simply the truth. Do you imagine he will take you home to his parents, introduce you to his friends? Johanne, darling, your Mutti used to scrub the floors for people like this! You surely don't think you could become part of such a family?"

I wanted to scream at her. Slowly I pronounced one word after another: "We...are...going...for...a...walk...that...is...all." But her words, ja, they rang true. They made my stomach churn. When it came to breeding, the German upper class closed ranks and chose from its own. That I knew. But how hard my aunt was to offer no hope, no word that I was desirable, no sense that I was special or worth anything! Just a good cook who happened to be pretty, that's what I was. Never would I tell her another thing! Never! I hated her and her old-fashioned common sense.

"The world is changing," I said as I left her.

"Not that much," she replied.

On leaving I kissed her briefly and reluctantly. She spoke from love, that I knew. But it was not her love I was interested in.

As I walked along the Hofjagerallee I could see him waiting, casually talking to another officer. When he caught sight of me, he spoke briefly to his companion, who turned to look towards me. He then made some remark that made Sturmbannführer von Steiglitz nod his head and smile. As I approached them I felt that I would melt from self-consciousness. But immediately on reaching them, von Steiglitz took my gloved hand

and kissed me on the exposed skin of my wrist. He then introduced me to his friend as if he were introducing a princess. The fellow officer also kissed my hand and, with a casual remark about the beauty of the day, left us.

I have told you enough already about my feelings for this man. We'd hardly spoken and, ja, it was pure chemistry, but soon it became more than that. For three Sundays we met for coffee, went for walks, and once went shopping on the Kurfürstendamm for some perfume his mother liked. "Mitsouka," he told me, adding with a short laugh. "It's the only perfume she's ever worn." Mitsouka! I treasured the magical name, this little snippet of family knowledge, repeating it like a mantra. Mitsouka! Standing with him at the counter in the perfumerie along the Kurfürstendamm, I felt like I was sharing part of his family life with him.

Everything he did and said made me fall more in love. Kurt's love for the Fatherland was in the marrow of his bones. He would willingly give up his life for the Führer and for the Führer's vision of a Thousand Year Reich. He explained to me about the cruel Treaty of Versailles, how it had humiliated and destroyed the old Germany. It was his job with others to restore Germany to its full and former glory.

All this happened long ago, nein? More than a half century ago, but I remember it as if it were yesterday. I hung on every word my man said. Everything about him impressed me as superior, noble. "He's no ordinary man," I told myself, and without hesitation I adopted his thoughts as my own. "We both come from the same rich soil," he once said. How that flattered me, a cook, and he, a von Stieglitz, whoever they were, for, despite my subtle attempts, he rarely spoke of his family. "We both understand authority, obedience, order, self-sacrifice," he said, and I nodded, feeling those words made us one. "These are the disciplines that will help us rule the world."

I wasn't interested in ruling the world, only in conquering Kurt. When we walked side by side, he in grey tailored uniform, buckled and booted he emanated power and strength. I could not help but notice other women glancing at me with envy. To me he was like a priest. He was connected to our new god, Hitler. He was my own very intimate connection to this new god. He could see through to my heart like God did and he could define my worth.

The same fire he lit in me, I felt I lit in him. Of that I was sure. When, on the fourth Sunday, he suggested we go to his apartment, I was ready.

We became lovers. I knew this would happen long before we reached his second-floor apartment on a narrow side street in the Hansa district. We had been strolling in that direction when a sudden shower drove us into a doorway. We huddled together, and with his arms around me, Kurt said, "I think it's time for me to get that recipe out of your head." I looked at him. He was staring at me intensely as if assessing something—what, I was too naïve to imagine. "My apartment is just around the corner. We can wait the rain out there, and you can finally give me your Tafelspitz secret. And perhaps any other secrets you would like to share, eh, *mein liebling?*"

Together we ran to the apartment, one of several in a solid stone building where the dark paneled foyer and elegant staircase seemed strangely deserted. A couple of weeks later I realized that most of the apartments, which billeted SS officers, had been the homes of Jewish families. I didn't ask but thought they'd been sent to work camps. By then I was used to the thick carpets, the fine furnishings, and the large comfortable bed in which Kurt and I sported for hours every Sunday. I had no time nor inclination to think of those who had once lived here. They'd vanished. The world was ours.

⚬

I look at the matronly body, the motherly breasts, the grey hair and pasty skin, the faded blue eyes glittering not with tears but sheer joy at the memory of those shameless, magical days, a time of self-revelation and total liberation. It's hard to say nothing as Johanne speaks so joyfully, shamelessly. She might have been ignorant then about the fate of the Jews, but she certainly isn't now. Yet what she is remembering and describing now is the magical chemistry of sex aroused, a sexuality heightened by her lover's authority, the fearful power invested in his crisply tailored uniform, his didactic attitude towards the value of discipline. How easily the rigid, respectful, churchgoing, authority-loving servant child from Świdnica moved over to give room to the authentic Johanne. In the passion she experienced and the freedom to wallow in sexuality and luxury, she got in touch for the first time with her true self, a self very different from the self-sacrificing child who always gave her bakery treat to Vati and allowed him to take her hard-earned wages without expressing the profound anger she felt.

Now I like her; she's had the courage to show herself. At the same time I detest the fact that she doesn't seem to care that their lovers' nest was stolen. "Didn't you say you loved children?" I ask. "Surely you asked Kurt what had happened to the family who'd lived in that apartment? And all the other families and apartments like them?"

She turns slightly pink and effortlessly replies, "I was young and my love affair was the only thing in the world. Nothing else mattered to me. Selfish—have you never heard the young called selfish? Of course, you might not have experienced such a thing as I had."

Meow, meow. I want to say, Oh, come off it, Johanne. You think you're the only woman in the world who's been crazy in love? Instead, the depth of erotic passion in Johanne's remembrances and the frankness with which this old woman, a picture of ramrod respectability, stuns me into silence. I'm reminded of the American feminist who once said that if women told the truth the whole world would split apart, and once again I bemoan the fact that most of us don't.

⚬

Such joy there was between us! I had not imagined it and describe it I can't. That day when we had huddled out of the rain, that Sunday before we became lovers, he had been assessing me, he later admitted. Was I a virgin? Had I been to bed with a man before? How experienced was I? That question was finally asked as he slowly undressed me. When, burning with shame and desire, I confessed that I was a virgin, his face became radiant, his hands actually trembled. The most profound joy and pleasure seemed to suffuse his entire being, and I thanked God that I had the gift of my virginity to give to this princely man.

⚬

Good God! Pictures of Johanne as a teenage blonde beauty jump into my imagination. She is creeping into her stepmother's room and filching one of those romantic novels so dearly loved by lazy Magda. Now she is hunched in the backyard laundry room, guiltily devouring every titillating

191

line, no doubt learning that the heroine who had a future was the heroine with an intact hymen.

＋～＋

That was the beginning of the great love of my life. I was twenty-two years old. Soon Kurt was taking me to dinner and parties at the officers' club near Stauffenbergstrasse. Ach, with what pride he showed me off to his friends and superiors! I felt as stately and beautiful as a swan. I looked at the women around me, not obviously, of course, but a little secretly. I saw the way they sat, held their heads to the side when they flirted, forced the men to lean far forward for the honor of lighting their cigarettes. Sometimes Kurt would point out a great lady to me: "That is the Countess Margarete Karlsruhen. Having a bit of a fling with the general while her husband's in Vienna," he'd add with a chuckle. Or: "There's the Baron, under the weather again. Too much cognac. Tut, tut, so early in the evening."

Ach, it was magical for me to move in such circles. I thanked God I was blessed with such pure Aryan looks: they opened the gates of heaven on earth for me. Ja, that is how I felt: grateful, always grateful. Much of my small savings went on elegant clothes, beautiful shoes, manicures, and the hairdresser. I lost even more weight, and, under Kurt's guidance, bloomed in and out of bed. I felt like a woman for the first time, like a real woman, a somebody.

＋～＋

I'm wondering how the Lachmanns felt about their cook fleeing the kitchen coop and taking off with one of their guests. I ask.

＋～＋

At home I said nothing about Kurt. The Lachmanns were aware that I was seeing someone regularly because often during the week I went downtown at night, and on Sundays I disappeared completely. Frau Director had very sweetly probed and teased a little, saying she hoped she and Herr Director would not soon be looking for another cook. I assured her no, although that was precisely what I hoped for. Despite Aunt Maria's fears, I now knew Kurt was not married. One night while he showered I'd gone through his identification papers, and under marital status all were stamped "Unverheiratet." (Single.)

192

You did not know those times, so you can't know what it was like for me to be the chosen love of an SS officer, a man who saw Hitler, if at a distance, on a regular basis and had even, on one occasion, spoken to him. That made me feel equal to everyone, even a distinguished family like the Lachmanns. I had learned that the dinner visit from the Ober-gruppenführer—with Kurt as his aide—had signalled the Nazi takeover of Herr Director's factory. Herr Director remained in charge, but now his factory produced instruments for armaments rather than tools for times of peace.

This takeover was the cause of the stress I'd noticed between this lovely couple. I don't think the Lachmanns were ever Nazis. I admit—I said I would tell you the truth—that my feelings towards Frau Direc-tor cooled when I sensed this. She and Herr Director should have been honored to work for Hitler. One must be patriotic. I'd also noticed that the last thing Herr Director did as he left in the morning was put on his swastika armband, and it was the first thing he took off at night as he walked through the door, throwing it—as if angry—onto the hall table. These things I did not mention to Kurt.

By now our Führer and the Wehrmacht, which had already taken over Austria, had seized all of Poland. These victories, and the bond be-tween Kurt and I, consumed our lives. All our Führer had promised was coming true! The future unrolled before us, sparkling and brilliant. The officers at the club glowed with a sense of power and triumph, and ja, we, the women, were infected too. So proud we were to be in the middle of it all, to be the chosen mates of the conquerors.

I've said I will tell you the truth. This is it. The last thing I thought of was the Jews and their fate. They never entered my mind. I remember, one time I did wonder about the family whose apartment I now regard-ed as ours. Once when I was hurrying to go out I dropped an earring in the bedroom. Feeling under the dressing table, I drew out a wooden spinning top that children play with. I knew then that a child had lived in our apartment, a child perhaps three or four years old. Where was that child now? The rumors about the work camps for Jews were being replaced by uglier stories. That night I asked Kurt what happened to the Jews. He put his finger on my lips as if to stop my questions and then kissed me lightly. He said that sometimes duty asked things of the good German soldier that were hard to do, things that went against one's nature. But one must harden one's heart and do them for the Fatherland to be pure and victorious.

Ask again I did not. The hard things these soldiers had to do, things that could go against their nature—I did not want to hear about them. Taking everything the Jews owned and throwing them out of their homes was surely part of it. Sending them to work camps, separating families, were other parts. Beyond that I made myself deaf. I was happy, and I had never been fully happy before. Other people's misery spoiling my happiness, that I did not want.

One night in late August 1940, British planes bombed Berlin for the first time. I was at home, asleep, when the sirens wailed. For weeks they'd wailed on and off in practices and false alarms, so I simply snuggled deeper into my eiderdown. Then there was a pounding on the door and the voice of Herr Lachmann shouting, "Anna, Johanne, sofort in den Keller! Das ist nicht ein falscher Alarm! Die Englischen sind in der Luft!" (Get into the cellar! This isn't a false alarm! The English are on their way!)

I scrambled into my dressing gown and, followed by a red-faced panting Anna, ran down the stairs into the concrete bunker built under the house some months previously, replacing the old root cellar. Herr Director locked the double steel doors as the first bombs exploded, and for the first time we felt the earth around us tremble. Happily for us we didn't know that this was the beginning of four years of living like terrified rats in a hole.

The following week I missed my period. I knew that many women missed a period or two following a loss or a trauma. A month later I missed my period again. I knew I could not be pregnant. Kurt always used condoms. But as days passed and my period still didn't come, I remembered that once or twice Kurt had declared he was fed up with them. He wanted "all of me," and I wanted to give him what he wanted, so we made love anyway. Surely I couldn't be pregnant because of this once or twice! I felt well, ate as heartily as usual, and never felt nauseated. Yet my breasts had a certain weightiness and my nipples seemed a

194

little tender.

I made an appointment with a doctor on the other side of town. I wasn't the young countrywoman who'd arrived in Berlin two years earlier in sturdy shoes and thick lisle stockings. I slipped into a department store to buy a cheap ring for my right hand. And I took out a few marks so I could pay the doctor by cash. He examined me and offered congratulations.

I was two months pregnant.

This fact gradually sank in during the hours that followed. I was to be the mother of Kurt's child! I would give Kurt a beautiful son or a daughter, the perfect deutschblutig Aryan child. Then I realized we would now be married! Now his family would accept me! And the Führer—this is what he wanted of us women: to bear babies for the sake of Germany and the Thousand Year Reich. My heart overflowed with joy. I could not wait to tell Kurt.

At last Sunday arrived. I all but ran to our apartment. Lying in bed with a weak winter sun filtering through the sheer curtains of the window, I told my lover I was going to have his baby. I was in his arms, his face close to mine. He turned his head and kissed me on the lips. "Say that again, slowly," he said.

I laughed with delight. "You're going to be a father!" I announced. "I'm going to have your baby."

"Are you sure? Absolutely sure?" he asked quietly.

"Two months," I cried triumphantly. "I'm two months gone. It'll be a perfect baby. I know it will be perfect. So proud I feel, Kurt! Like a true German woman." Love and happiness overwhelmed me. Now he would speak of marriage, of his family, of the discussions that must take place, the date that would be set. But no, he remained silent. Well, I thought, men aren't like women. It's a woman's thing, having a baby. And Kurt had so much to consider with the war on, the possibility of transfer even to the front. Small wonder he seemed a little taken aback.

"It's all right," I said. "Please don't worry about me, darling. I'll manage. I'll make do whether you are in Berlin or not. We'll get through this somehow. It'll be so worth it, and when it's all over we'll laugh about it."

He tightened his arms around me. "It's too much for you, my darling.

I could be transferred away at any time. To be alone…I don't want that for you." I started to ruffle his hair, to playfully kiss him all over but he stopped me gently, saying, "No, listen to me. I'm serious." For a moment he hesitated, "Now don't be angry. I just want to ask you—because I don't like to think of you going through this alone, here in Berlin, without support—have you thought of an abortion?"

"An abortion?" I was dumbfounded. I pulled myself up and, resting on my elbow, stared into his face. "What are you saying? This is our child! This is what the Führer wants: perfect Aryan children! This is my role, Kurt, just like yours is in the SS." I was disappointed that he thought my role as a child-producer for the Reich was less important than his role in the SS. I started to cry. "Abortions are illegal. How could you even suggest it?"

"Oh, my darling." Kurt took my face in his hands. "I didn't suggest it. I just mentioned it, whether that's what you wanted. I know they're illegal, but I happen to know…well, it doesn't matter." He kissed me all over my face. "Here, let me kiss your tears away." Again he said, "I only suggested it because it would be so hard for you if anything happened to me."

"But you want the baby, don't you?" I wailed.

"Johanne, liebling, what do you think? Of course, of course. A child that looks like you, ah, it will be beautiful. Ja, beautiful. Now, wipe your eyes." He searched for his handkerchief under the pillow and gently dabbed my face. "Now smile. Big smile. Good girl." He went on dabbing and then asked, "Have you told the Lachmanns?"

"What a funny question!" I said. "What does that have to do with it? Have I told the Lachmanns? Of course not. I've never told them anything. Not a thing about you and me. They know I have a man, but he's a mystery man." I imagined their surprise when I announced the name of the man I was marrying, their marveling at my discretion, my proud ability to keep a secret.

Again Kurt kissed me all over my face. He seemed near tears. "My sweet girl," he said. "My sweet Johanne."

We lay in silence. Kurt seemed overwhelmed with emotion. I waited for him to speak of marriage, to come up with some arrangements, make a commitment. I was the woman he took around town, partied with at the officers' club, danced with, made love to, slept with. In one way we were already married. He was mine and I was his.

"Kurt," I said, "we've got to make arrangements. You know what I mean, don't you?"

He put his face close to mine and whispered in my ear, "Marriage, ja, by an arrangement that is what you mean."

"Of course," I laughed. "What else? We are going to have a baby, Kurt. It is a surprise, even a shock. But a beautiful shock, nein? Anyway, my love, it's happened."

"Ja, it's happened." He sounded thoughtful. Speaking openly of marriage was the right thing for me to do. It would prod him into making a decision that was now unavoidable. And it worked because he said, "Just give me a few days to think things through. The best way to handle it, ja, the arrangements that must be made." He remained silent for a moment, gently massaging the back of my neck. And then he came to a conclusion. I'd seen his lips in that thin line before—tough, focused, determined. Immediately he seemed relieved. "I'll look after things, sweet girl. In a few days, just give me a few days."

I went home happy.

I never saw Kurt von Steiglitz again.

ŚWIDNICA

MAY 19, 2002

We didn't finish last night till nearly midnight, and I'm still lying in bed when the phone rings. It's only 8:00 a.m., but Johanne, husky voiced, says she wants to see me early as she will be ill at ease until she finishes her story. I realize that today is almost our last chance, that tomorrow—although Johanne is unaware of it—we will all meet at Reichenbach camp.

So I tell Johanne that I'll meet her in an hour at a coffeehouse down the street and lie brooding for another few minutes while I turn over all she has told me. She was raised to be passively anti-Semitic, if it's possible to describe any unexamined discrimination as passive. She came from an impoverished family that accepted authority as the natural order. She was intelligent but uneducated, likable but moulded in a time when virtually all values were based on interior and exterior discipline. Being "resolute" was a condition of economic survival in a time when the Treaty of Versailles had crushed Germany and reduced its people to near starvation. Being silent in the face of injustice was a condition for social survival. This was Johanne's formation. Did it lead her to becoming an SS guard? And if she was the guard who saved Mania, will she simply say so and let us all go home?

Obviously Johanne is not only telling me her story; she's telling herself a story, and like most stories we tell ourselves about our past, it's likely a mix of truth and myth. The myths are laced with chunks of truth, and the truth is made more interesting with fragments of myth. And both myth and truth reflect an invisible, interior reality. Why is she doing this? Maybe she's struggling to work out who she really is, what her life has really been about. Maybe because I'm a stranger and a good listener, I'm helping her do this. Or maybe Johanne is leading me by the nose—or thinks she is. Whatever it is, my job is to separate the facts from the fantasies, the truth from the lies, and so far I don't seem to be doing very well.

I pick up a light jacket—it's another perfect Polish spring day with a little frost, and the air is fresh as a vast bread basket—and go to the coffee shop. We edge into last night's revelations after a lot of chitchat, a pot of boiling coffee, and two crusty rolls slathered in pure creamy butter and topped with ham. I remark that this beats granola and grapefruit any time.

Then I ask, "You never saw von Stieglitz again? Never? That must have been tough. And how old were you? Twenty-four? I can only imagine how you felt, Johanne."

༲

Twenty-four I was, but that is not like twenty-four today. It was hard. Painful. Not only in my heart but…like hot steel it was, seizing my neck so I could not turn my head, running across my shoulders like a red-hot bar. But not at first. No, not at first. I was too in love, too naïve to know he'd dumped me. I expected to hear from Kurt that first week, but when no word came I went to our apartment on Sunday as usual, full of joy and confidence, and knocked on the door. I expected he'd open it, seize me in his arms, ask me lovingly how I was feeling. Then he would sit me down and tell me what arrangements he'd made. Ja, that is what I was like, as naïve as a child.

I thought nothing of it when nobody answered. I waited in the foyer, confident that Kurt had been delayed at work, until the cold and dark drove me home. Two nights later I returned. I tapped, I knocked, I pounded. I imagined he was inside, deep in an exhausted sleep. Then the door across the hall opened and a neighboring officer emerged. Was I looking for Sturmbannführer von Steiglitz? Ah, too bad, the Sturmbannführer had been transferred.

"Transferred? What do you mean, transferred? From Berlin, you mean?"

"Ja, transferred. No longer in Berlin. Banging on the door won't help, Fräulein."

Why was Kurt's neighbor lying? To stop my knocking? He didn't know what he was talking about. He didn't know what there was between us. Kurt would never leave Berlin without letting me know. He was solicitous and well organized and orderly. If he'd been transferred, he would have gotten through to me somehow—a note or a friend or a telegram. The post offices were still working despite the increased bombing. There wouldn't be total silence.

You can say I was a stupid girl, but I was just a woman in love. Maybe that's the same as being a stupid girl. At home I waited for a note that never came. A terrible fear was beginning to stir at the back of my mind. Maybe Kurt had fallen ill or been injured? He couldn't possibly be in any political trouble. Where could he possibly be that he couldn't contact me? As the days passed I started going downtown at night, tramping through the snow from one coffeehouse to another, searching for some-one, something—I don't know what—perhaps someone who would say, "Ah, Fräulein, the Sturmbannführer is on a secret mission, but soon he will be back." That's what I hoped for. Funny, nein?

Finally one night I went to the officers' club, and of that I remember every detail. The snow snapped under my boots, and an icy wind cut through the corners of the stone buildings. All my courage it took to go there. I cast from my mind memories of other women I'd seen arriving alone, searching, disbelieving, demanding entrance, and being turned away. How I'd pitied them and despised their lack of dignity!

A corporal stopped me at the door. I could not enter without an officer escort, he said firmly.

This man had seen me coming and going on Kurt's arm a hundred times. Rigid with attention he'd been, saluting as we passed. He dare not fool with me, I thought.

"I'm aware of that," I replied. "I will wait in the foyer."

"That will not be possible, Fräulein." The clipped words came smartly from tight lips. "Single women are not admitted unless the host officer has left instructions at the door. I have received no such instructions for you, Fräulein."

Did I imagine it, or was there a gloating tone in these last words? I wanted to slap the man's face. He knew me. He knew who my man was. For a moment I hesitated. Couples pushed by me. I searched their faces for some sign of recognition and tried to keep my tears back. Soon this bastard of a corporal would tell me to move on. I turned and left.

Weeks it took for me to realize that Kurt had dumped me. When Aunt Marie hinted at it, I hated her. What did she, with her pale, dumpy little life know about us, about a love like ours? She was jealous—that was it. It was insane to suggest that Kurt wanted me out of his life. When I'd left the apartment he'd kissed me tenderly and told me he'd make arrangements. No hint had he given, no look or word that suggested we'd never be together again. The possibility that he was gone, that there'd be no marriage, that he had gone out of my life—that I could not grasp. I still had not told my aunt of my pregnancy. I couldn't bear her foreseeable reaction—the tears, the sympathy, the long silence that would let me know that this was what she had warned me about, this was just what she had predicted.

I finally understood that Kurt wanted rid of me. This is how the message at last sunk in: I was in the city, perhaps a month after Kurt's disappearance, when in the distance I saw Ernst, one of Kurt's fellow officers, striding in my direction. We'd often partied together. But when Ernst saw me, he veered course and hurriedly crossed the road. Even from a half block away I could see his embarrassment. But I couldn't stop myself. My heart rose with hope. I ran after him, stumbling in my high heels, calling, "Ernst! Ernst!" like a madwoman, smiling and waving. I felt with every step I was degrading myself, because he was desperate to avoid me. And still I kept going!

Ernst finally stopped, half turned, and looked at me. There was nothing an SS officer despised more than lack of personal discipline, and in that moment, in his annoyed, half-pitying, half-condescending look, I saw that Kurt had not been transferred, was not on a secret mission, was not injured. I saw that the news of my pregnancy and expectation of marriage had done the round of his friends. I saw that Kurt had everyone's sympathy. I saw that I'd been jilted. I saw that everyone knew it but me.

Ernst said he had no idea where Kurt was. I knew he was lying, knew I could never penetrate the protective circle that Kurt's male friends had built around him. And still I couldn't stop myself, couldn't shut up, couldn't let go of the last traces of my dream.

"You're lying," I shot back. I was standing in the gutter, shouting like a druggie. "Don't lie to me, Ernst. Tell me where he is. I've got to see him."

Ernest looked at me with pity. "Go home, Johanne," he said and hurried on.

I grew up that night, became a real woman, starting to learn the ways of men. I understood that I had no way of ever finding Kurt. But he knew exactly where I was. Ernst was simply doing what powerful men did for one another: ensuring his friend was inaccessible to the woman he'd dumped. It's just as true today, nicht wahr?

The Lachmanns realized my relationship was over. I spent every night and most of Sundays upstairs in my attic room. Frau Director said nothing. There was no need to wonder how I spent the nights; my red eyes told everything. Now I could never tell them who my lover had been. Ja, I'd looked forward to that, the chance to show off my real worth beyond being a valued maker of Tafelspitz and tasty sauces. But I'd been put back in my box: in the kitchen, where I belonged, serving others.

My big secret I kept to myself.

One day about three months into my pregnancy I opened my wardrobe and took out every piece of clothing I'd worn to the officers' club. The dark-blue suit, the evening dress with a silver lamé bodice, the black crepe dress with the low square-cut neckline on which I'd spent a month's wages, the two pairs of high-heeled dainty shoes. I packed everything into a box and marked it "Trash." Then I kicked it into a dark attic corner, ready for a trip to the secondhand store. I kicked it and kicked it until it fitted where it belonged.

Did I ever consider an abortion? Nein, never! I had part of Kurt in me. That, he could not make disappear. But shame I felt. Not because of my sexual life with Kurt nor that I was single and pregnant. Never did I regret the lovemaking we'd had. I had that—something most women never have. I thought of my stepmother, Magda. Ja, that is why she'd read all those romantic books, searching, searching for something she knew was there but she had never had. But I had had it.

The truth—for that's what you want, nein?—is that even after being dumped, if Kurt had come back I would have crawled on my hands and knees to welcome him. It wasn't only love that possessed me. I'd been branded, my body, my soul. Never had I made love before. No man's hands had touched me, no words of love had ever been whispered in my ears, no tongue had curled itself around my tongue. Kurt opened a world of magic for me and never, never, did I regret it.

"I'd never known it could be like this," Kurt had often said while making love. And I, like all the women he'd probably said it to before, believed my lovemaking was wilder, more daring, than anything he'd known before. It made me work harder, which he'd counted on. It took me a few years to realize what a smooth and practiced seducer my lover had been, what a pack of little lies he had on hand to please. But even realizing all this, my heart warmed at the memories, and I couldn't keep a smile from coming to my lips. Some of us women are like that, nein?

❧

Johanne pauses for a breath and looks at me. My mouth is dry. It's hanging open. She repeats, "Some of us women are like that, nein?" and I should be supportive, so I nod my head while thinking, "Count me out on that one."

❧

Ja, these were the things that caused my shame. At twenty-four I was still dreaming the dream I'd had when I was twelve and played the princess in the school play at Schweidnitz. I was the beauty who would be adored by the prince. Why am I telling you these things? That's what you're wondering, isn't it? I want you to know I am telling you everything—everything. I am hiding nothing. I am telling the truth of my life.

In the Lachmann household there was much to do. Poor Anna had fled after the first air raids, returning to a small town in the southern mountains where there was no railroad or industry to attract the bombers. "Lots of flowers and peace," she wrote on the only postcard we received. Not long after she was killed when a British plane, unable to find its target, unloaded its bombs on the town en route home.

My life in Berlin developed a new routine. In the morning I walked for miles, searching shops for particular luxuries the Lachmanns were used to—certain soaps, for instance. Apart from that, Herr Director was able to get whatever we needed by way of food and oil. Then I prepared the main meal of the day with whatever we had. In the afternoon I prepared supper and cleaned the house with Frau Director, who was more of a nuisance than a help.

About my pregnancy I still said nothing. Before I told them, I wanted to make sure they counted on me to the point they felt they couldn't do without me. With time I'd worked out all the details of keeping my job and the child. At first a cradle upstairs. Then as the child grew a bassinet and a little caged area in the kitchen. I knew Frau Director would allow this; in fact, she might be pleased to have some young life in the house.

I gained little weight, and it was not until my seventh month that Frau Director remarked, "Johanne, you are so big. Is anything up?"

"Ja," I said, feeling a surge of pride and joy. "I am going to have a child."

Frau Director almost fell off her chair.

"*Mein Gott*, Johanne. When?"

"Six weeks or so," I said.

"Six weeks or so? But where is it?"

Now I laughed with happiness, the first time I had laughed aloud for months. Apart from Aunt Maria and my family back in Schweidnitz, I had told no one. What a joy and relief it was to say it aloud! I had always felt I carried the baby in my back, for it was almost invisible. But now I patted my stomach and said, "It's here, Frau Director, right here in my little belly." Such love I felt. This child would be the love of my life.

At least four nights a week now we spent in our bombproof shelter because the raids had become heavier and more frequent. Fortunately, my labor pains started during the day. Frau Director took me to the hospital by tram.

Two days later my son was born. Perfect he was and beautiful, fair-haired and blue-eyed and strong. I lay in bed and held him to my breast and wept in joy and pain.

⁓

Sixty years have now passed, but Johanne's tears insist on falling. She takes off her glasses and wipes her red eyes. I feel disabled by this sudden spurt of sadness and remember the birth of my own son and the insane, transcendent joy when, through a fog of pain and Demerol, I saw his sweet, fair face and held him in my arms for the first time. Suddenly I feel connected to this woman through things far beyond politics and nationality and old wars, and I think how much women everywhere have in common and how they could renew the face of the earth if only they had the political will.

I pull myself out of my reverie and ask, "Johanne, did you think about Kurt during this time in hospital with your baby?"

I struggled against daydreaming but failed. If Kurt could only see him, I thought, he'd want us both. He could never close his heart to such perfection. I would say to him, "Kurt, just think, this might be the only son you'll ever have." Ja, I still loved that man. Just thinking of him made the milk drip from my breasts and soak the coarse gown in which I lay.

Hours after my son's birth Herr and Frau Director arrived with a huge bouquet of flowers. They peered at the baby in my arms, smiled, and remarked on his perfection. They asked no question about his father, and my heart warmed to them for this.

The following day Frau Director visited me again.

"So what will you do with the baby, Johanne?"

"Do with it?" Her question flustered me. "At first in the attic, a little crib, and then later—"

"Johanne!" Frau Director jerked her chair closer to me, scraping it across the wood floor. "You cannot keep the child! You can't be intending that! We can't have a baby in the house. Johanne, dear girl. But such an idea! It's out of the question!"

I must have turned white because Frau Director stood up and leaned over me so close I could smell the powder on her face and feel the warmth from her well-corseted body.

"Johanne, you cannot have thought it could stay in our house? You have never said anything to us. The Herr Director and I, we thought your family would take it. But for it to stay in our house! Nein, nein, such a thing is out of the question."

Why did she call my son "it"? I wanted to protest, but her words had drained all strength from me. I wanted to say, "Then the baby will go and I will go with it!" I started to cry. I felt weak and alone. Perhaps if I told her who the father was, ja, that would make a difference, no ordinary little bastard as they thought but the son of an aristocrat, the son of an SS officer.

I said quietly—my anger I could not hide—that I hoped that Frau Director did not believe "it," my son, had been conceived under a hedge in the city park. "He was conceived in great love, Frau Lachmann, and in his veins is the pure blood of an old and distinguished German family.

Never have I told you who my lover was but—"

Frau Director jumped to her feet and held up the palm of her hands to stop me. "Don't, Johanne. Don't say it. I don't want to know."

I wouldn't stop. How could she refer to my son as "it"? I was pleased to see her distress, pleased that my love affair with Kurt had awakened my sense of self-respect.

"You don't want to know, but I want to tell you."

Frau Lachmann covered her ears with the palms of her hands. "Johanne, stop. I beg you to stop. Never have my husband and I wanted to know. Don't put this burden on us. You are not yourself. You've been so discreet all this time. Don't spoil it. Please, Johanne."

I leaned back on my pillow and wept. The Lachmanns and their home were all I had. I explained that months earlier I'd asked my father to take the baby at birth, but he'd said he could not feed another, that he was already feeding ten mouths. Aunt Maria could not help me. When I knew this I'd created a plan to keep my baby with me.

Frau Director sat rock-still in total silence. Then she announced, "In that case the child must be given up for adoption."

Never, I thought. Never.

I stayed in hospital for two weeks. In those days this was normal after childbirth. The authorities were aware of my situation and allowed me to leave my son there when I returned to work. I rode my bike to the hospital early in the morning, breast-fed my son, rode home, prepared lunch, returned to the hospital and fed my son, went home and prepared dinner, and then rode once again to the hospital to nurse my beautiful boy. I wrote again to Vati and Magda, but again the reply was the same: "We are still raising our own families and we cannot take more on. You must care for him yourself."

After a month the hospital authorities said they could not keep the child, that I must take him. I took him to the Lachmanns and started searching for a place for him in the neighborhood. I planned to use my wages for his care and visit him as I wished. But there was no place for him to go. I felt so utterly betrayed. I was a proud and fertile pure-blood Aryan woman. I had produced a perfect male child, a child the Führer himself would have been pleased to father. Yet nobody would help me.

After a few days Frau and Herr Lachmann told me once again that I would have to put the child up for adoption. They were very firm. They knew of a couple in the neighborhood who wanted a child but could not have any. Only if you have been in my situation can you imagine the state of my heart.

The following morning I told the hospital I would freely give up my child for adoption. Within two days they told me they had found a suitable couple—an SS officer and his wife. This couple turned out to be the same couple the Lachmanns knew. I felt so bitter when I realized it had all been discussed and arranged behind my back. Things went quickly. I was asked a lot of questions about my family, and was forced to reveal in confidence the name and status of my child's father. The hospital authorities had to make sure there was no "impure"—that is, Jewish—blood in my child.

A nightmare it was, planning to give up my son.

It happened when he was four weeks old. The pain was indescribable. To this day I cannot dwell on this time. I met the SS couple—let me give them the name Burchert—and they congratulated me on producing such a perfect child both for them and for the Fatherland. Before I signed the papers I demanded one condition: that I could visit the child whenever I wished. They agreed. It sounds commonplace to say my heart was broken, but it was. My throat, too, for at times I could hardly breathe. My breasts, bound tightly in cotton strips to stop the flow of milk, were on fire with pain.

Five days later I was working in the kitchen when there was a knock on the side door. To my astonishment there stood Vati, a small flower in his hand, a smile on his lined face, and his best suit, shiny and old, on his back.

"I've come for the baby," he smiled. "I've already raised ten kids, so I thought, what's another one?"

Ach! Don't ask me to tell you how I felt then. My breasts were still bound in cotton cloth to stop the milk from coming. I was physically in pain and now in my heart and soul. I howled like a whipped dog. Vati wept too. We sat at the kitchen table and cried together. He wept for me, for his lost grandson, and ja, for our whole sad lives.

I went back to my life of cooking. On Sundays I didn't go strolling down the Kurfürstendamm or enjoying the Tiergarten. I stayed at home and visited my son, but even that I could not do as often as I'd wanted. Frau Burchert really did not want me there. She wanted my son to herself. She always opened the door, was always polite, always handed me my son in a kindly manner. But she never left us alone, never let me change his diaper or give him a bath, and when I brought little gifts for him she never unwrapped them but put them aside as if they carried germs. Once I put a little spit on my finger and curled the soft down at the nape of his neck, and when I looked at Frau Burchert she was sitting still and straight, just looking, not smiling as I was. I saw she disliked my being there, but she never refused me entry. So I saw my son, whom they had named Evert, crawling and then taking his first hesitant steps. The arrangement worked well, the pain of separation lessened, and I assumed it would go on forever.

One day the front doorbell rang. I hurried to answer it, but Frau Director was already there, staring, immobile. Two uniformed men stood there with a letter in hand. For the death or missing in action of an ordinary soldier the government sent a letter. But for an officer or someone important, the news was given personally. I see it still today, the two men in their uniforms, one rattling the paper and then reading aloud, "In the name of the law, Konrad Lachmann died for Germany." And I can still hear Frau Director screaming, and me closing the door, and her half falling down, and me dragging her upstairs to her bedroom and laying her on the bed, and fumbling in the cupboard for the brandy but there was none. And then Herr Director came home ashen-faced, and he closed the bedroom door, and I could hear them both sobbing. Konrad was a navigator, shot down in England, although I can't remember where.

☙

As Johanne speaks I also hear the sound of sobbing. I am in the hall of my home in a Melbourne suburb and the doorbell rings. I am home from school on holidays. It is a hot day in January 1944, and I go to the front door. A boy of about sixteen is standing there with his hand holding a thick beige envelope. He is dressed in navy blue and has a peaked cap on his head. He hands me the envelope without looking. I open it and it says that 416830 Pilot Officer Robert Norman Allan is missing following a raid

209

over Magdeburg, Germany, on the night of January 21.

I go down the hall and through the kitchen to the back door. I can see my father at the back of the yard near an old gum tree. He is doing something with a long-handled shovel. It looks like he's making a compost heap. I walk towards him. I'm fifteen and fully aware that I am about to destroy his life, aware that from the moment I speak he will never spend another day of his life without deep pain. "Dad," I say, handing him the envelope, "Bob is missing."

He says, "Oh dear. I must go to your mother."

Later I go back into the house and block my ears at the sound of sobbing in my parents' bedroom.

⁖

The day we heard of Konrad's death, I hurried to see my own son. The grief, the Lachmanns' sobbing—it was so unbearably familiar because night and day I held back the same sounds and felt the same pain for my own son. Now I felt desperate to hold him in my arms, smother his face with kisses, croon over and love him. I ran to the Burchert house, but nobody answered my knocking. I hurried down the narrow side path to the back and banged on the kitchen door. I peered into the house. It had been stripped. The Bucherts had left, and my son was gone.

I ran home, but there was no one there to talk to because the Lachmanns were still locked in their room, so I ran back to the Bucherts' neighbors. Ja, ja, the woman next door told me. She did not know Hauptsturmführer Buchert or his wife, but they and all their belongings had moved two days earlier. She did not know where.

That spring of 1943—that's when I lost my son and started a search that took most of my life. ↦

ŚWIDNICA

We break for lunch. I want to walk about Świdnica with Johanne. She says she's going for a walk but would rather be alone. I watch her stride away, determined and steady as she weaves along the medieval street, a walking bank vault of old secrets from a life deeply lived. I watch the blue pantsuit disappear in the throngs and take off hesitantly in the opposite direction. I try to enjoy the beauty of the day, the medieval buildings, the history-soaked streets, but it's hard to completely shut out the Lachmanns' hopeless sobbing, which seems to intermingle so effortlessly with the muffled bedroom sounds that arose from my parents' broken hearts. Again I have an irresistible feeling of identity with the whole human race, the whole fucked-up human race with its fateful inability to change, let alone sanctify, the human condition.

When Johanne and I meet again, this time in my cramped bedroom, I have to work to remind myself that I'm in Poland for one reason only: to determine if Johanne Müller, cleaning woman, was the guard who saved Mania's life.

"You were speaking of the terrible bombings," I say to Johanne to get her going. All I feel in saying those words is pity for those in the air and those on the ground who are about to become victims of a madman's dream. ↦

1943 — 1982

The weeks went by. More and more bombs, the English and Australians at night, the Americans by day. In August all the children, and adults not required for essential work, were evacuated from Berlin.

Early one evening in July 1943 Herr Director came into the kitchen and told me that I must soon go to the bunker. My sister Trudi was staying with me that night. She didn't want to go to the bunker. Often I did not go. But this night Herr Director was insistent. "A big English invasion will come this night," he said. He spoke as if someone high up had warned him.

Like hell it was that night. On and on the bombing went, with the earth shaking and trembling. Then suddenly the earth beneath us rose and heaved like it was dying and giving out one long, last breath. In the morning the gardener opened our bunker door. He said, "It's all gone." Herr Director stepped out and then he collapsed. We had taken a direct hit. We crawled out beside him. The house had vanished. No walls or roofs or windows or garden—just a blue summery sky with a few wisps of cloud above and rubble below. All we had was what we had on our bodies.

We walked to Herr Director's office and factory. The air was filled with dust and smoke and people. Like ghosts they were, hardly able to move. The district was mostly in rubble, but the administrative offices were intact. My sister and I went back to the site of the Lachmann home and with Herr Director's help dragged a couple of torn and blackened mattresses to the office. Directly above Herr Director's office was an attic. We lay the mattresses on the floor, and that is where Frau Director and I slept. The director slept on the floor of his office. A cleaner and his wife slept on the ground floor, and Herr Director's chauffeur slept in a little hut by the side of the building.

There was a small kitchen in the building, and I did the same work as I had done before. For two years I worked on that little stove and served Frau and Herr Director whatever food we could get, and never did I leave Berlin. We were like a little family; I was like the daughter. Once—yes, I remember now—once I went back to Schweidnitz. Vati was ill and I went back to care for him. My stepmother, Magda, and my sister Elise had moved to Bahmstadt, but Vati could not leave his work at Fremds and Freudenburg, the big iron foundry in Schweidnitz. When he became very sick, permission was given me to leave Berlin to care for him. The spring of 1944 it was.

᙭

This doesn't sound right. Almost every woman and child was evacuated from Berlin at this time, and yet for two years Johanne stayed with the Lachmanns, cooking over a tiny stove in the rubble of an office? And the Nazis did not order her to work in some wartime capacity, leaving Frau Director Lachmann to whip up the schnitzels herself? I say nothing because the date 1944 is like a handle that opens a chute, and my own memories fall out in a torrent. Mania, young, sick, alone, and terrified in Birkenau extermination camp. Johanne, a new childless mother, a true believer in Hitler, a dutiful daughter back in Schweidnitz. And I am going back to boarding school.

Before leaving home I ask my parents to tell me themselves if there is any news of my brother Bob. I insist I don't want to be told by anyone other than a family member. Standing at the Spencer Street Station in Melbourne, I make my older sister promise that, whatever the news, I will not be told by a nun. Back at school the weeks go by. I study, play cricket, go to Mass, and sing in the choir at Sunday Vespers. And all the time I hope and dream that my brother had safely parachuted to ground, is walking across Europe, hiding in German forests, and being helped by the French resistance. I dream this until one night I am called down to Reverend Mother's study and told that my brother's body has been found and identified. I ask if they are sure it is my brother. Reverend Mother says, yes, the identification was made by the Swiss Red Cross. The tail of the plane bore the insignia "M for Mother." Two members of the crew were identified, five were not.

I thank Reverend Mother, leave the room with the required curtsy, and go back to my studies. There is no letter or phone call from home for two weeks. A decision has been made at home that it is best not to disturb

214

me. No one tells me this was the reason for no contact. I learn of it forty years later.

The spring of 1944. I snap out of my reverie, and Johanne is saying she was in Schweidnitz then and…

⁜

Few men there were in Schweidnitz. All had gone to fight the Russians. Maureen has told me that she'd learned all the strong, healthy women in town were recruited as prison guards. That's probably true, but of it I knew nothing. Of slave labor camps in the countryside nearby, I knew nothing. I was in Schweidnitz simply to help Vati. All the other time I was in Berlin, cooking on a stove in a bombed-out office. Strange things happened in the war. I have nothing to hide. I always tell the truth.

⁜

I'm hanging on to every repetitious word, hoping for some slip, some breakdown, an admission—I don't know what. But Johanne doesn't waver. Stone-faced, she holds herself erect, her thick-veined hand in her lap, her voice soft but insistent. For the fifth time she returns to the story of her dying father, adding bitterly that with "all the kids he had I was the only one sitting with him in our old apartment."

⁜

Dieter, my elder brother, had been killed in the Wehrmacht, and Harrer, my younger brother, had disappeared at Stalingrad. I held Vati's hand when he died. I had a small stub of a candle and lit it by the bed and stayed on for a while, alone. Ja, the same bed it was that Mutti had died in, and that Vati had shared with Magda. Ah ja, Magda! Not even there when Vati died!

Then I went back to Berlin and the Lachmanns. And then the first Russians arrived in Berlin. We were in East Berlin, right in their path. The war ended, and what hell that was because we got the worst of their hunger for women. We had a bunker that we hid in with a small side room that had two bunk beds, and we took turns sleeping in them. There was an old couple—eighty years old—also in the bunker. They got fed up and went out, and the old woman was raped and then they were both shot. The Russians were like animals. We could hear them yelling,

215

"Ladies, ladies, come sleep with us!" They raped every woman and female child they could lay their hands on.

Frau Director and I were lucky. One day we heard them coming, shouting, "Come out, Fräulein, come sleep with us!" and laughing. We got through the small window and into the next little section. When the Russians opened the bunker door they saw nobody and left. For weeks after they arrived we hid in that bunker from these animals. And to this day I should love the Russians? Should be nice to them? Another person might say it doesn't matter. Let them! Not me!

But Frau Director I loved. Ja, she would not let me keep my baby in the house, and I lost my son because of her. But I loved her. She was a lady. While we were in the bunker she said to me one day, "When something happens, when the Russians come, I can't...Johanne, I can't." I knew what she meant. She was speaking of those disgusting Russian devils. And I loved her so much that I said, "I will give myself instead of you, Frau Director." You can only understand what this meant if minute by minute for weeks you've lived in fear of gang rape.

As Johanne says, "I will give myself instead of you," her voice rises, her shoulders slump, and tears roll down her cheeks. Memory overwhelms her, but she struggles to sit up, and with one hand in the air, pointing a finger towards me, she says emphatically, between tears, "I wasn't raped, though. I swear I was not raped. I had luck."

⁕

I don't tell her I have just finished reading *A Woman in Berlin: Eight Weeks in the Conquered City*. The anonymous German author claimed that very few females, old women or young girls, escaped being raped by Soviet troops. Ironically, for years German critics dismissed this book on the grounds that it "besmirched the honor of German women"—a further wounding for the victims. I want to touch Johanne lightly with a comforting gesture but she speaks again, and at her words I pull my arm back.

⁕

Ja, I had luck. Others did not. The Jews were not the only ones who suffered. But no compensation do we get.

Because I was strong and healthy, the Russians put me to work clean-

216

ing the rubble off the streets of Berlin as a Trommel frau. We had to hammer the concrete from the bricks, clean the bricks with our bare hands, and then place the waste in a big steel drum. No gloves. We weren't allowed to wear them. We were guarded by a Russian female who walked back and forth, armed with a rifle with a bayonet fixed. After three months all the skin was off my hands. When I could do it no longer, the Russians let me go.

I hunted for other work and again found it with the Russians. There was an airport near Straussberg near Berlin. Three times a day at a Russian camp I cooked with other German women for 450 Russian soldiers, men and women. We served twenty-four hours on, twenty-four hours off.

In between I kept looking for my son. When the war was over, all the SS took off their uniforms and fled this way and that. None remained by Hitler. Nobody knew each other anymore. The biggest guys from Hitler, nobody knew them anymore.

There were several search agencies because so many people were missing, so many families broken. I learned that the parents of Frau Burchert were in Berlin. I contacted them, and they gave me their daughter's address in Hamburg. Do you know what a coal wagon is? A big wagon for transporting coal. No toilet, no water. All of us squeezed together, and off we went to Hamburg.

I found the house. I stood in front of it, and a woman I didn't recognize came out. I asked, "Does the family Burchert live here?" and suddenly a little boy came out and stood behind this woman. Oh my God, I thought, that is my child.

"Who owns this little boy?" I asked. It had been more than three years since I had seen my son.

The woman said, "He's mine," and shut the door in my face.

Where could I go? What could I do? I went to a place across the street, a cellar bar, a place today we'd call a disco. Refugees could sleep there for fifty pfennig a night, and you got breakfast and a cup of coffee. I watched the house, but nobody came or went. I tried again, but no one answered. I waited and watched for a day and a half, and then I had to get back to work. I had no money, no resources. I had to eat. Was that little boy my son? Had the Burcherts moved in the hope of erasing Hauptsturmführer Burchert's SS past? Every SS soldier who could was doing it because the Russians were either putting them into prison or sending them back to a slave labor camp in Russia.

I started a search through agencies in all the big cities, but my letters kept coming back stamped "Person Unknown." After a couple of years many search places were closed because people had been found.

The rest of my story, except for one thing, is ordinary enough. I married in 1947 a good man. Thirty-one years old I was and had learned what a good man was. We had both saved our money and rented and ran a small hotel with a restaurant near Straussberg. We were there for three years. But the Russians, who rode our back on everything, decided to send my husband to Russia because he spoke the language. We fled overnight by bicycles, going to Wittenberg through the border, with nothing except what we had on our backs.

We started all over again. In 1950 we moved to Soest. In 1953 the Canadians arrived, and soon after that I started work with them. They liked my cooking and knew I loved children, so soon I was working for a very high-ranking officer. We lived on Möhnesee, high on the mountain, in a beautiful villa that the Canadians had taken over. Every two years the Canadian officers were changed, but they always kept me on. Then after some time the Canadians moved down to the Black Forest. I wrote to the office in Lahr. They had my papers, and that's where I went.

My husband died in 1965. I worked, but my real life was searching for my son. Years passed yet not one day went by that I didn't think, "Where is he? What does he look like? What does he do?" And last I wondered, "Does he look like Kurt?" My love for Kurt, all tangled up into the war, never died. I loved my husband, but a woman never forgets her first love, nicht wahr?

The last search office was in Berlin. I wrote there, and the miracle happened. Two weeks later I received an answer that the family Burchert was living in Friesland up north. After almost forty years I had found my son.

Through letters—too nervous I was to speak on the phone—my son and I arranged to meet. I was to go to his apartment. How I trembled, how I fussed about my hair, my clothes! I drove there. Sick with tension I was. He opened the door. He was a tall, fair-haired man, almost middle-aged but slim and fit. Ja, I could see Kurt in him. We stared at one another. Stupidly I blurted out, "Your mother, your stepmother, I told her when you were small that I was allowed to see you whenever I wanted. This was agreed at your adoption. That I want you to know, black and white." Why, why did I even then have to apologize, excuse myself, after all that had been done to me?

He stood there. Then he put his hand on my arm and said, "Come in, Mother."

How did I feel? My uppermost concern was how Frau Burchert might feel at my sudden reappearance. I cannot explain why I felt so strongly about this. And it was hard to associate this big stranger with my baby boy. More than anything I was too nervous to enjoy the moment I'd dreamed of for forty years. My son suggested I might feel better if I spoke to his adoptive mother. She lived near the border of Holland, and we drove to her that day.

I wanted everything to be in order. I said, "Frau Burchert, I have one question that my son must know the answer to. Is it not true that it was agreed I was allowed to see my son whenever I wanted?"

"Yes, Evert, what she says is true."

My son and I were both relieved. Now I could relax. Afterwards we sat in Evert's apartment. He talked and talked. "Mother, now I can imagine it. Whenever my parents were away, there was always a locked container with my mother's jewelry, papers, and so on. Always locked, and they never said what was in it. One day they were away and I got nosy and opened it. That's how I learned I was not their son. I was adopted."

And then he gave me a great happiness. "For years," he said, "I have been searching for you. But I was searching under your family name, not your married name."

That he had searched for me! Such joy to know that. Soon after this visit Evert came to my apartment in southeast Germany. How I scrubbed, cleaned, and cooked in anticipation! Such happiness I had not known for years. Like a girl I was, giddy with joy. "Cooking for my son," I told myself. "Ja, my son, my own child, is coming." I had always loved kids, and as a young woman I had dreamed of having my own. If no man married me, I thought I would adopt one if the law allowed. Now my dream had come true. I was in my own home awaiting the arrival of my own son. I planned to tell him everything, of my love for his father, of his father's high-class birth and rank in the SS, of his ultimate betrayal. My son was a gracious man. He deserved the truth; he would deal with it the right way.

At first it was a little awkward with my son in the apartment, although lovely it was to hear him call me "Mother." Each time he said the word I felt its sweetness, so long had I waited. Evert had been well raised, and all that he said and did reflected an air of social ease. But after so many years, what to say? Where to start? So we chatted of little things: where he went to school and what subjects he was good at, what work did he for a living.

We had finished dinner and were sitting over coffee when he remarked he had had very few friends at school because his parents moved quite often.

How could I have realized the impact, the consequences of my next words?

"Ja, it was like that for some of the officers in the SS," I said. "Your father must have attained a high rank if you and your mother could go with him."

Evert stared at me. I could feel his shock. What had I said?

"Nein, nein, Mother, you're mistaken," he said. "It cannot be. You are saying my vati was a member of the Schutzstaffel? My vati? In the SS? Is that what you said? That this is true?"

Then I understood that he had never been told. He was only three when the war was over. Why would the parents have told him? I hadn't taken into account that it was now 1982. The swastika was now evil, the SS despised. For forty years his parents had successfully hidden the truth, and in one second I'd thoughtlessly destroyed their whole façade.

"I took it for granted you knew," I said.

He sat very still, looking at me. The look on his face had changed from denial, to shock, to repulsion.

"When I was very little, my father went away. I learned later he was in prison. I never knew why. Muti said it was all a terrible mistake, that I was not to think any more about it. But…but…if he was in the SS, and of high rank, that would explain it. Ja, ja." He grew very thoughtful. "That would explain so much."

Every detail of my son's life I was longing to know about. You understand that for years I wondered: what is he doing, what does he look like, are they good to my little boy, teaching him right, loving him, holding him as I would have done? Ja, I was curious. But I tried to hide this; one does not like to appear greedy for information. So I managed to say simply, "Oh? How do you mean? Explain."

"I could never get close to Mutti and Vati," my son said. "I loved them. They were very good to me, but I always felt a silence, a secret between them I was not allowed to share. I grew up with this silence. And I've read, Mother, that the children of the Holocaust victims also grew up with this silence. Something huge in their parents' lives, something monumental, that they were shut out from."

While my son spoke, I could listen with only half my heart. It registered that he was saying something about the Jew children of survivors, that he had suffered from silence as they had suffered from silence. But I hardly understood because his words were a terrible shock. Such bitter disappointment I felt! I realized never could I tell him who his biological father was, that his real father had been a high-ranking SS officer and how proud I had been of that. Never could I explain all that happened then, the way it happened. If he felt so shocked—ja, repulsed—that his adoptive father was in the SS, how would he feel about his real father? How would he feel about himself, his own blood?

Nein. Evert would not have understood. The Germany that made him, my Germany, was not his Germany. He would never understand all that his true father was. He left me, but still he was the love of my life. Silly of me, ja, but I needed to share a little of my real life with my son, wanted him to know what love he had been conceived in and in what a great time, what great glory there was in those days.

But risk it I could not. I felt like weeping. And I felt anger. I saw time had dug a big black hole between us: neither of us could cross it. So proud I was of his—what do you say—genes? Ja, genes. So proud of the heritage that flowed in his blood. This was the secret I was bursting to share with my son. But I saw I would have to die with it. And I was right. Once on a later visit I said to him, after some black people moved into the apartment next to mine—I wanted him to know that I am tolerant, that I understand that Germany is not the same old Germany—I said, "I suppose black people can't help being black any more than Jews can help having Yiddish children." But Evert looked at me very strangely. I knew then there were things I'd never understand about this new Germany, knew I'd made the right decision to shut up. Some things just can't be set right.

٭

This is Johanne. She moves my heart one moment and infuriates me the next. She stops at this point, looks straight at me, and repeats, "Some things can't be set right." The emphasis she puts on things that "can't be set right" puzzles me. I understand that she is closing down, shutting tight. Her words have a blunt muted sound, like the thud of dirt onto a coffin.

Hers was a mother's love: wild, unconditional, passionate. A simple love, like the love for a child held at the breast, the spontaneous love and laughter that spills out when a pouty little mouth opens and reveals the first tooth. It was also a love that would symbolically put her back in Kurt's arms, a love that would keep the door of memory open to those heady, magical days when the world of wine and roses and territorial conquest made every day golden and nothing impossible. Unrealistically she had dreamed of revealing everything and, in return, receiving unconditional love from her son. But few adults can give unconditional love: that's the reserve of children. None of this has happened. Evert has grown up in a German world that Johanne barely recognizes, has never known, doesn't understand, and definitely does not like.

She says she has finished her story. There is nothing more to say to me. But why has she so willingly told me her story? Why has she bothered to put herself through such an ordeal of memory? Surely not just to ask, what was my life all about? Is there any meaning in it, any meaning in what I have been and all I've been through? Who am I really?

No. Such questions are not the sort of questions that bother Johanne. She is resolute, disciplined, hardworking, capable of passion and maternal love, at times charming, at other times sour. She is an ordinary human being. She is not into philosophy or metaphysics. She has told me her story for some other reason. And I don't know what that reason is.

In two days the group will leave Poland. I fear it will it be with the same lack of proof of Johanne's alleged past as a guard as when we arrived. It seems likely. I'm afraid we've all been caught up by the power of fantasy, the seductive allure of myth, the stuff of every enduring play and piece of literature since the time of the early Greeks—the noble human being choosing at great risk to act for good in the face of terrible evil and sure punishment.

I tell Johanne that I'm happy she found her son. She smiles and volunteers a personal note by saying she sees Evert three or four times year, and that he is gentle and kind to her. I remark that that's great, that I know a few parents in Canada who are lucky to see their children once a year. Of politics and of all the "strange new people" who've immigrated to Germany, she says, of things like that she and Evert do not speak.

We say good night, and I go down to the desk and make arrangements to leave Świdnica late the following afternoon. This will allow ample time to witness the meeting, and reacquaintance, of the two women at Reichenbach camp. Despite the consistent denials and the almost total lack of proof, I find myself still harboring fantasies of Johanne breaking down, embracing Mania, and admitting, "Ja, it was me. I am the guard who saved you! I am the guard who wanted to adopt you. I had lost my son, I loved children, I wanted my own child. I wanted you."

I phone Maureen and go to her room. I take a bottle of mineral water with me—Maureen, for unknown reasons, prefers water—and find myself telling Maureen that Johanne was not the guard. Maureen says she believes she is. And Mania is more certain than ever. Why would Johanne have been allowed to stay in Berlin, cooking when Germany had conscripted every other able-bodied person into useful national service? And was she in Świdnica in 1944 solely to visit her father? There were no men left in that area, and yet Gross-Rosen comprised a series of slave labor camps all needing guards. What a work opportunity for a strong young

223

woman anxious to stay in her beloved hometown!

I persist as devil's advocate. Just what are the odds of a Toronto housewife, formerly a child Holocaust victim, hiring a cleaning woman and the cleaning woman turns out to be the former Nazi guard who saved her? It's time we saw Mania's identification for what it is: a case of mistaken identity fueled by a mix of desire and a strong moral sense of gratitude and survivor's guilt. We've accepted Mania's word about all the bizarre incidents that led to her survival. We should accept Johanne's word.

Maureen comes back swiftly. "There were thousands of work camps in the Third Reich. What are the odds that the hometown of that cleaning woman would be a few kilometers from the labor camp Mania was in?"

I return to my room and start to pack. Looking at my pile of now useless interview notes, I'm tempted to ditch them. After a moment's hesitation, I tuck them in my suitcase. ↔

MAY 20, 2002

It's another spring morning bursting with life. Maureen has gone ahead in a car with Mania, Elzbieta Gibokova from the Gross-Rosen Archives, and a second cameraman. A little later, accompanied by archivist Aleksandra (Ola) Kobielec, I follow in a car driven by Magdalena Zajac. A short time later Piotr, Neil, translator Sylke Plaummen, and Johanne leave the hotel to meet us at the camp.

Johanne still does not know where she is going, but that's her fault. When she had agreed to participate in the project, she knew her role would be to accompany Mania, a Jewish survivor of the Holocaust whose house she had cleaned in Toronto. But this morning she is in a sour mood. All the blunt, sweet, sad memories voiced over the last few days have left her drained, and all that remains is dark, like the residue in a bottle of vinegar. When Maureen enthusiastically asks her, "Are you interested in knowing where we are going today?" Johanne turns on her and spits out, "Es ist scheiss egal." (It's all the same shit to me.) Taken aback, Maureen says nothing.

We take another short drive through the rich, lush Polish countryside. The site of the former slave labor camp is in an isolated area, although only about five kilometers from Reichenbach's town center, an elegant area with fine old homes and broad, shaded boulevards. Here the land is flat, and although the area surrounding the camp is covered in grass and crops, the site itself, surrounded by a five-foot stone wall, is dry and stony.

After the war the camp, with its fifteen three-story buildings, was used in part as a pig farm. Several stone buildings remain; others have been reduced to a few piles of weathered grey stone half covered in weeds. There are some indentations in the rough ground, as if earth had once been removed and things buried there. In the distance is a mountain range, and I suppose this is what Mania saw as she left the camp to march to work. This and the frozen fields and the guards around her.

We stand outside the gate, waiting for Johanne's car. Mania is nervous, looking around in obvious confusion. Ola discreetly comments that confusion is common to most prisoners who return to the site of their imprisonment. "In 1992 we had a group of one hundred male survivors, all former prisoners, return to this camp. About half of them were instantly confused, and none agreed on anything. They were all quarreling within minutes."

Despite her disorientation, Mania remains Mania. In her hands she holds several small, expensive, luxury gifts carefully chosen for Johanne: perfume, scarf, rouge, lipstick. "Everything Christian Dior," says Mania proudly. "And a lovely color, the lipstick. Today I will definitely be able to tell yes or no by her expression."

She doesn't have long to wait. When Johanne arrives she steps out of her car, looks around at the nearby woods, the wall and gate of the former campsite, and turns to us and smiles. She is gracious, cool, and perfectly controlled, the bad temper, the coarse words of the morning now vanished. Butter wouldn't melt in this lady's mouth.

Mania has gone ahead into the camp and is sitting on a pile of rocks, waiting. The cameras, set up, begin to roll. At the sight of Johanne, Mania goes forward and greets her warmly. "Johanne, do you remember me?"

Johanne looks bemused, "No." She looks again at Mania, smiling, puzzled, says vaguely that Mania seems somehow familiar. She puts her hand to her face in a show of trying to remember.

Mania launches into the story of her life and the kind guard at Reichenbach who gave her food and clothes while she worked at the Telefunken factory.

"You know, it's hard to talk about my life," she says, to which Johanne briskly replies, "Well let's not talk about our lives, yours or mine."

But Mania is insistent. "I was just a little girl. The guard said my name was not Mania, it was Marie." The words that sketch out her anguished life fall out repetitiously, almost desperately. "And when I saw you for the first time in Toronto, I lost my voice."

Johanne retorts smartly, "Why didn't you ask me then if it was me?"

It's an odd reply. Johanne has denied she knows Mania, but doesn't this remark suggest she did? Or is her sharpness nothing more than an unkind put-down? I look at Maureen. Her expression is like an alert fox, ears pricked up, waiting to hear which way the dogs will run.

The pair wanders off in and out of earshot, an incongruous couple in that forsaken setting, one woman small with reddish hair, wearing a brown dress with a pink cashmere shawl flung over her shoulder, the other with glossy white hair, tall, straight, and strong in her sky-blue pantsuit. I have no earphones and have to stay out of the camera's way, hanging about in the background, catching snatches of their conversation.

They speak in German, occasionally in English. Johanne insists she does not recognize Mania, and certainly had never cleaned her home in Toronto. Now my ears prick up: the latter statement isn't true. It's a matter of record that Johanne worked briefly for Mania. After her return to Germany, Johanne sent Mania a Christmas card and included a photograph of herself. Maureen had taken Johanne's address from this card and made a copy of Johanne's photo. So why is Johanne lying?

This denial, however, doesn't make Johanne the guard. Like most older people, she probably forgets things. She worked for Mania very briefly, and that was more than a quarter century ago.

Mania isn't making such allowances. She looks exasperated, once again totally certain. She turns to the camera, conveying the fact that she is fed up. Johanne remains composed, dignified, allowing only an occasional expression to sweep across her placid face: affronted one moment, amused the next. As the two women move across the yard towards a standing building and are forced to step over rubble, they once or twice offer each other a hand, an offer that on either side is tartly dismissed.

Together they wander up the stairs of what was likely a former barrack. They warn each other, like bossy older sisters, to be careful on the staircase. They look at the end wall where some neo-Nazi thugs have recently painted the jagged lightning sign of the SS, a swastika, two gibbets, and the words "White Power" and "Ku-Klux-Klan."

All the while the camera rolls, recording images and sounds. There are three main sounds: the word "guard" in Mania's softly supplicating voice, Johanne's tenacious, sometimes amused, denial, accompanied every so often by her favorite expression: "Beat me to death, I'll deny it."

Outside in the warm sunshine, the smaller woman sits on a large stone and lights a cigarette. She seems tired and defeated. The larger woman continues to walk around in the early summer sunshine like a senior on a delicious day's outing. When the smaller woman asks her yet again if she's certain this is her first visit to Reichenbach camp, the larger woman looks a trifle scornful, as if to say, How could anyone be so mistaken?

But then a little later Johanne says, in a tone of gracious compromise, "When I think back, it could be possible that someone from my family somehow came into this camp and watched over you. It's not me personally. I swear on that."

On and on it goes as the two women stroll over the gritty soil. Mania's voice coaxing and pleading, Johanne's voice calmly denying. I know now it will go on for eternity. So when my taxi arrives in the late afternoon, I take it and say good-bye, once and for all, to this fabulous journey through the lives of two different women, through two different countries, and through the most fascinating period of time in the last century. A fabulous journey and a classic wild-goose chase. Since Mania questioned Johanne in her Toronto kitchen twenty-five years ago, there has been not one iota of change in the beliefs and statements of both women.

I am uncomfortable not being straightforward with people, and my relationship with Johanne has been colored by this fact. If I had to say whether Johanne has been straight with me, I would have to say yes and no. If I had another card up my sleeve, so did she. But the real source of my basic discomfort is elsewhere. I loathe the mystique that surrounds the hideous Third Reich, yet feel, in attempting to unravel an intriguing secret of the human heart, in part intrigued by it. It's time to pack up and go home. ↔

JUNE 2, 2002

I have family in South Carolina, so I stopped there en route home for a short visit. I'd barely stepped into my apartment in Vancouver when Maureen phoned and said she wanted to see me as soon as possible. How soon? Now, she said. Maureen is habitually enthusiastic, but this time her voice was red hot.

Within an hour she was at my apartment and, ignoring all my questions, sticking the roughs of her film into the television. Roughs are first-take, unedited film. In a second we were back at Reichenbach. I see what I've seen before, the women strolling together, going into the barracks, sitting on a pile of broken rock in the sun. But now I have the sound of both voices, and as they stroll Johanne is saying, "You look familiar somehow. Ah…it's been over twenty years since…"

Mania: "That's correct because I lost your address. And when Maureen wanted to know something about my destiny, I explained to her…it's very hard to talk about my life."

Johanne: "So you've said…so let's not begin to talk about it because then my tears will fall also."

They walk in silence and Mania says: "I was here, and from here we went to the Telefunken factory."

Johanne: "Telefunken. Here in this area?"

Mania: "This is a camp."

Johanne: "It reminds me of a camp from the old days, from Hitler."

Johanne says nothing as Mania continues: "We went to the Telefunken factory, through forests. It was cold. There was snow. And we slipped and fell. It was dark. This guard, she was always careful to walk beside me. When someone fell they were shot."

"Shot," says Johanne. "That's true, that's true."

Mania: "This is my wish, to tell you. When I came here there was a guard. In the evening we had a counting." (At the word "zell appell" Johanne nods her head. She knows what a zell appell is.) And next morning a guard called me over and said, 'What's your name?' and I said, 'Mania,' and she said, 'You are not a Jew; your name is Marie.' She was always beside me. Also, in the factory she always brought me a special soup and a piece of bread. And she said to me, one day when she took me to the clothing building, 'Marie, I am not married and I have no children and I would like to adopt you after the war.'"

Mania continues to explain all the good things this guard did. "She was not like the other Nazis, you understand. Lots of people understand that not all were Nazis. They had to work."

Johanne: "They had to be in the party. They had to."

Mania: "When I saw you for the first time…this guard, she was not a Nazi. She was so good."

Johanne responds, "Thank you." Smiling, she curtsies.

Mania: "You were like an angel. And since then I can see your face."

Johanne: "Still."

Mania: "Still."

Johanne: "I understand you."

Mania: "My wish…I hoped you'd worked here."

Suddenly Johanne becomes terse. "I had absolutely nothing to do with it."

For a while there is silence. The two women walk towards the barracks and Mania asks: "Do you want to go in?"

"I want to see inside," says Johanne, adding, "I've never been in a place like this before."

They go inside.

Johanne repeats herself, emphasizing that she is "seeing this for the first time." And for good measure she adds, "I've never been in a place like this before."

Mania: "Here" (pointing across the room) "they used to have beds here."

Johanne: "Amazing." And says again, in case there is any mistake: "I'm seeing this for the first time. I've never seen anything like it before."

But when Mania asks: "Where is the clothing warehouse?" Johanne points to the barracks behind Mania. She then suggests that, because there are bars on the windows, maybe it was a prison.

Mania: "Yes, looks like it, but it's been changed."

Johanne: "Then there was the light and telegraph."

I stare at the film, move closer to the screen to peer at Johanne's face better. It's as if memories are flooding back, overwhelming her, making her incautious and unaware.

"If someone tried to get out, then they would be automatically filmed and then…" Johanne makes a clicking sound.

Mania makes no comment on Johanne's staggering self-revelation. Without a trace of excitement on her face, Mania points at a few stones and the outline of a building on the ground.

"What was that?" she asks. "There was something…here. It's exactly the same."

Johanne: "But there is a wall in between."

Mania: "But it's the same barracks."

Johanne: "Yes."

Mania: "I'm looking for the clothing warehouse."

Both wander around, both enthusiastic, both back sixty years in time, both old women, one a former child prisoner and one a former guard, but both now bound together by place and memory. From time to time they wander arm in arm. Now they stop and look at a certain spot.

Johanne muses: "Maybe that was the warehouse."

But Mania doesn't think so. "It was behind the barracks."

Johanne pokes around a bit more. "There's something there. It's very old. It could have been an ammunitions bunker."

Mania: "Yes."

Johanne: "The prisoners wouldn't have known."

Mania: "Yes, they [we] wouldn't have known."

Johanne stands, thoughtfully looking at the ground. "Usually they would use little hills, remove the inside of the hill, and put the ammunitions inside."

They wander further. "There was a men's camp somewhere here," says Mania, "but I don't know where."

"Oh, they were separate," Johanne says matter-of-factly.

Mania wanders towards the gate. "I'm not sure what exit we went through to walk to the Telefunken factory."

Johanne points to the wall and says, "Wouldn't you agree the wall was higher then and there was barbed wire?"

She adds something the microphones can't catch, and Mania turns to

231

the camera and says, "The wall was higher…and she says electric—"

"Yes," says Johanne, "electric wire."

"I can't remember where we washed." Mania looks puzzled. "We got up very early for counting and then we had to go, and then we came back extremely tired."

Johanne: "That must be there, where there are no windows."

Mania: "Or maybe over there."

As they walk towards the gate, Johanne spontaneously observes, "The wall has been completely rebuilt." Mania looks at the camera as if to say, "Did you get that?"

The film ends soon after with Mania and Johanne holding hands and walking through the exit.

I'm too stunned to speak. I sit, frozen. I feel like I've been hit in the solar plexus with an SS baton. Little feisty Mania, with her teeth into the truth like a terrier, had been right. Johanne was the SS guard who had saved her life. Johanne was the bereft woman who, having lost her own child, had wanted to adopt the lively little orphan of whom she had charge! Johanne, who always sent money home because she could not bear to think of her little sister, Brigitte, being hungry!

Oh, Johanne, what a clever old lying trickster you are! What a bravura performance! What a manipulating, double-dealing actress! Eighty-five years of age and she almost pulled it off! Then why not? She'd deceived the SS right under their noses, marching around while her comrades spoke of wiping out the seed of Israel while she was sneaking food on the side in the wild hope of saving one of them. "A born actress," her director had told her vati seventy years earlier. Brother, did he speak the truth!

I look at Maureen, who is positively oozing triumph.

She tells me that later that night in Świdnica when she had asked Johanne her full name, Johanne had proudly announced it was "Johanne Marie Margueretta," adding that her mother's name had also been Marie. The words of the camp guard speaking to the Jewish child fly back to my mind: "No, you are not Mania, you are Marie. Say your name is Marie."

When I recover my voice, I ask what Johanne had to say for herself regarding her seeming familiarity with the layout of the Reichenbach camp. Maureen said that on being asked, Johanne slipped back into denial. She'd scorned the notion that her words meant she had any particular knowledge of the Reichenbach camp, claiming she'd learned all about high fences, electric wires, cameras, and the fate of the Jews by watching television after the war's end. Day and night German television had broadcast scenes of the death camps and labor camps, and this she had seen for the first time in person. She said, "Es war ein ungeheuriger Scheck." (It was an enormous shock.)

Mania had been deceived by her dialect, Johanne insisted. All the guards who worked in the camp had the same dialect. As an aside she added, "I could get into trouble if people thought I'd been a guard."

Still sticking to her guns! Still denying it! But why? It's absurd to say she'd get into trouble if people thought she'd been a guard. What people? No authority would now bother prosecuting an old former guard. If they did, Germany would have to build a series of Special Facility Prisons for Grannies. At a stretch the authorities might go after an outstandingly brutal guard, but not one who had saved a Jewish child. So why, even after all her revealing statements at Reichenbach, did Johanne keep denying her relationship with Mania?

Then the answer hits us. All the time it had been an inch away from our nose, so simple, so obvious that we were crazy not to have seen it. Johanne could never, never admit to the truth.

We phone Mania, who is ill, mystified, and exhausted by her experiences, and fly to Toronto to be with her. In the living room of her West Finch Avenue apartment, we wait while Mania, dressed and made-up to stylish perfection, finishes making us chicken soup, deaf to our protests that she sit down and rest. "Never have you tasted chicken soup like this before," she says, as if we were the ones who were ill.

Then we talk, and the mystery of Johanne's intransigence is resolved.

When Johanne had told Evert that his dead adoptive father had been in the SS, he had been shocked, repulsed, and mystified. How would Evert have reacted had she told him that she, his mother, had also been in the SS, a prison guard in a slave labor camp? Johanne was not about to do anything that would risk losing the love of her son. Nor did she want to lose the only link she had with the dominating passion of her youth, Kurt von Stieglitz, a link that still sustained her with some twisted sense of glory and pride even as she faced the onslaught of age. Johanne would go to heaven or hell denying she was at Reichenbach, and whether others considered her a good guard or a bad guard meant nothing to her.

In this matter she despised the opinion of others, hence her occasional bursts of temper and annoyance when we insisted that she had been a good guard. At all costs she had to keep her past secret. She'd boasted of the necessity to be always "resolute." She'd made a good job of it. Her dominate "resolution" was that her son forever think of her as a cook, a respectable, politically innocent cook who had never forgotten her lost baby boy.

Mania listens to me in silence. When she speaks, what she says is unexpected but oh so typical of Mania. "You've got to forgive people. Evert should forgive her. There's no other way. A child...no one can break your heart like a child, no one can even begin to touch it the way a child does." She starts to reminisce. "When my husband, Micha, was dying, his mother, Ruth, flew over from Israel. He was a good, gentle man born on a kibbutz in Upper Galilee. He'd been raised in a kibbutz nursery. Neither one of us knew what a normal marriage was like.

"Anyway, Ruth came, old and broken and skinny, and she started to stroke Mike. And Mike said, 'Don't do that. I don't want it now. Where were you when I was a child? Where were you when I had my tonsils out and was discharged, waiting, waiting in the hospital to be picked up and finally walking home? Where were you then?'

"I stood outside the room and heard it all. All those years he had carried it in his heart and never said a word to me, all that pain. Now he could speak. I stood and wept both for Mike and his mother.

"Ruth, too, was a victim. She had no choice. I had no choice." Mania lights a cigarette and laughs. "But we mustn't think about things that make us sad. Just forgive, don't forget, but always hope. Wherever there's life there's hope, remember? We must choose life, not death. Remember my mother's words?"

I look at Mania and see the terrified nine-year-old running through the fields at night, believing an angel is at her side. I see the eleven-year-old walking into Auschwitz-Birkenau in the remnants of a Shirley Temple dress. I see a child prisoner who wants to "go on the wire." I see her young mother kneeling beside her, desperately seeking the words to sustain her child's life. "Listen, listen Manuska, never forget. God created you. He gave you life. As long as you live, you have to appreciate it. As long as we live, we have hope." Yes, I remember.

I ask my final question. "You've always said your life was a mystery, a puzzle, Mania. Did you feel better about it now that you lived when so many others died? Do you feel there might have been a reason?"

Mania shakes her head. "No. I don't think there was a reason," she says. "That is, it's not like God said, 'Oh there's Mania. I've got to save her. All the other kids can die.' No, it wasn't like that. I created the reason, not God. I created the reason, but it wasn't there until after I'd survived. We all must do that. We must create our own lives. No one else will do it. It's up to us."

She stops, pulls out a packet of cigarettes, and lights up. Her cancer is back, her heart is weak, I love her but not enough to put the lid on my irritation.

"Will you put that damned cigarette out?" I say. She throws me a look that hammers me to my chair and goes on talking as if to herself.

"Yes, I feel that's it. I had to tell whoever would listen about all the mysteries in my life. After I survived, I, not God, created a reason why I survived Johanne had mysteries, too, different from mine. That spark of goodness that wouldn't die even when she was living in an SS sewer. Yes, I think telling my story has created a reason why I lived. It's finished now."

She takes a long draw and, throwing me a glance, stubs out her cigarette.

"Let some believe, let some not believe." ↺

EPILOGUE

Mania Fishel Kroll died June 21, 2007. She died believing as she always had that all organized religions have proven to be cruel and dangerous, that trust is the closest word for God, that heartfelt forgiveness is essential to being fully human, and that life is a precious gift that must be celebrated daily.

Johanne Clausen Müller died in Germany in the fall of 2006. Her last name and those of her family members have been changed for the purposes of privacy.

Maureen kept contact with Johanne almost to the end.

It is not known what her thoughts or beliefs were at the time of her death. She was eighty-nine years old.

mitted in their concentration camps and villages. Many stories are woven together in this book—the survival of the child, Mania; the love affair between an attractive domestic worker and a dashing SS officer: and the reunion between Mania and her alleged rescuer, Johanne. While learning about the lives of Mania and Johanne we also become privy to the delicate interviewing skills and brilliant editorial commentary by Lisa Birnie. A gripping, meticulous and fearless book."
Vancouver Holocaust Education Centre

"As the library technician for Patrick Henry High School, San Diego, I was asked for recommendations for something new and insightful for two different departments, History and English. In *Mania's Memory* was exactly what we needed. Over 50 copies were ordered. It is unique, informative, and well written, one of my favorites in quite a long time. "
CARE KELLY, Library Technician, Patrick Henry High School, San Diego, California

"Lisa Birnie's In *Mania's Memory* is the remarkable story of a Polish Jew named Mania and a German Christian named Johanne. Mania was imprisoned in Auschwitz at age seven. Fast forward to 1976 and she is living in Toronto when she hires a cleaning woman who appears to be the same Nazi guard (Johanne) who protected her and gave her special food so she could survive in a work camp called Reichenbach. The guard was hoping to adopt Mania by war's end but they were separated. But the Toronto cleaning lady denies she is Johanne. Lisa Birnie tries to unravel the truth. We learn Johanne was a beautiful young German woman passionately in love with an officer of the Third Reich. Is Mania deluded? Are memories reliable?

For a documentary film, Birnie accompanies Mania and the woman who continues to deny she was the Nazi guard back to Auschwitz, where they roam the grounds. Birnie has added some of her own experiences of war to this fascinating story."
BC Bookworld

"In *Mania's Memory* (Read Leaf) is a fascinating read. . . Birnie deftly melds the interviews she conducted with Kroll and Müller, who have both

since died, as well as her own observations and feelings about what she learns. With so many threads, it's surprising how easy it is to follow, and how the tension builds to the moment when the truth finally is revealed. It really is a case of fact being stranger than fiction."
The Jewish Independent

"Countless memoirs have been written about the atrocities of the Holocaust, but a new approach helps capture the lives of two very different women in the new book, In Mania's Memory. Written by Australian native and journalist Lisa Birnie, the author shares her personal prejudices of Germans, while telling the story of a survivor and her former guard. Birnie's writing style is almost like an interview that slowly evolves into a narrative. The author asks Mania questions about her childhood while Mania's voice slowly takes over. In and out, Birnie weaves a tale through Mania's voice of a girl who survived brutality, but still managed to forgive . . . Finding the truth takes readers on a page-turning trail. Is the woman Mania met in the 1970s the former guard who saved her? And if so, why won't the woman admit it? Birnie doesn't stop at Mania's tale, though. She looks into the life of her captor, Johanne. Sharing Johanne's crude upbringing gives readers a glimpse of what life could be like for poor Germans before the war. Johanne states that many were excited for Hitler's rise, and the new opportunities Germans found."
The Oakland Press

"It's a thorough and satisfying exploration of how two people on opposite sides of a great divide survived an unspeakably grim period of human history . . . Readers will feel sympathy for Kroll and probably for Muller, too. The narrative keeps readers guessing as to whether Kroll was right when she told Birnie, "My cleaning woman [in 1976] was former SS Corporal Johanne Clausen, guard at Reichenbach slave labour camp [in 1944-45]." On the phone, filmmaker Kelleher made this trenchant observation: 'It's not so much whether or not she was a guard, it's that the war was really bad for women on both sides.'"
The Vancouver Sun